BETWEEN REASON AND HISTORY

SUNY series in the Philosophy of the Social Sciences

Lenore Langsdorf, editor

BETWEEN REASON AND HISTORY

HABERMAS AND THE IDEA OF PROGRESS

David S. Owen

State University of New York Press

Published by
State University of New York Press, Albany

Printed in the United States of America

For more information, contact State University of New York Press, Albany, NY
www.sunypress.edu

Production by Judith Block
Marketing by Jennifer Giovani

Library of Congress Cataloging-in-Publication Data

Owen, David S.
Between reason and history : Habermas and the idea of progress / David S. Owen.
p. cm. — (SUNY series in the philosophy of the social sciences)
Includes bibliographical references and index.
ISBN 978-0-7914-5409-1 (alk. paper) — 978-0-7914-5410-7 (pbk. : alk. paper)
1. Progress—Philosophy. 2. Habermas, Jürgen. I. Title. II. Series.

HM891 .O94 2002
303.44'01—dc21 2001049779

10 9 8 7 6 5 4 3 2

For Diane

Contents

Acknowledgments

When I began my graduate study in philosophy my interests generally concerned issues of social justice. I worried, however, that critiques of "grand narratives" and of the reification of human nature undermined the possibility of grounding the normative stance of any critique aiming at social justice. In one of my first seminars I encountered the work of Jürgen Habermas, which immediately resonated with me. I found in his work a carefully nuanced attempt to provide a grounding for social critique, without collapsing into either foundationalism or relativism. That seminar was taught by Sandra Bartky, and since that time she has provided invaluable guidance, encouragement, and criticism for both my career and this project. There is no doubt that without her regular encouragement I would not have completed this project. I also want to thank David Ingram for his helpful suggestions throughout the entire manuscript, and for proving to be an important resource, guiding me through the labyrinth of Habermas's work. Others who have read the manuscript and provided valuable feedback include Jürgen Habermas, Richard Kraut, Charles Mills, and Leo Shelbert. I would also like to express my appreciation to Thomas McCarthy, who graciously took the time to discuss this project with me and confirming for me its importance during the early stages.

Throughout the writing of this study I have had many discussions and conversations with colleagues and peers that have helped me to clarify and strengthen my arguments. I especially want to thank Paola Kindred, Christopher Zurn, Vic Peterson, and Amy Allen for their immensely helpful insights and comments. And I would like to thank the participants of the Critical Theory Roundtable, who over the years have provided a crucial intellectual community to discuss these ideas with.

There are two people without whom I would not have been able to write this book. Beth Wagner, my mother, both encouraged and supported my studies so that I could arrive at a place where this book could even be a possibility. And Diane Marschang, who has been at my side from the very beginning of this project, offering encouragement and support throughout its writing, and who deserves much of the credit for its completion.

I also want to thank Jane Bunker, my editor at State University of New York Press, for her advice and dedication to bringing this work to publication.

A portion of chapter 4 was previously published as "Habermas's Developmental Logic Thesis: Universal or Eurocentric?" in *Philosophy Today* 42 (1998): supplement, 104–111.

Abbreviations

In citing works by Jürgen Habermas, the following abbreviations have been used:

BFN	*Between Facts and Norms: Contributions to a Discourse Theory of Law and Democracy*
CES	*Communication and the Evolution of Society*
HE	"History and Evolution"
KHI	*Knowledge and Human Interests*
LC	*Legitimation Crisis*
MCCA	*Moral Consciousness and Communicative Action*
PDM	*The Philosophical Discourse of Modernity*
RCA	"Remarks on the Concept of Communicative Action"
RHM	*Zur Rekonstruktion des Historischen Materialismus*
TCA I	*The Theory of Communicative Action*, Vol. 1: *Reason and the Rationalization of Society*
TCA II	*The Theory of Communicative Action*, Vol. 2: *Lifeworld and System*
TP	*Theory and Practice*
WAR	"Wahrheitstheorien"
WB	"Walter Benjamin: Consciousness-Raising or Rescuing Critique"

Introduction

Karl Marx famously asserted that "[t]he Philosophers have only *interpreted* the world, in various ways, the point is to *change* it," and with this practical conception of philosophy he inaugurated what can properly be called critical social theory.[1] Marx's point was not that we should abandon philosophy for political polemics, but that we need to reconceive philosophy in fundamentally social terms. This is because, as Hegel had shown, thought is sociohistorical in essential ways. On the one hand, our understanding of ourselves, of our relations to others, and of nature shapes our judgments, practices, and institutions. And on the other hand, our judgments, practices, and institutions shape these self-understandings and our knowledge of our place in the world. A significant consequence is that the rigid separation of fact and value, of theory and practice, traditionally maintained by philosophers and scientists alike, is no longer tenable. From Hegel on, any adequate philosophical account of human nature, and any adequate scientific description of social reality must incorporate this insight—that human needs, interests, and values are tied up with social practices and institutions.

Critical social theory was born out of this insight. But critical theory is not concerned merely with describing social reality; rather it seeks to synthesize a scientifically respectable description of social reality with a critical or normative orientation. In other words, the Enlightenment tendency to hold theory rigidly apart from practice must be rejected in favor of a new approach, one that recognizes the fundamental interrelatedness of theory and practice. It should be evident that the basic guiding value for critical theory is freedom. Critical theory is critical just because it has an interest in emancipating persons from unnecessary domination, and this presupposes a conception of freedom that contrasts with domination.

To be sure, the idea of freedom is fraught with misunderstandings, misuses, and abstraction. Critical theorists do not understand freedom in the colloquial and liberal sense of freedom from external constraint. The conception of freedom as being able to do what I want to do without anyone or anything interfering or constraining me from doing so is far too thin a conception for the purposes of critical theory, and moreover it is incoherent given the conception of the relation of thought and practice by which they are guided. If thought and practice are mutually constitutive, then the conception of freedom as freedom from external constraint ignores those forms of unfreedom that inhabit thought, constraining action from the inside as it were. Critical theory is concerned not only with emancipation from external constraint, but also from forms of internal constraint. Thus, the conception of freedom with which critical theorists operate is a more substantive one that can be traced back to Hegel, which explains why critical theory is understood as an attempt to retrieve some of the Hegelian roots of Marxism. Hegel argues that modern individuals see themselves as having "abstract right," that is, an abstract freedom of the will in general to make choices, and modern social institutions must protect this abstract right. However, while abstract right determines persons, *subjects* are persons who also possess subjective freedom, which is the freedom to give meaning to one's life through one's choices. When I express myself through my actions I am subjectively free and I find satisfaction in the action, and this results in my happiness.[2] What this means for critical theory is that the emancipation sought is not grounded on a liberal freedom of choice, but on a more substantive conception of freedom, one that also includes a freedom to express and realize one's own aspirations and vision. For critical theorists, genuine freedom involves being able to satisfy one's physical and material needs, self-determination, and happiness that derives from self-realization.

Jürgen Habermas has been seen as a second generation Frankfurt School theorist, although he arguably has moved away from these roots.[3] The Frankfurt School of critical theory—only so named in the 1960s—was represented by such thinkers as Max Horkheimer, Theodor W. Adorno, Walter Benjamin, and Herbert Marcuse. Significantly, they hardly constituted a "school" of thought, but what they shared was an interest in formulating a scientifically and philosophically adequate critical theory. Habermas's magnum opus, *The Theory of Communicative Action*, is an explicit attempt to clarify the normative foundations of critical theory, and his important contribution to this is to steer critical theory around the linguistic turn that has occurred in philosophy in the course of the twentieth century.

However, although there is an extensive and growing literature concerning Habermas's critical theory, what is missing from those discussions is a sustained and careful discussion of the theory of social evolution. It is my aim in this study to contribute to filling in this gap. In this study I will locate this theory, both within the context of critical theory itself and within Habermas's particular conception of it, I will systematize and clarify its key provisions, including that of the concept of a developmental logic, and throughout I will critically assess the theory's basic claims. This is not intended to be the final word on the subject; rather, it is intended to lay the framework for further inquiry and debate, in other words, to be a contribution to an on-going research program.

I think at this point it would be helpful to provide the reader with a general idea of Habermas's conception of social evolution in order to provide a perspective on the arguments to follow. When one hears "theory of social evolution," one typically thinks of the totalizing, universal histories of the nineteenth century. But the theory of social evolution need not be conceived as a universal history. For if we distinguish, as suggested by Jürgen Habermas, between the logic of development—as a universal of societal development—and the dynamics of history—the contingent "content" of the historical process—we can then conceive of a theory of social evolution that has a universal moment (the logic of development), but is not properly characterized as a universal history. On this model of social evolution, the logic, or pattern, of societal development is a postulated universal; that is, every society that develops (and this is a contingent matter) will universally progress through the reconstructed stages of the developmental logic. Distinguished from the logic of development is the dynamic process of history, in which the innumerable contingencies of the historical process have effect. This will be clarified, but for now the important point is that an adequate theory of social evolution—that is, one that avoids the stigma of an applied philosophy of history—can be conceived by separating the pattern of development from the dynamics of history.

This characterization, however, remains somewhat obscure until we clarify what is meant by a logic of development. One might think of a staircase (the developmental logic) upon which an individual (a determinate society) travels. The individual can proceed up or down the stairs, or can even remain on one particular stair, but it is not possible to skip stairs (perhaps they are too far apart). When and why the individual steps up or down is a strictly contingent matter; it depends upon innumerable variables. But when she is sufficiently motivated to step up or down, she *must* follow the contours of the staircase. But what do the stairs themselves represent? Pursuing the metaphor further, we can see that when the individual steps up to a higher stair, she can see for a greater distance, and when she steps down, the distance of her vision is reduced. The same can be said of societies that develop. When they "step up" to a higher level of development, they have expanded their consciousness, in the sense of an expansion of learning capacity; and when they step down, they constrict their consciousness, or their learning capacity. On this model of social evolution, then, the developmental logic is constituted in a hierarchical series of levels of learning that manifest themselves as collective horizons of consciousness. And within each learning level, or collective horizon of consciousness, many different social formations are possible. So while two determinate societies may occupy the same learning level, they may appear on the surface to be significantly different.

The fundamental assumptions involved in this claim are that there are underlying structures of consciousness that determine the horizon or range of possible contents of consciousness, that these deep structures are a universal property of the human species, and that these structures of consciousness have an internal development. Such a theory of social evolution is properly characterized as developmental, since it explains only the *structure* of the horizon-constituting structures of shared consciousness, and the explanation is formulated from a third-person perspective. This contrasts with a theory of universal history, which seeks to explain the *particulars* of a society's history in a narrative form.

While Habermas's theory of social evolution is not a universal history, neither is it a speculative philosophy of history, which seeks to identify the universal and necessary determinants and form of world history. There are two key distinctions that Habermas maintains must be made if the theory of social evolution is both to explain the empirical historical facts, and to avoid the problems inherent in philosophies of history. First, a distinction needs to be drawn between two types of structures of consciousness. There are cognitive-technical structures that determine the horizons of our empirical knowledge about the objective world. These should be distinguished from moral-practical structures that determine the horizons of our practical know-how in relation to the social world. Accordingly, we can reconstruct the developmental pattern associated with each of these dimensions. Habermas's thesis is that the dimension of moral-practical insight possesses its own developmental logic that is independent of the developmental logic of cognitive-technical knowledge. In contrast to Marxism, which maintains that the two are either causally or functionally interrelated, in his theory of social evolution Habermas postulates that each dimension follows its own autonomous developmental logic. The second key distinction is implied by Habermas's use of the concept of developmental logic. For this concept, which is borrowed from developmental psychology, refers to a developmental pattern of structures that delimit the logical space of possible determinate contents. Thus, Habermas explicitly makes the distinction between the logic of development of structures of consciousness and the empirical content that is the result of the contingencies history. Just as the cognitive and moral competencies of individuals mature through reconstructable stages, societies likewise develop through reconstructable stages. As in the individual, each society follows its own unique path, although that path is constrained by the abstract logic of development. The metaphor of the staircase that was mentioned above is again useful here. The developmental logic is represented by the staircase; in stepping up or down, all stair climbers must follow the contours of the staircase, and each can occupy only one stair at a time. But, why a given individual steps up or down, or remains on one step, is a strictly contingent matter. Moreover, each individual follows a unique path, again dependent upon contingent reasons, up or down the staircase. No two individuals will likely follow in the same footsteps (though unlikely, it is not ruled out a priori). Thus, Habermas postulates that societies will develop in accordance with a universal developmental logic, each individual society following its own path insofar as the determinate contents of its history are concerned.

Given these distinctions, we can now sketch Habermas's conception of the *process* of social evolution. Societies are said to evolve to a higher level only when learning occurs with respect to their normative structures. Whether or not societies learn in this dimension is contingent on circumstances. The pressure to develop in the normative dimension, however, arises from the base of society, that is, from the development of the productive forces. An increase in cognitive-technical knowledge potential which cannot be implemented because of normative limitations determined by the prevailing learning level generates a crisis situation, which is experienced as an identity crisis. Only by developing a new form of social integration—advancing to a developmentally higher learning level—can a society progressively overcome a crisis. The thesis that each dimension of social reproduction, the material and the sociocultural, follows its own developmental logic, however, entails that there is no causal or functional relation between the development of the two. Problems generated in the base can only be overcome by a development of the normative structures of society, but how they develop is independent of the base. Accordingly, Habermas conceives of social evolution as a bidimensional learning process, which is constituted by a logically independent rationalization of the structures of consciousness in both the cognitive-technical and the moral-practical dimensions.

Perhaps the most fundamental thesis of Habermas's theory of social evolution is what I call the developmental logic thesis. This is the claim that societal evolution occurs according to a certain pattern, and that pattern can be reconstructed in terms of a developmental logic. The concept of a developmental logic and the meaning of the developmental logic thesis require considerable analysis and clarification, tasks that are tackled later in this study. Briefly, Habermas understands development in this sense as a rationalization of the structures of consciousness. Here rationalization should be understood as a decentering of perspective, in which partial and provincial perspectives are replaced by more comprehensive, and universal perspectives. Thus, as Lawrence Kohlberg has shown in the development of moral consciousness, a highly egocentric perspective, in which the child associates right and wrong with immediate pleasure or displeasure, becomes replaced by a conventional perspective, in which right and wrong are socially determined by convention and tradition. And finally, the conventional perspective is replaced by the postconventional perspective, in which the adolescent reflects upon the justifications themselves of the moral principles. In the mature adult, then, a universal moral point of view is said to have been achieved. This is an example of the sort of rationalization process Habermas maintains occurs in social evolution.

Rationalization on this conception is understood as a form of a decentering of perspective. Thus, development refers to a society achieving an increasingly decentered perspective, with the significant consequence that capacity for learning embodied in the society's lifeworld is expanded. That is, as a society evolves, its structures of consciousness become more rational, allowing the society increasingly to interact successfully with its environments (both objective and social). And this rationalization process produces the happy effect of expanding the learning capacity of the society. The expansion of the learning capacity is a consequence of the developmental logic. As a society advances to a higher learning level, or stage of development, its structures of consciousness are transformed: there is a reordering of the contents of the previous level in a new structure. This higher level is a developmental achievement because it allows the society to function with a greater degree of stability, and to adapt better to reproductive challenges (that is, those societal problems that generate systemic crises).

Once I have examined the details of these arguments, as well as various objections and criticisms, the next questions becomes, Does Habermas's theory of social evolution entail an adequate conception of progress for the purposes of critical theory? It seems that it both does and does not. On the one hand, explaining development by reference to a developmental logic of structures of consciousness provides a necessary explanation of social change from the internal, or participants', perspective. Only by incorporating both internal and external explanatory perspectives can a theory of social evolution adequately explain the possibility of progressive social change. And Habermas's developmental logic thesis, by postulating a developmental logic for the normative-practical structures that is independent of the developmental logic of the cognitive-technical structures of consciousness, explains the possibility of progressive structural change independently in both empirical knowledge and practical insight.

On the other hand, a theory of social evolution that accounts for progress in only the dimensions of material need and freedom from oppression cannot preclude the possibility of a prosperous and free society that lacks happiness and fulfillment. In other words, it is blind to the possibility of progress in terms of self-realization. Is it then possible that we might achieve social conditions which are free from material need and oppression, but are meaningless? Habermas acknowledges this possibility in an early essay, but he argues for pragmatic reasons that we must first focus on progress in the dimensions of material well-being and self-determination. Consequently, his later construction of the theory of social evolution emphasizes cognitive-technical and moral-practical progress to the exclusion of progress in the dimension of self-realization. I would suggest that a constructive contribution to this research program would be to draw on Hegel's conception of subjective freedom to develop a better understanding of what it means for a society to progress—or even regress—in the dimension of self-realization. Consideration of individual happiness and satisfaction has always been an integral part of critical social theory, and the focus on material well-being and self-determination should not overshadow a concern for meaningful happiness and fulfillment.

Chapter 1

The Idea of Progress and Critical Social Theory

In this first chapter I am interested in the significance for critical social theory of the idea of social change that is progressive. The intention is to lay the groundwork for my later examination of Habermas's theory of social evolution, which I will argue is an integral part of his critical theory. In other words, before going into the details of this theory and of its relation to Habermas's conception of critical theory, it will be useful to clarify the general relationship between the concepts of progress and critical theory. Thus, I will take the broad view here of critical theory in order to make a case for the claim that an adequate critical social theory must include an account of progressive social change.

Critical Social Theory

In reviewing the current literature in critical social theory one might wonder just why a critical theorist should be at all interested in a theory of social evolution. For example, in the literature on Habermas, while there is much talk of whether or not a consensus concerning normative claims is possible, and if so, how it might be achieved, and whether such a consensus is even desirable, there is comparatively little discussion of the broader social and historical context of these questions, especially with respect to the specifically modern presuppositions on which they rest. In particular, any concrete consensus, whether real or hypothetical, is already embedded in a sociohistorical context, and it is the particulars of this context that the theory of social evolution is intended to illuminate.

In this section I will situate the theory of social evolution with respect to the theoretically informed practice of social critique. I will attempt this through both historical and formal analyses. In order to establish the historical importance of the theory of social evolution, I first will locate the intrinsic role played by the concept of progress within the Frankfurt School tradition of critical theory. My discussion will focus on Max Horkheimer's seminal essay, "Traditional and Critical Theory," which served as an informal manifesto for critical theory.[1] In this historical analysis, I will attempt to show how the original idea of a critical theory of society entails the need for an account of progress (which is provided by a theory of social evolution). Next, in a formal analysis of the idea of social critique, I will argue that any conception of the practice of social critique that does not give an account of progress is inadequate. In other words, it is essential to the practice of social critique that the social critic operate with a notion of progress. It follows that a nondogmatic, or reflective, social critic will seek to make explicit and clarify that notion of progress.

Max Horkheimer first explicitly formulated the concept of a critical theory of society that became the guiding idea of a group of thinkers collectively known as the "Frankfurt School." Horkheimer became the second director of the *Institut für Sozialforschung* in 1931.[2] The *Institut* was established in 1923 with the financial resources of Felix Weil, the son of a successful Frankfurt businessman. Weil arranged to finance an institute that would be associated with the University of Frankfurt with the idea of furthering the development of Marxism.[3] He had several goals in mind: to provide the means for the independent theoretical development of Marxism; to increase the scientific respectability of such research; and to develop Marxism as a serious academic discipline. Weil insisted on complete independence in regard to the direction and content of research to be carried out at the *Institut*, and he retained nearly absolute power to appoint the director, who possessed, in turn, near dictatorial powers over the research conducted by the *Institut*. Thus, Horkheimer, throughout his term as director of the *Institut*, from 1931 on, exercised considerable control over the research program of the *Institut's* members. The term "Frankfurt School" is typically identified with the general approach to social inquiry adopted by the diverse group of philosophers, sociologists, political scientists, psychologists, and economists who were members of the *Institut für Sozialforschung*, although this particular label was first applied to this tradition only in the 1960s, despite the fact that this tradition consisted of anything but a unified, coherent body of theoretical work, or a monolithic approach to social critique.[4]

Following John Rawls's distinction between a *concept* and a particular *conception* of that same concept, I will refer to the general idea of a critical theory of society as the concept of a critical theory of society.[5] The concept of something contains the core features that are shared or presupposed by the various individual conceptions of that thing. The concept of a critical theory of society consists of those features that define what a critical theory of society is in general. Critical theorists may have different and unique conceptions of critical social theory, but they would agree on the features essential to the concept of a critical theory of society itself. The distinction between concept and conception is important in a study of critical social theory since historically there have been many particular conceptions of social critique, both within and without a narrowly conceived critical theory tradition. The work of the Frankfurt School is unified primarily by its "aversion to closed philosophical systems."[6] The "vulgar" forms of Marxism had predicted that revolution was an inevitable result of capitalism, but the expected revolution did not occur. The Frankfurt School theorists attributed this, in part, to the overly scientistic development of Marxist theory, which engendered a more closed system than had been envisioned by the early Marx. Thus, the Frankfurt School attempted to overcome problems stemming from the scientism of vulgar Marxism through a reconsideration of the Hegelian inspirations of the early philosophical Marx.[7] As the theoretical work of the members of the Frankfurt School developed, however, theoretical differences present at the beginning gradually grew wider. The work of the core members, Horkheimer, Theodor W. Adorno, and Herbert Marcuse, did however converge in the early 1940s on a critique of instrumental reason.

My exposition here will detail only the essential features of the concept of a critical theory of society that Horkheimer conceived as the organizing approach to the social inquiry of the *Institut*. His writings on these issues came at a time when he was most optimistic about the potential of critical social theory. During the period between 1931 and 1937 Horkheimer produced several studies in which he explained and elaborated his understanding of the concept of a critical theory of society and the ways in which he believed that this concept could be put into practice. In his inaugural address as director of the *Institut,* entitled "The Present Situation of Social Philosophy and the Tasks of an Institute for Social Research," Horkheimer sketched what he considered to be the fundamental overarching theoretical approach for the members of the *Institut*.[8] In this, which has been called the *Institut's* "manifesto," he argues that contemporary social philosophy finds itself in a dilemma that derives, on the one hand, from its commitment to methodological individualism, and on the other hand, from the increasing specialization and isolation of its diverse disciplines.[9] It is in the methodological individualism of social philosophy that Horkheimer locates the primary source of its difficulties: "Now, it is precisely in this dilemma of social philosophy—this inability to speak of its object, namely the cultural life of humanity, other than in ideological *[weltanschaulich],* sectarian, and confessional terms, the inclination to see in the social theories of Auguste Comte, Karl Marx, Max Weber, and Max Scheler differences in articles of faith rather than differences in true, false, or at least problematic theories—it is in this dilemma that we find the difficulty that must be overcome."[10] The difficulties arising from methodological individualism contribute to the gap between social philosophy and the empirical social sciences, which both refuse to cross:

> The relation between philosophical and corresponding specialized scientific disciplines cannot be conceived as though philosophy deals with the really decisive problems—in the process constructing theories beyond the reach of the empirical sciences, its own concepts of reality, and systems comprehending the totality—while on the other side empirical research carries out its long, boring, individual studies that split up into a thousand partial questions, culminating in a chaos of countless enclaves of specialists. This conception—according to which the individual researcher must view philosophy as a perhaps pleasant but scientifically fruitless enterprise (because not subject to experimental control), while philosophers, by contrast, are emancipated from the individual researcher because they think they cannot wait for the latter before announcing their wide-ranging conclusions—is

> currently being supplanted by the idea of a continuous, dialectical penetration and development of philosophical theory and specialized scientific praxis.[11]

Horkheimer here finds the solution to the dilemma of social theory in interdisciplinary cooperation between social philosophy, which is able to reflect upon the conditions and limits of social theory and guide empirical research, and the empirical social sciences, which are able to provide the data to either confirm or falsify the general theories. The task for social theorists (including social philosophers), he says, is to "pursue their larger philosophical questions on the basis of the most precise scientific methods, to revise and refine their questions in the course of their substantive work, and to develop new methods without losing sight of the larger context."[12] Horkheimer emphasizes that this concept of social research cannot be fulfilled by the lone researcher, whether philosopher or sociologist. This concept of social theory requires the cooperation of a variety of researchers from the widest possible range of disciplines. Thus, he also urges social theorists to make the very process of social research a more social process, and not a process of individuals in isolated and highly specialized disciplines. Moreover, Horkheimer urges social theorists to focus more on structures of social relations, rather than individual actions of social agents, as the object of their inquiry. Thus, in this essay, Horkheimer first sketches the initial outlines of an idea of critical theory: it is interdisciplinary, empirically grounded, and systematically reflective.

In a programmatic essay from 1937, "Traditional and Critical Theory," Horkheimer explicitly attempts, once again, to explain the concept of a critical theory of society.[13] It should be noted that in this essay Horkheimer discusses his ideas concerning critical theory at two levels, which are not always clearly distinguished. At the first, metatheoretical level, he provides an explicit formulation of the concept of a critical theory of society, and at the second theoretical level, he articulates his own particular conception of critical social theory. As I have indicated above, my interest is in his metatheoretical considerations of the essential features of the concept of a critical theory of society. Horkheimer's approach to the concept of critical theory is through the distinction between the notion of a critical theory and the hypothetical-deductive model of theory presupposed in the sciences, which he refers to as "traditional theory." According to Horkheimer, the scientific model of theory can be defined as "the sum-total of propositions about a subject, the propositions being so linked with each other that a few are basic and the rest derive from these."[14] A theory is considered to be more explanatorily adequate the fewer basic propositions it has, and the validity of a theory is evaluated according to its capacity to explain the totality of facts derived from empirical research. If the facts do not match the theory, then the validity of either the theory or the facts must be reexamined. Thus, traditional theories, and the propositions contained by them, have only hypothetical status, since they are always open to experimental falsification.

Horkheimer's understanding of traditional theory in this essay derives from the hypothetical-deductive model, which, as he sees it, structures theory construction in the natural sciences. Although the conception of scientific theory construction as purely hypothetical-deductive is certainly an oversimplification, especially in light of the various criticisms of this model that had been generated by that time (for example, by Mannheim's sociology of knowledge), I think that this claim is justified, historically speaking, since the hypothetical-deductive model of science remained the dominant conception in such groups as the Vienna Circle. Nevertheless, Horkheimer goes on to argue that the social and the human sciences typically conform to this scientistic model as well: "There can be no doubt, in fact, that the various schools of sociology have an identical conception of theory and that it is the same as theory in the natural sciences."[15] This scientistic theoretical structure is not affected by whether the fundamental propositions of the theory are inferred from empirical facts, or are gotten by selection, intuition, or stipulation, since the hypothetical character of the fundamental propositions is retained, and thus remains open to theoretical revision based on further evidence: "The way that sociology must take in the present state of research is (it is argued) the laborious ascent from the description of social phenomena to detailed comparisons and only then to the formation of general concepts."[16]

Horkheimer goes on to make the Hegelian argument that the basic theoretical propositions are not derived from logical or methodological sources, that is, these basic theoretical propositions are not motivated by strictly logical or methodological reasons. The inference to basic theoretical propositions can be properly understood only within the context of real social processes.[17] What this means is that the criteria of theory choice, that is, whether theory X or theory Y best explains the phenomena under investigation, whether these criteria are either logically or methodologically motivated, are themselves products of social processes. For example, according to Horkheimer the choice of the Copernican heliocentric cosmology over the traditional geocentric cosmology in the seventeenth century exemplifies this thesis since it involved criteria that were inextricably bound to the social processes of the period: "In the seventeenth century, for example, men began to resolve the difficulties into which traditional astronomy had fallen, no longer by supplemental constructions but by adopting the Copernican system in its place. This change was not due to the logical properties alone of the Copernican theory, for example its greater simplicity. If these properties were seen as advantages, this very fact points beyond itself to the fundamental characteristics of social action at the time. That Copernicanism, hardly mentioned in the sixteenth century, should now become a revolutionary force is part of the larger historical process by which mechanistic thinking came to prevail."[18] What appears, in this example, to be a strictly logical criterion—greater simplicity through fewer explanatory propositions—in fact reflects the historical trend of the seventeenth century towards a mechanistic worldview in which simplicity is a virtue. Copernicanism explains cosmological phenomena with relatively simple mathematical formulae, thus increasing the rationality of the explanation over Aristotelian explanations. Moreover, Horkheimer argues that not only does the social context influence theory construction, but the application of the theory to further empirical observations is also a social process. Empirical confirmation or falsification of a theory is necessarily a social process, since the validity of a theory is determined not by the assertions of one scientist, but by the repeated confirmations of the scientific community.

The consequence of the scientistic understanding of traditional theory is that the "scholar and his science are incorporated into the apparatus of society. . . ."[19] This general unreflexivity of traditional theory (as characterized by Horkheimer) results in it typically being a conservative force in the building and renewing of social bonds, in a phrase, social reproduction. That is, society ensures its own continued existence through the reproduction of its key institutions and structures, and traditional theory typically contributes unreflexively to social reproduction. Since social reproduction is accomplished through social action that is conditioned by institutions and practices, and since scientific inquiry is inherently social, scientific inquiry manifestly contributes to social reproduction. This is not what Horkheimer finds problematic. What he objects to is that the contribution of science to social reproduction remains largely unexamined, due to the general unreflexivity of the traditional conception of theory. Thus, since traditional theory does not reflect on its own inextricable involvement in the reproduction of the social, it participates in the process of social reproduction in a nonrational way. As traditional theory blithely goes about its business under the existing division of intellectual labor it contributes to the continuation, justification, and expansion of the existing categories and conditions of social existence. This leads Horkheimer to characterize traditional theory as (typically) a conservative force in social reproduction.

Moreover, progress in traditional theory is measured according to ever greater accumulation of knowledge, which in turn generates increased technical efficiency of social reproduction. Greater technical efficiency, in either the natural or the social spheres of action, means greater control over the object of knowledge, since only through the achievement of a comprehensive and detailed understanding of objects can we manipulate them in accordance with our needs and desires. Thus, complete domination over both external and internal nature is the telos of traditional theory. However, since theoretical activity is circumscribed by the division of labor within society as a whole, its end, which is the complete domination of its object, is concealed from it: "In this view of theory, therefore, the real social function of science is not made manifest. . . ."[20] Herein lies its greatest fault; traditional theory's unreflexive attitude towards its own function encourages a conservative approach to the increase in knowledge. The traditional conception of theory can now be seen as a single moment in the total process of enlightenment: "To the extent that [traditional theory] conceives of reason as actually determining the course of events in a future society, such a hypostatization of Logos as reality is also a camouflaged utopia. In fact, however, the self-knowledge of present-day man is not a mathematical knowledge of nature which claims to be the eternal Logos, but a critical theory of society as it is, a theory dominated at every turn by a concern for reasonable conditions of life."[21] Traditional theory needs to be replaced by a conception of theory that is progressive, and self-reflective concerning its grounding in the social world; this Horkheimer refers to as "critical theory."

The unavoidable social character of scientific inquiry, however, does not invalidate the knowledge it produces. Horkheimer argues that a more adequate theory necessarily will be a social theory and critical; that is, it will be scientific, yet also actively reflective about its own social origins and functions, and about the consequences of this social character. The key flaw of traditional theory is that it absolutizes the positivistic notion of theory such that it appears to be immanent in the very nature of knowledge as such. Once the social function of theory is recognized (and critically engaged), then the validity of the positivist concept of theory is undermined. But this need not result in a loss of confidence in empirical research. On the contrary, empirical knowledge that has been critically engaged by social critique can be considered to be more valid than it is within traditional theory. An important consequence for theorists, though, is that theory construction must remain an open-ended process, such that critical theories possess an irremediably hypothetical status.

Horkheimer argues that an adequate conception of critical theory could not be successfully co-opted by society in the way that traditional theory is co-opted. A critical theory of society takes society as a whole as its object, and doing so involves the recognition that the totality of the world, that is, the objects of science, are themselves a product of social activity: "The facts which our senses present to us are socially preformed in two ways: through the historical character of the object perceived and through the historical character of the perceiving organ."[22] For example, we have learned to distinguish and recognize the sounds of grammatically structured propositional speech, just as phonemes developed into distinct units. Moreover, the relationship between these two ways that facts are conditioned is dynamic. The categories of our understanding are historically conditioned, while at the same time the objects of our perception are in part socially constructed. As Horkheimer claims, even facts about the natural world are categorized as natural only by contrast to the category of the social. Horkheimer concludes that the unconscious consequences of individual human action determine (in part) both the subjective moment and the objective moment of perception. A critical theory of society does not want to overthrow the traditional conception of theory, rather it simply wants to expose that conception as overly simplistic and incomplete. Traditional theory is incomplete precisely because it hypostatizes aspects of social life that are only moments in a more complex historical process. Action based on these hypostatized moments, then, cannot fulfill the conditions of rational action, since that action is based on a distorted (ideological) understanding of social reality. A more adequate social theory would still be scientific, but it also would be self-reflective.

According to Horkheimer, the concept of a critical theory of society can be characterized as a sociohistorically informed *critical theory of the present.* The aim of critical social theory is to achieve a comprehensive understanding of the present social order, such that social action can be oriented in a rational manner. This involves: (1) a theory's reflecting on its own social origins and function in the present order; and (2) aiming for an adequate theory of the social order, without attempting to achieve a closed theoretical system. The purpose of critical social theory is practical, to change present social conditions—and its methods are both philosophical and empirical.

Since the aims of this study are analytical and systematic rather than historical, I will attempt to generalize from Horkheimer's specific discussions to a general concept of critical social theory. The analysis that follows is intended to distill out the essential features of the idea of critical social theory. The essential features that are implied by Horkheimer's early writings are:

1. The objective of a critical social theory is a comprehensive, open history of present social conditions.
2. The purpose of a critical social theory is to rationally orient social action in order to change present social conditions with the intent to reduce unnecessary domination.
3. A critical social theory is critical in the sense that it reflects on the social conditions of its own formation.
4. The methods of a critical social theory involve a dialectical synthesis of philosophical and empirical approaches.

To say that a critical theory of society is a history of the present means that, at the most basic level, it constitutes a historically sensitive explanation of the origins and prior development of the normative structures and institutions of the present social order; that is, it seeks to answer the question, How did the elements of our present society historically develop into their present form? This involves reflecting upon the social conditions and functions of theories and concepts.[23]

Critical social theory attempts to generate a comprehensive explanation of the historical development of the present social order. But it is explicitly open-ended, and so does not constitute a closed theoretical system; also, the unavoidably historical situatedness of critical social theory itself implies at least that it is open and fallible, in the sense that its representations of the history of the present and its normative orientations are always and interminably open to revision based on new evidence, perspectives and arguments. Thus, critical social theories should always be seen as ongoing accomplishments of self-reflective social agents.

The openness of critical theory of society will become especially important in my discussions of both Habermas's unique conception of critical theory and his theory of social evolution. He is often misinterpreted as offering transcendental groundings for his critiques. While this interpretation may be justified with respect to his earlier work—especially *Knowledge and Human Interests*, where he asserts a "quasi-transcendental" grounding for the knowledge-constitutive human interests—it is not justified with respect to his work since the early seventies.[24]

Despite Habermas's propensity to construct systematic theories (including the theory of social evolution), he reminds his readers that these are emphatically programmatic, meaning that they are intended to serve as frameworks for empirical research. Their ultimate justification rests solely on their usefulness in our projects of self-realization and self-determination, and also in their fruitfulness for organizing empirical research.

Further, the open-endedness of critical social theory suggests the practical orientation central to the concept of critical theory. As Horkheimer reminds us, the proper aim of Marxism (of which critical theory is a variation) is "the transformation of specific social conditions, not knowledge of a "totality" or of a total or absolute truth."[25] Critical social theory does not simply desire to describe and explain the present social order; its primary intention is to change social conditions such that the unnecessary domination inherent in those conditions is reduced and eliminated. This practical interest that is a formal property of a critical theory of society is expressed in norms and ideals, which possess a regulative, rather than a constitutive, function. Norms and ideals provide the normative orientation for the critical theory in such a way that they "serve to guide and evaluate thought and action and not to represent realized or realizable states of affairs."[26] Thus, a critical social theory does not necessarily seek to describe a utopia; it seeks to critique the present state of affairs with the aim of improving those conditions.[27]

A critical theory of society is more than just an historical description or explanation of the present. It is a critical theory of the present in the sense that it also consists of a reflection on its own sociohistorical conditions. A critical theory of society explicitly considers and accounts for its own development and its function in the social order. Nevertheless, to avoid a nonrational decisionism, it seeks to rationally ground its claims such that they possess universal (but not necessary) validity.

Finally, critical social theory proceeds through a dialectic interplay between philosophical and empirical methods. Neither alone is sufficient to generate a critical theory of the present. On the one hand, exclusive reliance on philosophical methods leads to speculative metaphysical theories that lack even the possibility of empirical confirmation or falsification. On the other hand, exclusive reliance on empirical methods leads to a fetishization of facts and an unreflective, and hence uncritical, theoretical process that tends more to support the present social order than to change it. A mediation of the speculative tendency of philosophy and the conservative tendency of empirical science is necessary to achieve an adequate theory of the present that is both empirically grounded and critical.

To conclude, where traditional theory (in both the natural and social sciences) aims at improving the functional efficiency of particular subsystems of the current social formation, critical theory takes as its object the current social formation as a whole. It seeks to illuminate the individual's real relationship to society: "Critical thinking is the function neither of the isolated individual nor of a sum-total of individuals. Its subject is rather a definite individual in his real relation to other individuals and groups, in his conflict with a particular class, and, finally, in the resultant web of relationships with the social totality and with nature."[28] The goal of critical theory is emancipation from ideological representations of these relationships, in contrast to the goal of traditional theory, which is domination (of both inner and outer nature). To be sure, this does not mean that the critical theorist has nothing to learn from previous thinkers. The critical theorist proceeds dialectically, seeking to preserve the moment of truth in prior thought, and rejecting what is false or ideological, for critical theory's aim is to unmask ideology in order that the individual, in her real relationships within society, can make fully conscious decisions.

Perhaps the most distinctive feature of critical social theory is the attempt to combine the normative orientation of social philosophy and the empirical orientation of the social sciences.[29] But critical social theory's attempt to encompass both descriptive and evaluative approaches generates the problem of the justification of its normative claims. This problem derives from the attempt to ground the normative orientation of critical social theory in a rational manner. More specifically, this problem can be formulated in the following way: How can a critical social theory ground its normative orientation in such a way that it is intersubjectively justified, and yet neither foundationalist nor relativist? In what follows, I will argue that by adopting an historical framework that can distinguish between progressive and regressive social change, critical social theory can rationally ground its normative orientation while avoiding both foundationalism and relativism (I shall discuss the disadvantages of foundationalism and relativism below). The phrase "progressive social change" as I use it here refers to directional changes in structures of social relations that increase the degree of, or capacity for, some specified human value or values. I am not assuming here any particular conception of progress; that is, I do not specify which value or values are the criteria of progress, only that some conception of progress is warranted. Here my aim is not to justify a particular conception of progress; I am arguing only that the satisfaction of the systematic claims of critical social theory requires some theoretical conception of progressive social change. Moreover, I want to suggest that it is not the case that merely adopting an historical framework of this type is one way that critical theory can satisfy its own intentions. I will also argue that for a conception of critical social theory to adequately satisfy its intentions, it must adopt an historical framework that gives an account of progressive social change. To be sure, the burden of proof for this stronger claim is substantial. Rather than providing a comprehensive defense of this claim, which would be beyond the scope of the present study, I will suggest some promising lines of argument that might be pursued in its support.

The question of how we can rationally justify social critique presupposes that rational justification in social theory is possible. But do the normative claims of social critique admit of rational justification? Critical social theory, of course, assumes that they do, but we need to justify this claim before we can go on to discuss how they can be justified.[30] The normative claims of social critique concern the norms and structures of society; hence they involve the individuals of a given society in their social relations to each other. In the modern era, however, factual propositions are typically distinguished from normative propositions. One way to understand critical social theory is that it aims to reintegrate these empirical and normative moments of practices of social thought that have become distinguished in modern history. That is, critical social theory wants to overcome the modern distinction between "is" and "ought." Despite the efforts of critical social theory to overcome the distinction in practice between fact and value, that is, between "is" and "ought," this distinction is a theoretical presupposition of social critique, since questions of the normative justification of given social norms only arise when conventional justification is no longer recognized as foundational: "[A]n ethical question first exists when the agreement of actions with the factually valid norms of a society are no longer recognized as the final instance of a 'justification' of these actions."[31] Thus, the is/ought distinction must still be made at a higher level of analysis when considering the justification of social norms. By this, I mean that we can (and should, when performing social critique) distinguish between de facto social norms that are justified merely by appeal to convention from social norms that are legitimately valid (TCA I, 287). In contrast to conventional norms, legitimate social norms deserve to be recognized as valid, hence implying the possibility of their being rationally justified. The practice of social critique, then, is interested in the legitimacy of preexisting social norms, that is, whether or not they are rationally justifiable.

Typically, social theorists respond to the question of the legitimacy of social norms in one of two fundamentally opposed ways. On the one hand, those who believe in the validity of the application of reason in practical matters enter into argumentation regarding the proper form justification of social norms should take. On the other hand, those who have rejected the validity of the notion of practical reason argue that social norms cannot be rationally justified. These skeptics typically argue that we cannot distinguish legitimate from illegitimate social norms (at least insofar as legitimacy makes reference to some notion of rational justification), because that very distinction presupposes an idea of practical reason that they reject. They argue that we need methods other than rational argumentation, such as genealogical critique, to identify those social norms that have repressive consequences. This is an important debate in contemporary philosophy and it will not be settled here. Nevertheless, I agree with those defenders of practical reason who maintain that norms and values are open to rational justification. So if a social theorist wants to practice social critique, then that social theorist must, when challenged, present and defend arguments in support of the normative claims necessarily embedded within the critique. Thus, assuming that norms and values can be rationally justified, the very practice of social critique pragmatically requires the use of some conception of reason, such that social critique necessarily involves practical reason.

To choose to abstain from rational argumentation with respect to social critique can have various results. Perhaps those skeptics who recognize and accept the lack of a possible rational justification for sociocritical claims simply refrain from engaging in social critique. Typically, however, the denial of the possibility of rational justification of norms does not prevent socially conscious individuals from practicing social critique. Many skeptical social critics (such as Rorty, or Foucault) will formulate a critique but justify it only on the basis of intuitive insight, or by reference to the norms of a tradition or culture, thus leaving the normative justification of that critique unexamined. This, of course, is little more than mere opinion, which some social critics have asserted is a perfectly legitimate mode of social criticism. Furthermore, many (if not all) of these socially conscious skeptics do engage in reasoned argumentation about the possibilities and limitations of the practice of social critique. The consequence is that they are caught in what Habermas has labeled a "performative contradiction." An agent commits a performative contradiction when asserting "a constative speech act *k(p)* [which] rests on noncontingent presuppositions whose propositional content contradicts the asserted proposition *p*" (MCCA, 80). Hence, if skeptics intend to practice social critique, then, if challenged, they must (in a pragmatic sense) enter into a process of rational argumentation in order to justify the normativity of their critique. This is not, however, an a priori claim about a metaphysical necessity. The claim that the practice of social critique necessarily involves normative claims that require justification is based upon the unavoidable (for us, here and now) pragmatic presuppositions of communication. Thus, I will adopt the position that in order to engage in social critique, one must make use of some conception of rational justification.

But what does it mean to rationally justify a normative claim? At a general level, the process of rational justification involves the giving and evaluating of reasons that purportedly support the claim that has been advanced. Following Toulmin and others' analysis, there are four basic elements involved in a justificatory argument: there is the *claim* in need of justification, the *grounds* that delimit the facts of the situation, the *warrant* that is the rule of inference from the grounds to the conclusion, and the *backing* from which the warrant is inferred.[32] There are two implications of this analysis that I am interested in here. First, the formal-pragmatic structure of the practice of rational justification involves the assertion of a claim and the giving and evaluation of reasons in support of that claim. So whether it is the validity of the facts of the case under consideration (the grounds), or the inference (the warrant), or the support (the backing) that is contested, the only way to make the case is by presenting further arguments with the same pragmatic structure in support of the contested claim. Second, I am interested in the various types of backing that are appealed to when asserting normative claims. So if the backing is conventional, say, "Given the present-day understanding of what the demands of equity in human relations require," and it is contested, the proponent might argue either that convention constitutes the final standard with respect to normative claims, or that there is a further standard to which we can appeal.[33]

Now there are various types of (final) backing that can be appealed to when making normative claims. To simplify matters somewhat, historically there have been two primary approaches regarding the (final) backing of social norms: foundationalism and skepticism.[34] The foundationalist appeals to a set of self-evident axioms from which the conclusion of the argument can be deductively derived. Don Herzog describes the salient features of foundationalist justification: "[A]ny political justification worthy of the name must be grounded on principles that are

(1) undeniable and immune to revision and (2) located outside society and politics."[35] In social theory this results in a form of foundationalism that claims to derive sociopolitical norms from a set of timeless and necessary first principles, for example a theory of human nature, or natural law.

The skeptic, on the other hand, rejects the very existence of foundational axioms. Skeptical arguments can take various forms, but perhaps the most popular currently is either cultural relativism or historicism. Cultural relativists take the position that sociopolitical norms can be justified only with reference to a particular culture, and that it is illegitimate to attempt to provide a justification for them that claims transcultural validity. Historicists take a parallel position, arguing that sociopolitical norms can be justified only with reference to a particular historical time frame, and that no sociopolitical norms can be legitimately justified transhistorically. To be sure, this is an oversimplification of the issues involved and of the possible positions with respect to normative justification. Nevertheless, it is adequate for my aims, since it represents the extreme antithetical forms of justification in contemporary sociopolitical theory. The truly challenging question facing the critical social theorist is whether a form of justification can be conceived that avoids these two extremes.

As I have indicated, the idea of a critical social theory has at its core a fundamental tension that derives from the intention of critical social theory to generate a rational critique. This rationality refers to the rational justification of the normative orientation of critique, and rational justification is fulfilled by the giving and the accepting of reasons for normative claims in processes of argumentation.[36] The results of this justificatory process are (ideally) rational because they are based solely on reasons. The idea is that any social agent who possesses basic speaking and acting competencies would under ideal conditions be rationally convinced of the rightness of the norm being justified. The implication is that the results of processes of rational justification are universally valid. This is important for critical social theory, since the systematic intentions of critical social theory are such that the normative claims it generates are universally valid, where the claim is not justified from a merely particular, interested perspective, but from an impartial, third-person perspective. In other words, universally valid normative claims are justified from the moral point of view.

But how are we to conceive of this moral point of view if we accept the claim (as critical social theory does) that the contents of our ideas are historically conditioned? If the way that we, as thinking and acting beings, relate to the subjective, the social, and the objective worlds is unavoidably conditioned by our sociohistorical contexts, then how can we posit a moral point of view that escapes the relativism and historicism that seem to follow from this fact? As Stephen White lucidly describes the problem, it is one of justifying the standpoint of the social critic within history, that is without appealing to ahistorical, transcendental groundings: "[I]f the prescriptions of critical theory are historically conditioned along with those of bourgeois ideology, how can one set of prescriptions be defended as more valid or rational than the other?"[37]

The challenge for a critical social theory, then, is to rationally justify its own normative orientation while being reflective of its own sociohistorical embeddedness, and at the same time to avoid relativism. In this section I defend the following claim, which I call the "Relevancy Thesis" (RT). RT states that one way that a critical social theory can rationally (and universally) ground its normative claims while at the same time avoiding relativism and historicism is by offering a theoretical model of what would count as progressive social change. In other words, critical social theory can rationally justify its own normative claims by making reference to a theoretical model that explains progress in social relations. I want to set aside for the moment the problem of determining what is meant here by social "progress." No doubt this will prove to be a highly controversial issue, but for my present purposes, I want only to focus on the idea of a theoretical framework that can give some account of social progress however progress might be defined. I understand this theoretical model along the lines of a theory of social evolution.

The objection might be made that we do not need a theoretical model to accomplish this task. We can (according to this objection) perform a kind of piecemeal criticism that relies upon a less totalizing conception of progress. We know, for example, that oppressing a group of people in order to satisfy our own interests is unjust, and that any social change that reduces oppression should be considered progressive. This notion of piecemeal social critique, however, implies an implicit claim that the critiques it generates are universally valid. If there is no such claim attached, it is not clear how this form of social critique can avoid the charge of relativism, that is, that its claims are relative only to a particular perspective, and thus, at least potentially, ideological. On the other hand, if the piecemeal critic acknowledges the universal claim attached to his or her critiques, then a theoretical explication of what counts as progressive social change seems to be needed. For only by generating a theoretical model can we clarify just what is intended when we claim a specific change to be progressive.

Typically, in sociopolitical philosophy normative statements are grounded with reference to a concept of the person. This is what grounds Kant's moral and political philosophy, and what, as some have argued, grounds Rawls's theory of justice.[38] However, critical theory reflects on its own origins and recognizes that even our current conceptions of the person are historically conditioned. That is, our very conceptions of ourselves develop and change throughout history; for this reason there can be in principle no ahistorical concept that transcends history. So it seems that the obvious conclusion is that we also cannot make sociocritical judgments that are universal, that is, that transcend the historical process, and thus our sociocritical judgments are necessarily relative to our historical perspective. Further, this historicist position would seem to lack any claim to rationality and rationality's concomitant claim to universality.

I suggest that it is unwarranted to infer that we lack any rational grounds for social critique from the premise that we are inescapably historical beings. If it is possible to reconstruct the history of contemporary social structures, then we should be able to identify deformations that result in social pathologies. Also, by knowing the historical trajectories of currently existing social structures, we could also identify the undeveloped potentials inherent in them, and thus which changes in the future are preferable to others. This conceptual model of progressive social change, then, would provide us with the means to justify rationally the normative claims of legitimate social critique. In other words, it is my claim that a general theory of social evolution can adequately ground the normative orientation of social critique. This approach possesses the virtues of not making a foundational appeal to a transcendental grounding of norms, but it justifies a universalist critique that avoids relativism. Let me emphasize that this theory itself does not claim any sort of transcendental status; it is itself fallible and open to revision since it is itself historically conditioned as well. It is a reconstructive theory such that it only reconstructs past historical developments, and has no predictive power. The function of this social evolutionary framework is to provide an interpretation of the genealogy of our social order, and to provide intersubjectively valid (in the sense of being impartial) grounds for making normative claims about alternative orderings of social structures. That is, the theory of social evolution would describe the history of the development of our self-understandings, and in doing so it would provide grounds for making rational judgments concerning which changes are preferable to others.

The difficulty that immediately presents itself has to do with the construction of a legitimate social evolutionary framework that does not impose historically conditioned categories as rational ones. In other words, how can we specify what counts as progressive social change without engaging in revisionist history writing, and how can we be secure in the claim that our understanding of the past does not simply idealize the present as the pinnacle of history? The tradition of the philosophy of history is full of examples of this sort of triumphalism, in which the present social order is interpreted to be the highest achievement of human society. To be sure, critical theory does not naively celebrate the achievement of the present as the highest stage in history, rather it notes the failures of the present alongside of its achievements. The difficulty with philosophies of history relevant to the present discussion is that they claim to have access to a uniquely rational understanding of the historical process, and based on this they derive an explanation of progress in history. Yet this explanation of the progress of history itself transcends historical forces. It is supposed to be rational, and thus not a result of historical forces. A critical social theory, on the other hand, explicitly recognizes the historicity of even its own categories, and thus cannot claim unique access to an ideal of objective reason. How, then, can we conceive of social evolution such that it itself is not ahistorical? I suggest (following Habermas) that rather than adopting an external perspective with respect to progress in history, as has been done in various philosophies of history, we adopt an internal perspective in order to account for progressive social change. We should attempt to explicate the historical conditions of our present situation from within the historical process itself. The question then becomes, can we give an account of progressive social change from the perspective of the historical agents and still justify a claim of universality? Since my aim in this section is to argue for the relevance and necessity of a conception of progress to critical social theory, giving a substantive conception of progress is beyond its scope. I will suggest, however, that from the internal perspective of the social agents themselves, progressive social change appears as a learning process. So what critical social theory is in need of is an account of this learning process that explains social progress.

In my discussion above I have made a case for the relevance of the idea of progressive social change to critical social theory. But now I want to present arguments in defense of a stronger claim, what I call the "Necessity Thesis" (NT). NT states that any adequate critical social theory (that is, one that can rationally ground its normative orientation) must incorporate a theoretical model of what would count as progressive social change. The necessity of this claim is not a metaphysical necessity. It is a pragmatic necessity relating to the practice of social critique. That is, insofar as we engage in argumentative practices concerning social norms, and those practices embody certain pragmatic presuppositions, we cannot avoid relying upon a conception of progressive social change. As I mentioned above, I cannot here provide a comprehensive defense of this thesis; I can only suggest a few promising arguments in support of it. First, since both the object of investigation (social relations) and the categories by which we understand them are historically conditioned (that is, they are embedded within history), an adequate critical social theory cannot justify its normative orientation by appeal to ahistorical, transcendental grounds. The consequence is that since critical social theory is itself historically conditioned, the only way to justify its normative orientation is to give an account of the theory's own historicity. Second, it can be shown that the pragmatic structures of the performance of social critique are based on an assumption of progressive social change.

As Hegel has shown, it is a characteristic feature of modernity that we have become increasingly conscious of our embeddedness in history. It is also characteristic of modernity that we come to reflect upon our own rational capacities, and a consequence of this is that we have become increasingly conscious of our power to rationally direct (to some extent at least) the historical process.[39] Even if we do not make our own history consciously and in a rational manner, we do affect its course. Furthermore, if we have learned anything from the critique of reason that was initiated by Kant, and completed by Hegel, it is that the very categories of our understanding are historically conditioned. We have come to recognize that there are mental structures that determine how we understand the world and ourselves, and that these structures evolve in history. Whether the structures of understanding evolve for biological reasons, or as a result of processes of social evolution, we have no good reasons to believe that these structures are ahistorical.[40]

This claim is supported by the linguistic turn in philosophy, in which we have come to appreciate the implications of the fact that humans interact with each other by means of symbols that represent meanings. Though the medium that dominates social interaction is language, other media carry meanings as well. The meanings carried by linguistic symbols, however, are ambiguous, so interpretation is required to understand their meanings. The consequence is that the nature of the object of social theory requires a hermeneutic methodology in order to understand social phenomena. But hermeneutics' fundamental principle is that the investigator brings his or her own worldview and set of beliefs to the interpretive situation, and thus can only understand a symbol relative to his or her own meaningful history. Thus, hermeneutic methodology results in contextualism, where the understanding of the symbolically mediated social world is relative to the self-understanding of the interpreter. So not only do humans make their own history, but the categories of thought by which we can understand that history are themselves historical. The unavoidable historicity of both the object (society) and the subject (human understanding) of our social existence demands that any adequate understanding of the social would take into account this historicity. It is not adequate, however, to merely acknowledge the historicity of both the subject and the object. Although critical social theory accepts the premise of the historicity of both the subject and object of social inquiry, an adequate critical social theory, in order to be critical, would need to be capable of distinguishing between progressive and regressive historical change. If critical social theory did not possess this capacity, then it would not be able to distinguish better from worse social orderings, as determined by some impartial means.[41] Critical social theory would be forced to become decisionistic, in the sense that once alternative historical paths were described, we could only choose between them. That is, there would be no principle of choice to which we could appeal. Perhaps in the end this is all that we can do. But for now, if we want to practice rational social critique, then we need to search for a criterion or a set of criteria that can ground a rational choice between alternative futures. For a critical social theory to achieve its ends, it must incorporate an account of progressive social change.

My second argument is a pragmatic analysis of social critique. I argue that the structure of the very performance of critique implies a notion of progressive social change. A social critic by definition aspires to do more than describe a given society or its parts. Social critics intend to critique the perceived injustice inherent in a particular social order. The statements of social critique, in criticizing the injustice of some social object, imply a more just ordering of social relations.[42] In pointing out the injustice present in social order A, the social critic implies that there exist possible alternative social orders, B, C, D, and so on some of which are better than social order A.[43] In what way some are better is not important here (they might be less unjust, or less oppressive), but what is important is the implication contained in the critique that real alternatives are possible. If social critics assert that in critiquing existing social conditions they do not mean to imply the existence of real alternatives, then their critical propositions are vacuous. Or, if social critics claim that their aim is merely to prevent conditions from worsening, then there is no implication of a better alternative. To begin, this notion of social critique explicitly relies upon a philosophy of history, for it relies upon the claim that progress is impossible. Given our current justificatory criteria, it is difficult to see how this philosophy of history could be justified with acceptable reasons. Furthermore, it is not clear in what sense this is social critique. At the most it is an extremely thin conception of critique, and at the least it is simply empty. Perhaps, though, they would concede that while their social critique implies the possibility of alternative orderings of social relations it does not take a normative position with respect to any one of those possible alternatives. This is a common claim among poststructuralists and postmodernists, who typically claim that social critique can best be understood as merely pointing out the injustices within existing social conditions, with no pretensions to making prescriptive claims. This seems mistaken from both internal and external perspectives.

Assuming with Marx that the point is not simply to interpret the world, but to change it, then the fundamental motivation of social critique is to reduce social injustice. It seems rather incoherent for social critics to claim that they perform social critique without any intention at all of reducing social injustice. Thus, internally the actual performance of public social criticism—that is, social criticism that is performed in the public sphere, and not done only privately—tacitly assumes the possibility of theoretically distinguishing between progressive and regressive social change. When one performs social criticism by expressing to a public some criticism of a social phenomenon, and subsequently gives reasons in defense of that assertion, there is a pragmatic assumption presupposed. Social critics engage in public discourse about social injustice with at least the implicit purpose of eliminating or reducing that injustice or oppression (or motivating others to do so), and changing social structures to eliminate or reduce injustice or oppression necessitates some understanding of the potentials and limitations of concrete social change. In order for us to reduce injustice, we need to know what the present social formation allows in the form of change, both in the sense of what the potentials contained by the present social order are, and what the limitations are that condition social change as set by the structure of the present social order. So despite the intentions of some social critics, the objective act of engaging in social critique implies at the least the possibility of progressive social change.[44] This holds for any conception of progress, so for the purposes of this argument it is not necessary to be more specific about what counts as progress at this point.

From an external perspective, the statements of social criticism are explicitly prescriptive. This means that in stating what ought to be the case, they imply that concrete social change for the better is at least possible. Publicly asserted statements of social criticism possess a normative function. Whatever the intentions of the critic, they are understood by others as prescriptive statements about present social conditions, whether or not the critic intended them that way. Statements of social criticism possess both negative and positive aspects; they negate the social order under investigation, while implying that real alternatives exist. So the statements of social criticism themselves make reference implicitly to some notion of progressive social change.

Critical Hermeneutics

While Habermas has been famously criticized for his defense of the power of reason, he has also been criticized for not taking history seriously enough.[45] David Hoy has argued that Habermas's move towards Kantianism and the accompanying "transcendental turn" led Habermas into a "transcendental narcissism" in which he claims a special status for the justification of his own theory. The implication of this transcendental narcissism is that the seriousness of Habermas's commitment to taking history seriously is brought into question. Although I would dispute Hoy's critique of Habermas, the question I want to examine here is whether it isn't possible to take history too seriously. According to Hoy, "[T]he primary intention of [hermeneutics] is to take history seriously," and "[f]rom Foucault's and Gadamer's points of view . . . Habermas has not taken history and a self-transforming, hermeneutical reflection seriously enough."[46] For Hoy, the choice seems to be between either a transcendental narcissism in which one's own theory is grounded in an ahistorical way, or a thoroughgoing historicism in which even one's own critical reflections are historically situated and radically contingent. In rejecting the first Hoy opts for the second, yet he claims that the historicism of hermeneutic reflection does not entail an invidious relativism. Hoy remains unclear, however, concerning how hermeneutic reflection avoids this invidious relativism, in part, I will argue, because he refuses to clarify the normative assumptions presupposed by hermeneutic reflection. Hoy is concerned to defend a conception of hermeneutics that is reflective only in the sense that it opens up the possibility for alternative self-understandings. But this limited understanding of hermeneutic reflection takes history too seriously because the generation of alternative self-understandings does not constitute an adequate form of social critique.

In order to gain a clear understanding of Hoy's conception of hermeneutic reflection it will be useful to look at his more recent debate with Thomas McCarthy over the proper conception of critical social theory.[47] In this debate Hoy articulates and defends a form of hermeneutic reflection that he calls "genealogical hermeneutics." Against McCarthy's more universalistic, and in Hoy's view ahistoricist, conception of critical theory, Hoy formulates a situated conception of social critique the primary virtue of which is its emphatic rejection of the universalizing tendencies of traditional theory. A primary objection that Hoy makes against the standard Frankfurt School conception of an interdisciplinary critical social theory is that it is preoccupied with theory, especially with a theory about what constitutes an adequate critical theory. By contrast, he claims that self-described critical theorists can engage in critical activity that is fully adequate without being in possession of a critical theory per se. He asks, "What makes a theory 'critical'? To be critical must one have a theory?"[48] He suggests that one need not have a theory to engage in the practice of social critique. Moreover, he argues that the very idea of a critical theory is in tension, since not only can we engage in social critique without a theory, but having a theory of social critique only hinders the practice of critical activity. He proposes that rather than constructing a metatheory about how theories can be critical, we should engage directly in critical activity, which he conceives as a critical history. Thus, he argues, "[W]hat is needed is the more concrete practice of critical *history*, that is, genealogical critiques of the specific, concrete ways in which we have been socialized subliminally."[49]

Although Hoy is especially concerned to emphasize that his conception of critical social theory, genealogical hermeneutics, is not a form of theory in any traditional sense, he objects to the application of the term "theory" to his critical history primarily because he conceives of theory in a hypostatized manner. As he argues earlier in his discussion, he does not see a qualitative difference between traditional and critical theory, at least as Max Horkheimer has drawn the distinction.[50] According to Hoy, Horkheimer's conception of the theoretical character of critical theory is found in its comparison of a totalizing comprehension of society with a more rationally organized possible social order. On this interpretation, social theories are totalizing and utopian, and Hoy objects to both of these characteristics. He argues that we can engage in critical activity without constructing totalizing social theories, that is, social theories that do not purport to explain systematically the totality of social relations and processes, and without postulating some utopian social order. Moreover, he argues that both of these characteristics of critical social theory (as they were formulated by Horkheimer) contradict, or at least are in tension with, the goals of social critique. Totalizing social theories typically distort social reality in their representation of it, and thus they legitimate ideological self-understandings. And projections of utopias can also mask ideological self-understandings, since they are often based on essentialist conceptions of the person. Thus Hoy concludes that elevating critical activity to critical theory is neither necessary nor desirable.

The difficulty with this argument is that Hoy appears to conceive of theory in a traditional, scientistic sense. He seems to not fully appreciate that which is distinctive about critical theory, as opposed to traditional theory: its reflexivity. Critical theory explicitly reflects upon its own social origins and social function. Assuming that we are in possession of a conception of critical social theory that adequately accomplishes this task, there is no reason to think that this conception of (critical) theory would unavoidably mask ideological distortions. To be sure, any social theory will contain distortions, but if the theory is critical in the sense of being self-reflective, those distortions themselves are at least open to being revealed. Moreover, it is far from clear how a critical history, as distinct from a critical theory, avoids this concern.

In contradistinction to traditional theory as Hoy conceives it, genealogical hermeneutics is conceived to be a critical methodology that operates by tracing the genealogies of concrete concepts, discourses, and understandings in order to unmask the contingency and arbitrariness of our self-understandings. For Hoy the essential difference between this conception and the traditional conception of critical theory defended by McCarthy and Habermas is that genealogical hermeneutics does not "construe itself as seeing through illusions and showing us how society really is."[51] It does not claim to generate disenchantment; it only seeks to illuminate our self-understandings as essentially contingent. It performs this task by formulating and constructing new perspectives from which we can understand ourselves, and as such it also presents alternative self-understandings.

On this understanding of genealogical hermeneutics, however, we would seem to be left with an invidious relativism of self-understandings with no principled way to choose between them. As Hoy notes in "Taking History Seriously," "both change and proliferation [of interpretations] are not necessarily for the better."[52] But Hoy has not made clear how the social critic who engages in genealogical hermeneutic inquiry might choose between the plurality of self-understandings that such a methodology generates. Nonetheless, Hoy seems to suggest that genealogical hermeneutics does offer at least some normative resources for assessing the relative value of alternative self-understandings, for he maintains that

> [a]long the way it may be unmasking previous interpretations. Since what is unmasked is self-interpretation, this unmasking through genealogical critical history can now be seen not simply in traditional epistemological terms as "revealing reality," but also modally as "deconstructing necessity." That is, genealogical research will show that self-understandings that are taken as universal, eternal and necessary have a history, with a beginning, and therefore, possibly, an end. Genealogy thus shows that self-understandings are interpretations, and it can bring us to suspect that conceptions of ourselves that we have taken to be necessary are only contingent. In making this contingency manifest, genealogy makes it possible for people to see that they could want to be different from how they are.[53]

But what is it that genealogical hermeneutics unmasks? Does it simply unmask the fact that our self-understandings are social and historical constructs and thus contingent and not necessary? Or does it unmask the truth about our self-understandings? Hoy expressly allows for both interpretations in the paragraph just quoted, so it is clear that despite Hoy's earlier claim to the contrary, genealogical hermeneutics does in fact seek to reveal our self-understandings as false or illusory and replace them with better, truer, less distorted self-interpretations.

These considerations point out what I see as a fundamental tension in Hoy's conception of critical theory, the tension between the refusal of genealogical hermeneutics to clarify or attempt to theoretically justify its normative stance and the unacknowledged yet unavoidable normative assumptions that are necessary for any practice of social criticism. This tension becomes manifest when Hoy attempts to explicate how genealogical hermeneutics is critical. For genealogical hermeneutics, the goal is no longer emancipation from oppressive social conditions; rather it is "inquiry," where inquiry is "the reinterpretation of what was already an interpretation."[54] But he is quick to note that this is not simply an agonistic model of argumentation in which the best argument wins. Instead, the goal of genealogical hermeneutics is to find "new descriptions of ourselves that locate new possibilities in our situation."[55] Given the description so far, it is not clear in what sense genealogical hermeneutics is a form of social critique since there is no attempt to integrate any sort of a normative stance with respect to the various self-understandings that have been generated.

The normativity of genealogical hermeneutics, however, is not absent; it simply has the status of an unacknowledged assumption. For Hoy goes on to state that "[t]hese reinterpretations [generated by genealogical hermeneutics] may even change what the premises are, . . . good interpretation can alter our conception of what is to be argued and what our premises mean."[56] This, of course, begs the question of what counts as a good interpretation: what are the standards for assessing the proffered interpretations? The giving of an adequate account of these standards will require more than mere critical activity; it will require a critical theory, that is, a theory that is self-reflective on its own conditions. Since genealogical hermeneutics is nothing more than a critical activity, it essentially lacks the capacity for self-reflection; it must simply assume some such standards for distinguishing those interpretations that are good and emancipatory from those that are bad and oppressive. It is this cryptonormativity that I find so troubling in Hoy's conception of critical social theory.

Another way to put this objection is that genealogical hermeneutics is ambiguous as to what role an account of sociocultural learning plays in the conception. Presumably Hoy thinks that sociocultural learning takes place when bad, or distorted, interpretations are replaced by good, or less distorted, ones. As I have argued, genealogical hermeneutics implicitly presupposes some idea of learning while explicitly rejecting it. Genealogical hermeneutics, as Hoy has described it, simply generates the possibility of alternative self-interpretations. To be sure, this is a necessary function of a critical social theory, but it certainly is not sufficient. Merely unmasking distorted self-interpretations does not in itself generate concrete alternative self-understandings. Indeed, describing the hermeneutic process as one in which distorted interpretations are unmasked implies a normative account of what count as undistorted interpretations. But Hoy's account of genealogical hermeneutics lacks the normative basis to justify this description of its own activities. The consequence is that genealogical hermeneutics does not, and cannot, justify its normative stance regarding which of the alternative self-understandings is to be preferred: it provides no normative orientation that is generative of emancipation. Without this normative guidance, genealogical hermeneutics is a hollow methodology that only abstractly negates its object.

But, as I have argued, genealogical hermeneutics does not, in the hands of Hoy, function in this manner. It does not simply abstractly negate given self-understandings, because it does imply that its own methods generate emancipation; after all, Hoy formulates this conception in the context of a debate concerning the proper understanding of critical social theory. Genealogical hermeneutics is supposed to simply generate the critical space for alternative self-understandings, yet Hoy asserts that we cannot choose to go back to unmasked self-understandings; they "are not real *alternatives* for us. . . ."[57] Once again the normative assumptions of genealogical hermeneutics are made manifest. Why are these unmasked self-understandings not real alternatives for us? Hoy is here relying on the ambiguity of the term "unmasked," for here he clearly means more than that the contingency of the self-understandings is revealed; he means that they are also revealed to be distorted, that is, deficient in some way. By asserting that genealogical hermeneutics reveals these self-understandings to be deficient, the unacknowledged normative assumptions of Hoy's project come to the surface. But since Hoy wants to maintain that genealogical hermeneutics only generates possible alternative self-understandings without making any normative judgments as to their quality, what prevents us from choosing an unmasked self-understanding over an alternative? When we come to understand the deformations inherent in a particular self-understanding, the deformed self-understanding does not present its deformity in some self-evident way. Rather, we recognize the deformed self-understanding as deformed only because we compare it to some normative standard. The normative orientations and values that are implicit in the background lifeworld in which we are all embedded color our perception of the unmasked, deformed self-understanding as deformed. Thus, the rejection of the unmasked, deformed self-understanding is grounded in a background framework according to which we order alternative self-understandings. Thus, Hoy's understanding of genealogical hermeneutics presupposes some notion of sociocultural learning, since he intimates that we emancipate ourselves from distorted self-understandings by seeing them as distorted, and thus deficient.

If the previous considerations have been persuasive, then it should be apparent that any adequate conception of critical social theory will necessarily be theoretical; it cannot be conceived simply as a critical activity, for an adequate critical social theory must be self-reflective, and while critical activity reflects upon its object, it does not reflect upon its own conditions. What this means in practice is that an adequate critical social theory will need to make essential reference to a critical theory of social change that can account for both what has been gained and what has been lost in processes of historical transformation. To be sure, this does not mean that we appeal to a philosophy of history, nor even to a theory of history. A critical theory of social change is a reconstructive science that seeks to uncover the deep sociohistorical structures that condition and shape historical change, and as such it is open and fallible. Thus, a critical theory of social change will engage in genealogical hermeneutics, but it will not conflate critical social theory as such with this critical activity. Hoy's conception of genealogical hermeneutics is a valuable instrument for social criticism, but it cannot function as an adequate critical social theory because it does not reflect upon its own normative assumptions, and this is a necessary condition of any adequate critical social theory.

Summary

In this first chapter I have examined the role that a notion of progress plays in the very idea of a critical social theory. I have argued on the basis of Horkheimer's early formulations of critical theory that such a notion is an essential part of any adequate critical theory. I further substantiated this claim by critically engaging the claims of critical hermeneutics, which shares the purpose of social critique with critical theory, but without, or so it claims, resorting to reifying theoretical constructs. I argued that critical hermeneutics implicitly presupposes a conception of progress, and that its refusal to make this explicit amounts to a dogmatism that is at odds with the fundamental self-reflective nature of critical theory. To further set the grounds for my inquiry into Habermas's theory of social evolution, in the next chapter I will sketch an overview of Habermas's conception of critical social theory. Part of my argument in this study is that this theory is an essential part of Habermas's critical theory, and that one cannot fully comprehend his critical theory on the basis only of the formal pragmatics of language. To warrant this claim I need to show carefully how his critical theory necessarily relies on a conception of progressive social change.

Chapter 2

Habermas's Conception of Critical Social Theory

In this chapter I will present a comprehensive overview of Habermas's mature conception of critical social theory. This serves a twofold purpose: first, a general understanding of Habermas's conception of critical social theory is key for my later inquiry into his theory of social evolution, since the theory of social evolution is an integral part of any adequate critical social theory (or so I will argue). Second, I want to emphasize the fundamental role that the theory of social evolution plays in Habermas's theory. This is important because this role is often overlooked or underemphasized in the secondary literature on Habermas. One reason for this, I believe, is that the focus of Habermas's *Theory of Communicative Action* (TCA I and II) is a bit confusing, and the rather unique organization of the book contributes to this confusion. Although the project of clarifying the normative foundations of critical social theory was a primary theoretical concern of Habermas's for two decades, I am here interested only in his mature statements that were developed throughout the 1970s and were systematized in his magnum opus, *The Theory of Communicative Action*, originally published in 1981. During this period his approach to the reconstruction of the normative foundations of critical social theory was explicitly guided by Horkheimer's original concept of a critical theory of society. In Horkheimer's early writings he found the intention of an interdisciplinary research program that utilizes the resources and methods of both sociopolitical philosophy and the empirical social sciences. Thus, it is worthwhile to keep in mind that Habermas does not claim to be constructing a completed theoretical statement of critical social theory. He attempts to construct a comprehensive, and open—hence, not totalizing—critical theory of society; he intends to be only programmatically elucidating the outlines of a critical social theory, the contents of which are intended to be further clarified and analyzed at both the theoretical and empirical levels. The programmatic framework itself is intended to be tested, clarified, and revised based on the results of further empirical research that is itself guided by the theoretical framework. In this respect, Habermas adopts Horkheimer's concept of a critical theory that is fallible. Habermas asserts that he is not providing a transcendental justification for critical theory, but that the ultimate validity of this particular conception rests on further empirical research that serves to illuminate various aspects.

Before discussing the details of Habermas's particular conception of critical social theory, it will be useful to begin with a sketch of its general contours in order to provide a general sense of the theoretical and conceptual terrain. Habermas's conception of critical social theory consists of two theoretical dimensions or frameworks: the synchronic and the diachronic. Both frameworks are necessary to adequately ground the normative claims of critical social theory. On this view, society in general can be viewed as being structured in both the horizontal, or synchronic, dimension and the vertical, or diachronic, dimension. For a critical social theory to justify its normative claims, it would need to provide an account of its normative grounding in each of these dimensions. Only by attending to both of these dimensions can critical theory ground its descriptive and prescriptive claims.

The synchronic framework provides a horizontal structural explanation of society, relying especially on a theory of communicative action which reconstructs the universal features of language use that are intuitively known by all competent speakers. Habermas's theory of communicative action postulates an idealizing component universally presupposed in grammatically structured speech, and this idealizing component provides a grounding for part of the normative orientation for critical theory. The normative orientation derives from the gap between the idealizing presuppositions implicit in language use and a comparison of these idealizing presuppositions with concrete discursive practices. The theory of communicative action is intended to explain the intuitive, pragmatic know-how of fully competent speakers. But Hegel impressed upon us the need to give an account of the historical character of consciousness. For this reason, the theory of communicative action needs to be complemented by an explanation of how these structures or competencies can change in the course of history.

Thus, the theory of communicative action needs to be complemented by a diachronic framework that explains the historical development of these universal features of language use. The theory of social evolution functions as this diachronic framework by explaining both the reproduction of society and how structures of consciousness undergo change. As we will see below, Habermas postulates that the structures of consciousness that determine the horizons of knowledge change according to a developmental logic, and that all societies share that same formal developmental logic of social change. Thus, the theory of social evolution involves a reconstruction of the universal stages of social development, and it interprets these stages as stages of a sociocultural learning process. It further distinguishes between the logic of development and the dynamics of development, so that while the logic of development is universal, the actual historical paths taken by societies are uniquely determined by contingent conditions.

The two frameworks are related such that the universal formal-pragmatic structure of speech that grounds the rationality inherent in communication gradually becomes realized in social institutions and practices in the course of historical development. From both the synchronic and diachronic frameworks, then, the normative orientation of critical theory can be justified both universally (that is, cross-culturally) and genetically (that is, historically).

Formal Pragmatics

The element of Habermas's critical social theory that has received the most critical attention by social and political philosophers is the theory of the formal pragmatics of language. As I mentioned above, the intent of *The Theory of Communicative Action* is perhaps a bit ambiguous, or at least multivalent. In this work Habermas's stated intent is to develop a first-order, well-grounded critical social theory: it is the "beginning of a social theory concerned to validate its own critical standards" (TCA I, xli). However, his focus, as the title suggests, is on development of a theory of communicative action, which I have shown is only one dimension, or element, of the critical theory of society. The theory of social evolution, which constitutes the second dimension, or element, plays a more implicit role in this book. Its details are largely assumed, and as such it is not substantially developed beyond the theoretical statements found in *Communication and Evolution of Society* (CES). Presumably it is this fact that has misled readers into interpreting the theory of communicative action (in its aspect as formal pragmatics) as the critical theory of society in its entirety, thereby neglecting to give the theory of social evolution its due. It is my intent in this study to correct this bias.

The theory of communicative action expresses the linguistic turn Habermas has given to his conception of critical social theory, in which he argues for a turn from the Cartesian conception of the subject, with its monological, subject-centered understanding of the knowing and acting subject, to a communicative, and hence intersubjective, conception of the knowing and acting subject. The theory of communicative action is not intended to be a metatheory about the methodology of social theory, but a substantive critical social theory (TCA I, xli). Moreover, the theory of communicative action is not merely an exercise in conceptual analysis, for it is conceived with the explicit intent to "make possible a conceptualization of the social-life context that is tailored to the paradoxes of modernity" (TCA I, xlii). The paradoxes of modernity that the theory of communicative action is intended in part to interpret are perhaps best expressed by Horkheimer and Adorno in the introduction to their *Dialectic of Enlightenment*, where they had "set [themselves] nothing less than the discovery of why [humankind], instead of entering into a truly human condition is sinking into a new kind of barbarism."[1] A few paragraphs later they explain this striking claim in Hegelian terms: "The dilemma that faced us in our work proved to be the first phenomenon for investigation: the self-destruction of the Enlightenment. We are wholly convinced—and therein lies our *petitio principii*—that social freedom is inseparable from enlightened thought. Nevertheless, we believe that we have just as clearly recognized that the notion of this very way of thinking, no less than the actual historic forms—the social institutions—with which it is interwoven, already contains the seed of the reversal universally apparent today."[2] So the problem that Habermas inherits from the Frankfurt School is the paradox between the increased technical rationality of the modern period, which seemingly should lead to a decrease in unnecessary domination since rationalization implies a greater conscious control over social reproduction, and the increased irrationality of social relations and historical events, which in fact result in an increase in unnecessary domination. The object of investigation, then, is the history of the present, or more specifically, the rationalization of modern society and the paradoxes involved in this process.

These paradoxes of modernity have consequences for both social theory and philosophy, as Habermas shows in the introduction to *The Theory of Communicative Action* (1–142). He argues there that rationality is internally related to social theory at three distinct levels (TCA I, xlii).[3] At the metatheoretical level of the proper understanding of social theory as such, social theory encounters the question of the rationality implications of its concepts of action. At the methodological level, social theory cannot avoid questions of the rationality implications of the unavoidable interpretive access to its object-domain. And at the empirical-theoretical level, social theory encounters the question of the meaning of the interpretation of the modernization of societies as rationalization (if it can be considered so at all). Thus, he argues that "*any* sociology that claims to be a theory of society has to face the problem of rationality simultaneously on the *metatheoretical*, *methodological*, and *empirical* levels" (TCA I, 7). In addition, Habermas argues that traditionally the question of rationality is addressed in the domain of philosophical thought. But within the past several decades the results of the empirical sciences and the self-critical attitude of philosophy have contributed to the lack of confidence in totalizing, a priori knowledge. However, philosophy remains interested in the formal conditions of rationality—despite the restriction of discourse to specialized spheres, for example, logic, science, language, ethics, and aesthetics (TCA I, 2). Under these conditions, then, the theory of argumentation becomes especially important, for "to it falls the task of reconstructing the formal-pragmatic presuppositions and conditions of an explicitly rational behavior" (TCA I, 2). Habermas concludes that in addition to social theory, postmetaphysical philosophy is also converging towards a theory of rationality.

Thus the concept of rationality and what it means to be judged rational need to be analyzed if we are to gain any understanding of the paradox of modernity. What do we mean when we say that X is rational? Habermas gives as first approximation the following. The subject of this statement can be either a person, or a symbolic expression that embodies knowledge (TCA I, 8). But what does "is rational" refer to? To begin, we typically think that something's being rational has some relation to knowledge, and Habermas claims that "the close relation between knowledge and rationality suggests that the rationality of an expression depends on the reliability of the knowledge embodied by it" (TCA I, 8). Rational assertions, Habermas argues, gain their rational status by being well grounded, and the well-groundedness of assertions is judged by the giving of reasons in their support. Thus, only through the social practice of argumentation are assertions rationally justified. In order to understand this social practice, then, it is necessary to analyze social action in general.

Communicative Action

Habermas begins his analysis of social action by defining action in general as "the realization of an action plan based on an interpretation of the situation" (RCA, 152; cf. TCA I, 96). An agent copes with a given situation through first interpreting that situation, and then, based on that interpretative accomplishment, acting so as to realize a plan. With this concept of action, Habermas rejects the conflation of actions with mere bodily movements: Actions and bodily movements and operations occur concurrently, but bodily movements are actions insofar as they are an element of the agent's interaction with the world (TCA I, 96–97). Bodily movements can be considered actions only in the derivative sense of being embedded in an agent's interaction with the world—for instance, in play or teaching practices actions can acquire independent status, but only by virtue of their being a part of an agent's interaction with the world. Furthermore, with this concept of action Habermas recognizes that all actions have a generally teleological, or purposive, structure, such that "[t]he actor achieves his aim or brings about a desired state by choosing and making suitable use of means promising success in a given situation" (RCA, 154). This means simply that any action is an intervention of one or more agents in the world to achieve some end: "With his actions the agent changes something in the world" (TCA I, 96). Thus, Habermas understands action as an intentional act that is aimed at bringing about some end.

Analysis of the social order requires an understanding of the coordinating mechanisms and influences between individual social agents: "The question in social theory of what makes social order possible has a counterpart in action theory: How can (at least two) participants in interaction coordinate their plans in such a way that alter is in a position to link his actions to ego's without a conflict arising, or at least without the risk that the interaction will be broken off?" (MCCA, 133). To begin, then, *social action* can be initially defined as the coordination of the actions of two or more agents in the accomplishment of a common plan of action.

Habermas distinguishes two fundamental mechanisms of coordinating social actions: *consent* and *influence* (RCA, 151–154). Consent coordinates social actions when there is an agreement between all of the relevant agents as to the interpretation of the situation. With this common knowledge in hand, the agents can pursue their common action plan. The action-coordinating function of consent is achieved through the intersubjectively valid understanding of the situation. The intersubjective validity of this common knowledge is what generates the reciprocal binding force between the participating agents. In order for José and Shanina to successfully accomplish a plan of action—the repair of their broken down tandem bicycle—they first need to come to an agreement regarding their interpretation of the situation at hand—the flat tire that is preventing their continuation. Agreement on this interpretation of the situation reciprocally binds José and Shanina together in achieving their common action plan. By contrast, influence coordinates social actions through the inducement of an understanding of the situation in at least one of the agents. Suppose two agents find themselves in a situation requiring coordination of their actions. A common interpretation of the situation can be achieved if one agent induces an opinion of the situation in the other (for example, through a lie). However, this common interpretation lacks the mutually binding and bonding effects constitutive of the interpretation achieved through consent. While the coordination of action may be successful, the common situation interpretation lacks the intersubjective validity that generates mutual obligations. From the perspective of the agent, the mechanisms of consent and influence are mutually exclusive means of coordinating actions.

Reflecting this distinction between action coordinating mechanisms, Habermas distinguishes between *action orientations*: actions oriented to success and actions oriented to reaching understanding. But, what does it mean to say that actors adopt certain orientations of action? From the perspective of the participant in social action, action orientations represent the two possible choices for coordinating action with other participants. In contexts of social action, the agent intuitively chooses between an orientation towards success and an orientation towards reaching understanding. However, from a third-person perspective, these two orientations, which now appear as action *structures*, can only be separated analytically (RCA, 173–175). The distinction between purposive and communicative action is only an analytic one because every given action involves elements of both. Action orientations are distinguished according to which of the two aspects is dominant. Communicative actions, which are oriented towards reaching understanding, nevertheless possess an underlying purposive structure, and teleological actions, which are oriented towards success, nevertheless rely on interpretive understanding of the action situation: "In strategic interactions, communicative means too are employed in the sense of a consequence-oriented use of language; here consent formation through the use of language does not function as a mechanism for coordinating action, as it does in communicative action. In communicative action the participants in interaction carry out their action plans under the condition of an agreement reached communicatively, while the coordinated actions themselves retain the character of purposive activity. Purposive activity forms just as much a component of consent-oriented action as of success-oriented action; in both cases the actions imply interventions in the objective world (RCA, 174)."[4]

Moreover, actions oriented to success can be further distinguished into social and nonsocial actions, and accordingly, there are two types of action that are oriented towards success: instrumental action and strategic action (TCA I, 285). An instrumental action is an action in a nonsocial action situation, is oriented to success, and utilizes technical rules to maximize the efficiency of its interventions in the action situation. Examples of such an action might include the hammering of a nail in the course of building a house, or Robinson Crusoe building a hut. In each case the object being affected is an inanimate object. In contrast, strategic actions, which are oriented towards success, aim at the manipulation of other persons. Thus, a strategic action is an action in a social action situation, is oriented to success, and utilizes rules of rational choice to maximize the efficiency of influencing the decisions of another. Examples include promising a fifteen percent across-the-board tax cut, which you know will be disastrous for the common good, just so you can be elected president, or commanding "Hands up!" to someone you want to rob. In these cases the fundamental aim is to manipulate another to conform to your wishes. Both instrumental and strategic actions are forms of teleological or purposive action that aim at success; they are simply different forms with respect to the type of object that is being affected.[5]

In contrast to actions oriented to success, Habermas distinguishes actions oriented to reaching understanding. The contrast here is primarily between strategic actions and communicative actions, both being types of social action involving the coordination of the action plans of multiple agents. On Habermas's model there are no nonsocial actions that are oriented to reaching understanding since reaching understanding entails at least two interlocutors. Now, whereas strategically acting agents are primarily oriented to achieving success, that is, effecting change in the world (including objects in both the so-called objective and the social worlds) such that their own ends are achieved, communicatively acting agents pursue their ends under the condition of cooperation with other social agents (TCA I, 286).

Before clarifying the concept of communicative action, let me recapitulate the basic typology of actions (TCA I, 333; CES, 208 n.2). There are two types of actions in general: social actions and nonsocial actions. Social actions can be further distinguished between two mutually exclusive types: strategic and communicative. In strategic actions, agents' plans are coordinated through influence, and in communicative actions, they are coordinated through consensus.

Habermas characterizes communicative action as "the attitude of participants when, in elementary cases, one person carries out a speech act and another reacts to it with 'yes' or 'no'" (RCA, 169). The relevant function of the concept of communicative action for social theory is the unique binding and bonding effects it produces between social actors: It both bonds them together in coordinated social action, and binds each to justify his or her validity claims if necessary. In order to understand what an "attitude oriented to reaching understanding" means, Habermas first analyzes the notion of "reaching understanding." The level at which this analysis is carried out is what he terms *formal-pragmatic*, which is distinguishable from the level of empirical description of the processes of everyday communication. Formal pragmatics seeks to describe the intuitively held competencies of social agents that condition the process of reaching understanding; that is, it aims to "grasp the structural properties of processes of reaching understanding, from which we can derive general pragmatic presuppositions of communicative action" (TCA I, 286).[6] This draws on the distinction originally formulated by Noam

Chomsky between *competence* and *performance*.[7] Formal pragmatics seeks to reconstruct the universal features of communicative competence, as exhibited by an ideal speaker-hearer relationship. It abstracts from such contingent conditions of actual communicative performance such factors as memory limitations, distractions, attention deficits, and simple errors of language usage. Another underlying assumption that formal pragmatics relies on is that certain pragmatic features of utterances are open to rational reconstruction.[8] And this, in turn, presumes the distinction between language, with sentences as its basic units of analysis, and communication, with utterances as its basic unit of analysis. The primary advantage of formal-pragmatic analysis over empirical analysis for a critical social theory is found in its capacity to identify the rationality potential contained in communicative actions.

Habermas begins his analysis of "reaching understanding" *(Verständigung)* by characterizing it as "a process of reaching agreement *[Einigung]* among speaking and acting subjects" (TCA I, 286–287). But not just any sort of agreement is adequate. The type of agreement that Habermas is referring to here is a communicatively achieved agreement, and thus is carefully qualified. A communicatively achieved agreement is not satisfied by a mere like-mindedness, but it is linguistically structured; in particular it is propositionally differentiated. The relevant consequence of this propositional differentiation is that communicatively achieved agreement is "accepted or presupposed as valid by the participants" (TCA I, 287). That is, the participants to the communicatively achieved agreement could under idealized conditions give their assent to the agreement. This precludes the possibility of a communicatively achieved agreement being imposed or induced by external forces, and it further precludes de facto accords. If an agreement is imposed through external force or inducement, then that agreement cannot meet the condition of being accepted as valid by the participants. In the same way, if an agreement between parties is merely de facto, then it does not (de facto) meet the conditions of being accepted as valid by the participants. This does not exclude the possibility that the participants could accept it as valid, but it merely points out the fact that they do not. This condition of the giving of assent by the participants points to the rational character implicit in reaching agreement through communicative action:

> A communicatively achieved agreement has a rational basis; it cannot be imposed by either party, whether instrumentally through intervention in the situation directly or strategically through influencing the decisions of opponents. Agreement can indeed be objectively obtained by force; but what comes to pass manifestly through outside influence or the use of violence cannot count subjectively as agreement. Agreement rests on common *convictions*. The speech act of one person succeeds only if the other accepts the offer contained in it by taking (however implicitly) a "yes" or "no" position on a validity claim that is in principle criticizable. Both ego, who raises a validity claim with his utterance, and alter, who recognizes or rejects it, base their decisions on potential grounds or reasons. (TCA I, 287)

Habermas further analyzes the concept of communicative action by way of the theory of speech acts. This theory provides insights into the concept of communicative action in several ways. First, a speech act analysis clarifies the distinction between actions oriented to reaching agreement and actions oriented to success. Second, a speech act analysis illuminates the peculiar binding and bonding effects communicative action has on participants in social action. And third, a speech act analysis clarifies the rational basis that underlies a communicatively achieved agreement.[9] An additional result of an analysis of action oriented to reaching understanding, and one that turns out to be significant (as well as highly controversial) is that it is said to show that the use of language oriented to reaching understanding is the original mode of language use.

Habermas adapts J. L. Austin's theory of speech acts developed in *How to Do Things With Words* for his formal-pragmatic analysis.[10] Austin distinguishes between *locutionary, illocutionary,* and *perlocutionary* speech acts.[11] The performance of a speech act, the act of saying something, Austin refers to as a *locutionary act.* When my friend Glenn says to me, "David, it is raining outside," he is performing a locutionary act. Locutionary acts are used to express a state of affairs, and as such express the content of propositions *(p). Illocutionary acts* are used to preform actions through saying something; they are speech-in-use: an illocutionary act is the "performance of an act *in* saying something as opposed to [the] performance of an act *of* saying something [locutionary act]."[12] My friend Glenn performs an illocutionary act when he goes beyond merely informing me of the weather and urges me, say, not to ride my bike in the rain: "You really should not ride your bike in the rain." *Perlocutionary effects or acts* produce effects upon the hearer and arise from the context of the speech act. Glenn brings about perlocutionary effects when he convinces me to not ride my bike in the rain, or when he bars my way to the door. Habermas summarizes each of these types of speech actions as "to say *something*, to act *in* saying something, to bring about something *through* acting in saying something" (TCA I, 289).

Habermas differs from Austin with respect to the conceptions given to each of these categories of speech acts. Austin and his commentators conceive of illocutionary acts as expressing the content of their meaning explicitly, and as possessing results that are internally related to their effects. Habermas, however, understands locutions and illocutions as distinguishable only analytically. In his view, every genuine speech act contains both locutionary and illocutionary components, where the locutionary component carries the propositional content *(p)*, and the illocutionary component M signifies the mode of the use of a sentence, and thus establishes an intersubjective relation between the interlocutors (TCA I, 289). So according to Habermas every genuine speech act is in the form M*p*, where M is the mode of sentence use, and *p* is the propositional content. Habermas also gives perlocutionary acts a unique interpretation. He understands perlocutionary acts as going beyond illocutionary acts to make reference to a context of teleological action, and as affecting consequences that rest on a basis other than strictly that of the meaning of the speech act. On his view, perlocutionary acts are simply success-oriented actions that incorporate elements that are (illocutionary) speech acts.[13] He argues that perlocutionary acts are "a special class of strategic interactions in which illocutions are employed as means in teleological contexts of action" (TCA I, 293). For (illocutionary) speech acts to be effective in this function, they need to be effective themselves; that is, the hearer needs to understand what the speaker is saying. Since illocutionary acts are essential to each type of speech act identified by Austin, Habermas concludes that illocutionary speech acts are the fundamental mode of language use. The establishment of an intersubjective relation with the aim of reaching understanding is the telos of language use (TCA I, 293).

In response to various criticisms of his speech-act analysis Habermas later clarified his understanding of the illocutionary/perlocutionary distinction.[14] Habermas now maintains a distinction between two senses of illocutionary success.[15] In the narrow sense, illocutionary success occurs when the hearer understands the utterance of the speaker. And in the broader sense, illocutionary success is achieved when the hearer accepts the validity of the utterance. Illocutionary success in the broader sense entails the establishment of an intersubjective relationship between speaker and hearer, which further entails certain obligations (such as the giving of reasons in support of one's validity claim). Habermas maintains that he understands illocutionary acts as applying only to those acts that achieve illocutionary aims in the broader sense, that is, that establish an intersubjective relationship with the aim of reaching understanding. Moreover, he understands as perlocutionary all those effects that go beyond these illocutionary effects, such as the effect (the conviction that forms in the hearer) that results from the strategic telling of a lie by the speaker. Habermas now also distinguishes two sorts of perlocutionary effects. There are those effects that result from the semantic content of speech acts (for example, a lie), and those effects that are a consequence of the contingent side effects of what is said—they do not arise from an intersubjective relationship that has been established between interlocutors (for example, the robber's command of "Hands up!").[16]

To be successful, perlocutionary actions must have the character of concealed strategic actions. In order to achieve the strategic end, perlocutions employ illocutions as means. For these illocutions to be successful, the hearer must understand and accept the offer contained in the speech act. But this must be achieved under the condition that the speaker not betray his or her strategic aims. Thus, the perlocution must be understood by the hearer as an illocution, and nothing more. For this reason, Habermas rejects perlocutions as adequate bases on which to explain the action coordinating and binding mechanism of speech acts.

Habermas suggests that a more adequate model with which to analyze action oriented to understanding is based on the concept of illocutionary speech acts. Speech acts that are pure illocutions provide the model for what Habermas has called "communicative actions": "I have called the type of interaction in which *all* participants harmonize their individual plans of action with one another and thus pursue their illocutionary aims *without reservation* 'communicative action'" (TCA I,

294). The "without reservation" condition refers to the claim that in communicative action participants interact only on the basis of illocutionary aims (*pure* illocutions; TCA I, 295). Based on this, Habermas distinguishes communicative action from strategic action (in social contexts). In communicative action participants are oriented to reaching understanding with the other participants, and they seek nothing more (that is, they do not also aim to produce perlocutionary effects in the other participants). In contrast, when participants are engaged in strategic interaction, they seek, usually implicitly through deception, to produce perlocutionary effects in other participants. Sometimes this involves the use of illocutionary speech acts in a deceptive way to achieve the desired effect. Thus, Habermas cautions that "acts of communication," which may involve actions oriented either towards success or towards reaching understanding, should not be conflated with "communicative actions," which involve only orientations towards reaching understanding.

Assuming, then, the validity of the distinction between communicative and strategic actions, speech act theory has the added virtue of possessing the resources with which to analyze the peculiar discursive binding and social bonding functions manifest in communicative actions. With this analysis Habermas intends to "explicate the conditions that have to be satisfied by a communicatively achieved agreement that is to fulfill the function of coordinating action" (TCA I, 296). Recall that the analysis of communicative action is a formal-pragmatic one, such that the objects of analysis are *utterances*, that is, sentences employed communicatively (TCA I, 297). Furthermore, the analysis is limited to action coordinating interactions that derive their binding power from neither the social force of convention (for example, in institutionally framed norms), nor the possibility of externally imposed sanctions.

Consider the following examples, and their affirmative responses, cited by Habermas (TCA I, 296):

(1) I (hereby) promise you that I shall come tomorrow.

(2) You are requested to stop smoking.

(3) I confess to you that I find your actions loathsome.

(4) I can predict (to you) that the vacation will be spoiled by rain.

(1a) Yes, I shall depend upon it.

(2a) Yes, I shall comply.

(3a) Yes, I believe you do.

(4a) Yes, we'll have to take that into account.

With each speech act and response an intersubjective bond is produced. By responding affirmatively, the hearer accepts the offer implied by the speech act and grounds an intersubjective agreement. Habermas distinguishes three levels of reaction to the utterance by the hearer (TCA I, 297). At the *pragmatic* level, the hearer takes an affirmative position with respect to the claim raised by the utterance thereby engaging the speaker and opening the space for reaching an understanding. At the *semantic* level, the affirmative response by the hearer signals to the speaker that the hearer understands the meaning of the utterance. And at the *empirical* level, the hearer's affirmative response acknowledges an agreement regarding the sequence of further interaction, and obligations implicit in that agreement.

In truth-conditional semantics the meaning of a statement, *p*, is determined by the conditions in which it would be the case that *p*. Habermas makes an analogous claim with regard to the meaning of a speech act: "*[w]e understand a speech act when we know what makes it acceptable*" (TCA I, 297). And since we are analyzing speech, that is, language-in-use, this condition is satisfied only intersubjectively. Thus, a speech act is acceptable only when it performatively satisfies the conditions such that the hearer can make an affirmative response to it. To understand a speech act, the hearer must know (a) the conditions under which the hearer could bring about the desired state of affairs; and (b) the conditions under which the speaker could give reasons justifying the validity of the content of (a). Condition (b) rests on the distinction between "the *validity* of an action or of the norm underlying it, the *claim* that the conditions for its validity are satisfied, and the *redemption* of the validity claim raised, that is, the grounding (of the claim) that conditions for the validity of an action or of the underlying norm are satisfied" (TCA I, 302). So in Habermas's speech act (1) the speaker produces a normative validity claim regarding the intention to bring about a desired state of affairs, and in (2) the speaker raises a normative validity claim regarding the imperative that the hearer bring about the desired state of affairs. In (3) the speaker raises a validity claim regarding the sincerity or truthfulness of an expressed subjective experience. And in (4) the speaker raises a validity claim regarding the truth of a proposition.

Thus, through the analysis of the assertion and redemption of validity claims raised in speech acts the binding effect of communicative action is revealed. In putting forth a validity claim, the speaker warrants that reasons could be given in support of that claim, if the hearer should choose to contest the claim's validity. In contrast to the motivating force of sanctions contained in imperatives, the coordination of actions—the bonding effect—derives from the rationally motivating force of accepting the speaker's warrant of redeeming claims of validity. Habermas concludes from this that only in those speech acts in which a speaker raises a validity claim can an intersubjective understanding arise, where the understanding is not dependent on external forces or sanctions.

Communicative action is now defined as "interactions in which those involved coordinate their individual plans unreservedly on the basis of communicatively achieved agreement" (TCA I, 305). I will now turn to a clarification of what

Habermas means by "validity claims" and their relevance to the critical theory of society. Recall that essential to a critical social theory is the incorporation and justification of a normative orientation. In the synchronic dimension, that is, when we analyze the structures of society in an ahistorical manner, Habermas locates this normative orientation in the validity claims (and their contestability) asserted in every speech act. In these validity claims, and in their capacity to be contested (and redeemed or rejected), the rational potential of speech is found that adequately (according to Habermas) grounds the normative orientation in the synchronic dimension of the critical theory of society.

In each of the speech act examples given above exactly one validity claim is thematized. But Habermas argues that every speech act raises exactly three validity claims: (1) the validity claim to the truth of the propositional content of the utterance; (2) the validity claim to the rightness of the speaker's action relative to a normative context; and (3) the validity claim to sincerity, or truthfulness, of the expression of the speaker's subjective experiences (TCA I, 307).[17] Consider the following example. In the course of repairing a friend's bicycle at no charge, a bicycle mechanic utters the following request: "Please bring me a number ten open-ended wrench." If the friend who is the intended recipient of the request understands it as a speech act oriented to reaching understanding, then she can either accept the validity claims made by the speech act or contest them. In principle she could contest any one (or several) of the validity claims. She could contest the existential presupposition that there is a number ten open-ended wrench within the shop: "No. We broke the last number ten open-ended wrench earlier, and all of the hardware stores in the area are closed for the night." Or, she could contest the normative rightness of the request: "No. You can't treat me like an employee." Or, she could contest the sincerity of the request: "No. You simply want to distract me so that I don't stand over your shoulder."

The consequence of the hearer's acceptance of a speech act is that an agreement (*Einverständnis*) is reached between the two participants. Habermas states that, based on an intuitive understanding of communicative action, a speaker produces a comprehensible linguistic expression with the intent of (a) stating something true about the objective world, (b) performing a normatively right speech act with respect to a given context such that an intersubjective relationship is established, and (c) expressing sincerely one's own subjective experiences. Thus, when a speech act is accepted, an agreement is established simultaneously at three levels: the speaker and hearer agree on the truth of the propositional content with respect to the objective world; the speaker and hearer agree on the normative rightness of the speech act within the given normative context; and the speaker and hearer agree on the sincerity of the subjective states expressed by the speaker. Furthermore, this trilevel agreement implies the tripartite function of speech acts: "As the medium for achieving understanding, speech acts serve: (a) to establish and renew interpersonal relations, whereby the speaker takes up a relation to something in the world of legitimate (social) orders; (b) to represent (or presuppose) states and events, whereby the speaker takes up a relation to something in the world of existing states of affairs; (c) to manifest experiences—that is, to represent oneself—whereby the speaker takes up a relation to something in the subjective world to which he has privileged access" (TCA I, 308).

Sociocultural Lifeworld

Communicative actions, however, are not performed in a presuppositionless environment; they are always already embedded in a determinate context, which Habermas refers to as the "lifeworld." The concept of the lifeworld is relevant to social theory because (1) it forms the horizon within which communicative actions are performed and (2) it is itself conditioned by the structural changes of society as a whole (TCA II, 119). For a communicative action to be successfully performed it must be embedded in a situational definition that is sufficiently shared by the interlocutors. If the understanding of the communicative situation is not shared to a sufficient extent by the participants, then the level of interaction is raised to the level of discourse (in Habermas's sense of communication that is free of exigent constraints) in which the problematic elements of the situation definition are explicitly discussed, and an agreement about the situation definition is the objective. However, the communicative situation is not a clearly delimitable context; it is centered on the theme of the interaction and thus has a shifting horizon that changes according to relevance to the theme: "A *situation* is a segment of *lifeworld contexts of relevance [Verweisungszusammenhänge]* that is thrown into relief by themes and articulated through goals and plans of action; these contexts of relevance are concentrically ordered and become increasingly anonymous and diffused as the spatiotemporal and social distance grows" (TCA II, 122–123). Thus the action situation is focused on a theme and it presents itself as a horizon of needs for mutual understanding and of options for action. It shifts with shifting themes, and it has a "horizon" that can be crossed at any time. Agents always act from within, and with respect to, an action situation, but the background of the situation is formed by the lifeworld as a whole. Yet the lifeworld itself cannot be thematized; only segments of the lifeworld are capable of being thematized and brought within the horizon of the action situation: "From a perspective turned toward the situation, the lifeworld appears as a reservoir of taken-for-granteds, of unshaken convictions that participants in communication draw upon in cooperative processes of interpretation. Single elements, specific taken-for-granteds, are, however, mobilized in the form of consensual and yet problematizable knowledge only when they become relevant to a situation" (TCA II, 124).

Habermas's analysis of the lifeworld up until this point is in line with the phenomenological conception of the lifeworld first proposed by Husserl and extended by Schutz. But to be consistent with his "linguistic turn" Habermas intends to give this concept of the lifeworld a communication-theoretic interpretation. Specifically, he proposes that we think of the lifeworld "as represented by a culturally transmitted and linguistically organized stock of interpretive patterns" (TCA II, 124). In other words, the lifeworld itself is constituted by structures of linguistically mediated modes of understanding that are maintained through cultural tradition. Language and culture, then, form the background context for action situations, and thus serve as the resources for particular thematized situations, but cannot themselves become thematized (just as the lifeworld as a whole cannot be thematized as a situation). Thus, the lifeworld itself is constituted by the totalities of language and culture, which provide the stock of knowledge from which action situations are constructed (culture) and the modes of intersubjective agreement about that knowledge (language) (TCA II, 125). Habermas emphasizes that the category of "lifeworld" is not at the same level as the formal world concepts discussed above (the objective, the social, and the subjective). Individuals interacting linguistically draw upon the resources of the lifeworld, but they cannot "get behind it" and thematize it as whole as an object of understanding: "Communicative actors are always moving *within* the horizon of their lifeworld; they cannot step outside of it. As interpreters, they themselves belong to the lifeworld, along with their speech acts, but they cannot refer to 'something in the lifeworld' in the same way as they can to facts, norms or experiences" (TCA II, 126). The lifeworld is a necessary condition of intersubjective understanding as such, while the formal world concepts (objective, social, and subjective) constitute the object about which intersubjective understanding is possible.

Habermas recognizes, however, that while the communication-theoretic conception of the lifeworld has been useful in reconceptualizing the lifeworld in terms of the philosophy of language, it remains too vague to be of much use for social theory. He suggests that the concept of the lifeworld can be made more serviceable for social theory if we adopt the *everyday concept of the lifeworld* (TCA II, 135–136).[18] The primary advantage of the everyday concept of the lifeworld is in its capacity to give an account of the narrative structure of social relations. This is important, according to Habermas, because individuals encounter each other both in the attitude of participants and as an audience to which they can present narrations of experiential events. Narrative presentations are based on an everyday concept of the lifeworld "which defines the totality of states of affairs that can be reported in true stories" (TCA II, 136). Simply put, the everyday concept of the lifeworld refers to the totality of sociocultural facts (TCA II, 136). But since this concept of the sociocultural lifeworld serves as the reference system for narrative presentation (and communicative action), it is important for purposes of social theory to explain the reproduction or self-maintenance of this linguistically structured lifeworld. Explaining the basic functions of language, considered as the medium of the sociocultural lifeworld, in that reproduction process will be key. Communicative action functions to reproduce the symbolic structures of the lifeworld in three ways. Through its function of mediating the achievement of mutual understanding, communicative action reproduces cultural knowledge. Through its function of coordinating the action of individuals' communicative actions, it establishes solidarity and generates social integration. And through its function of socialization, communicative action mediates the formation of personal identities. Thus, the lifeworld is reproduced and maintained in "the continuation of valid knowledge, the stabilization of group solidarity, and the socialization of responsible actors" (TCA II, 137). It is important to distinguish, however, between the reproduction of the *symbolic structures* of the lifeworld and the maintenance of the *material substratum* of the lifeworld. Reproduction of the symbolic structures of the lifeworld is accomplished through the means of communicative action, while maintenance of the material base of the lifeworld is accomplished through the medium of instrumental (and strategic) action. The material base has a certain priority, of course, since maintenance of the physical body of the individual is necessarily prior to symbolic interaction between individuals.

Associated with each of these dimensions of reproduction of the lifeworld (through continuation of knowledge, stabilization of solidarity, and formation of personal identities) Habermas identifies three linguistically mediated structures: culture, society, and personality (see TCA II, 137–140). *Culture* refers to the stock of valid knowledge which serves as a resource for social actors in their coming to an understanding about something in the world. The cultural reproduction of the lifeworld links up new situations with the lifeworld context as a whole in the semantic dimension; that is, the sociocultural lifeworld background supplies new situations with meaning. It ensures the continuity of tradition and the coherence of cultural knowledge (TCA II, 140). *Society* refers to the institutions by which individuals regulate their interpersonal relationships, and by which solidarity is secured. The social integration of the lifeworld links up new situations with the lifeworld context in the dimension of social space; that is, the sociocultural lifeworld supplies new situations with action coordinating functions by providing structures of legitimately regulated intersubjective relations (TCA II, 140–141). *Personality* refers to the competencies of speaking and acting, which enable the individual to engage in communicative action and in identity construction. The socialization of individuals links up new situations with the lifeworld context in the dimension of historical time; that is, the sociocultural lifeworld supplies new situations with participants who are generally competent speakers and actors (TCA II, 141).

So there are three reproduction processes associated with the three structural components of the sociocultural lifeworld.[19] Each reproduction process contributes to the reproduction of each of the three structural components. Primarily, though, cultural reproduction ensures the coherence and continuity of valid knowledge, social integration ensures the legitimate ordering of interpersonal relations, and socialization ensures the generation of generally competent social agents (see TCA II, 141–143). And as would be expected, pathologies develop when the reproduction processes of the lifeworld are disturbed. Specifically, a loss of meaning in the dimension of culture results from disturbances in cultural reproduction, anomie in the dimension of society results from disturbances in the dimension of social integration, and psychopathologies result from disturbances in socialization in the dimension of the personality (see TCA II, 140–143).

Habermas recognizes that this is an insufficient analysis of the concept of the lifeworld. Nevertheless, he considers it useful for social theory, where the question of the universal validity of this conception of the lifeworld will become relevant.

Habermas can now link up the sociocultural conception of the lifeworld with his earlier analysis of communicative action. The justification of the universal validity of this conception of the lifeworld is found in the analysis of the linguistic medium of which it is constituted. So if the theory of communicative action has universal validity, then the sociocultural conception of the lifeworld, which is constituted in language, will be universally valid as well. Note, however, that universal validity here does not mean timeless validity. The empirical forms that communicative action takes are historically conditioned, and so the theory of communicative action needs to be supplemented with a historical analysis of the rationalization of the lifeworld.

Communicative Rationality

The significance of Habermas's speech-act analysis for a critical social theory is the concept of rationality—namely, communicative rationality—that such an analysis entails. According to the formal-pragmatic analysis, when a speaker in everyday speech engages a hearer with a speech act, that speech act makes validity claims to which the hearer must respond, either explicitly or implicitly, with a yes or no answer. Typically, the hearer understands and agrees to the validity claims being made in the utterance, so no further elaboration is necessary. However, if the hearer does not assent to one of the validity claims it is incumbent upon the speaker to provide reasons backing the contested claim. Thus, contested validity claims are assessed through processes of argumentation, or, as Habermas refers to it, "discourse." The constellation of the initial making of validity claims, their acceptance or rejection by a hearer, and the need to attempt to redeem them in discourse, all imply that validity claims can be redeemed based solely on the convincing force of good reasons. Habermas refers to this as the "unforced force of the better argument." And this implies certain idealizing conditions under which the unforced force of arguments can be effected. The only way that a validity claim can be either rationally accepted or rejected is through processes of argumentation. In every speech act, then, there is an anticipation of the conditions necessary for a redemption of the validity claims made therein. If a speech act is contested, that is, if the hearer rejects the validity of either the truth content of the proposition, the normative rightness of the linguistic situation, or the sincerity of the speaker, then the interaction moves to the level of discourse, where the individual validity claims themselves are argumentatively examined. Keep in mind that this is only in cases of communicative action, that is, action oriented to reaching mutual understanding; cases of instrumental influence are excluded from this analysis. At the level of discourse, then, the participants are oriented exclusively towards reaching mutual understanding, so they are removed from imperatives of action. Moreover, the imperative of the discourse context itself (reaching understanding) implies that certain idealized conditions obtain. In order for the participants to reach an uncoerced understanding, all relevant and capable participants must be able to participate freely and openly. This, of course, is Habermas's controversial concept of the "ideal speech situation," though it is controversial largely because it is typically misinterpreted.

Although the notion of an ideal speech situation can be traced back to Habermas's 1965 Inaugural Address (KHI, appendix), he elaborated this idea most extensively in "Towards a Theory of Communicative Competence," and in "Wahrheitstheorien."[20] In "Wahrheitstheorien" Habermas defines an ideal speech situation as one "in which communications not only are not impeded by external contingent influences, but also not by the constraints resulting from the structure of the communication itself" (WAR, 255). In order to guard against unnoticed internal constraints on argumentation that originate in the very structure of communication, all relevant (and competent) participants must be able to interact symmetrically. This general symmetry requirement is the basis for deriving the specific formal conditions of the ideal speech situation. In a different context—a discussion of discourse ethics—Habermas adopts an analysis by Robert Alexy that expands upon Habermas's original ideas (MCCA, 87–89). It is here that he admits that his earlier analysis of the presuppositions of argumentation in "Warhheitstheorien" is unsatisfactory, but that the present study is not the place to undertake the elaboration, revision, and clarification necessary. For this reason he adopts Alexy's analysis as a "sketch or proposal." Following Aristotle, Alexy distinguishes three levels of presuppositions of argumentation: the *products*, the *procedures*, and the *processes*. The telos of argumentation is fundamentally to produce cogent arguments. Thus, at the level of product, participants in argumentation must follow the following rules:[21]

(1.1) No speaker may contradict himself.

(1.2) Every speaker who applies predicate *F* to object *A* must be prepared to apply *F* to all other objects resembling *A* in all relevant aspects.

(1.3) Different speakers may not use the same expression with different meanings.

At the procedural level of the presuppositions of argumentation participants adopt a hypothetical attitude in order to test problematic validity claims under conditions that are free of the imperatives of action and experience. Thus, at the level of procedure, participants in argumentation must follow these rules:

(2.1) Every speaker may assert only what he really believes.[22]

(2.2) A person who disputes a proposition or norm not under discussion must provide a reason for wanting to do so.

Lastly, at the level of process, in order to achieve a rationally motivated consensus (the goal of argumentation) participants must engage in communication that is free and open, that is, open to all relevant and competent participants, and free from all internal and external coercion. This last condition ensures that the consensus is a consequence of the "unforced force" of the better argument, and that the participants are motivated by nothing other than a cooperative search for truth. Thus, at the level of process, participants in argumentation must follow the following rules:

(3.1) Every subject with the competence to speak and act is allowed to take part in a discourse.[23]

(3.2) a. Everyone is allowed to question any assertion whatever.

b. Everyone is allowed to introduce any assertion whatever into the discourse.

c. Everyone is allowed to express attitudes, desires, and needs.

(3.3) No speaker may be prevented, by internal or external coercion, from exercising his rights as laid down in (3.1) and (3.2).

According to Habermas, these are the unavoidable pragmatic conditions of discourse that are anticipated in the formal-pragmatic structure of every speech act. Thus, whenever we engage in communicative actions, when we adopt the role of speakers and hearers in the exchange of speech acts, we unavoidably make these presuppositions.

One might have noticed that the theory of communicative action implies a coherentist theory of truth.[24] Habermas extends this to include, in an analogous way, normative rightness, so that what is true, or what is right, is determined by the converging consensus that results from a free and open argumentative discourse of all relevant participants. But not just any, contingent consensus or agreement determines what is true or right. It is important to distinguish rational consensuses from merely de facto agreements. The idealilizing presuppositions of speech function as just this sort of criterion. To the extent that any actual, empirical consensus is reached in accordance with the idealizing presuppositions of speech (that is, the rules of discourse), it is rational. And insofar as any given consensus is rational, its products are true or right. Habermas, however, recognizes that it is improbable that any empirical consensus would instantiate all of the idealizing presuppositions; nevertheless, this regulative ideal is still operative in distinguishing between a more or less rational and a coerced consensus. Habermas also addresses another concern, that it would be difficult, if not impossible, to empirically determine the fulfillment of the idealizing presuppositions in any empirical speech situation. He admits that there is no way to determine the actual fulfillment of these ideal conditions, even though we often do think that we can retrospectively decide whether a particular consensus is rational or coerced. He goes on to draw the conclusion that seems to be so often missed, and which he is at pains to emphasize in later writings. He concludes that the idealized presuppositions are not constitutive of discourse, but regulative: "The ideal speech situation is neither an empirical phenomenon nor a mere construct, but rather something we must unavoidably reciprocally impute in discourses. This imputation can, nay must not be contrafactual; but even if it is made contrafactual it is an operationally effective fiction in the process of communication. Therefore, I prefer to speak of an anticipation, a prefiguration of an ideal speech situation" (WAR, 258). Thus, the ideal speech situation should be thought of as a regulative condition of discourse, one that we ought to aim towards in actual, empirical discursive practices. But it is not externally imposed, requiring independent justification. Rather, it is anticipated in the very performance of speech acts themselves. It is implied by the assertion of the three validity claims unavoidably present in every speech act, and which can be called upon at the level of discourse to be redeemed. Every speech act implies the idealizing presuppositions of the ideal speech situation; not as empirically obtaining, but as imputing the possibility of adequate approximation if discourse is entered into regarding a disputed validity claim. Thus, Habermas claims that "[t]he normative foundation of linguistic communication is two-fold: anticipated, but as anticipated foundation also operative" (WAR, 258).

In his writings regarding communicative action and the ideal speech situation after the appearance of "Wahrheitstheorien," Habermas has repeatedly emphasized the regulative side of this description of the normative foundations implicit in linguistic communication. Since its introduction, Habermas has avoided using the phrase "ideal speech situation" just because of its many misunderstandings: "'Ideal speech situation' is somewhat too concrete a term for the set of general and unavoidable communicative presuppositions which a subject capable of speech and action must make every time he or she wishes to participate seriously in argumentation."[25] In addition, he wants to guard against the interpretation of the ideal speech situation as a prefiguration of an ideal society, such that it would be fully transparent. This, he argues, is not the role it is intended to play, and no concrete ideal society is meant to be implied by it.[26] This does not diminish, however, the normative import of the concept. It is intended to function as a normative standard against which actual, empirical discourses can be measured. By comparing these discourses with the regulative standards of the ideal speech situation we can determine the relative degree of freedom and openness of the real discourse, and thus we can judge the legitimacy of any consensus that might be its result.

So it is important to understand the function of the ideal speech situation within the larger context of critical social theory. The idealizing conditions of the ideal speech situation serve as the grounds of the normativity implicit in every act of communication. Since every speech act anticipates these idealizing conditions, as determined by formal-pragmatic analysis, this normativity is empirically grounded. Yet the ideal speech situation serves as a criterion against which we can judge the rationality of consensuses. Thus, the notion of *communicative rationality* that is associated with communicative action is grounded in these idealizing presuppositions: "This concept of *communicative rationality* carries with it connotations based ultimately on the central experience of the unconstrained, unifying, consensus-bringing force of argumentative speech, in which different participants overcome their merely subjective views and, owing to the mutuality of rationally motivated conviction, assure themselves of both the unity of the objective world and intersubjectivity of their lifeworld" (TCA I, 10). Communicative actions, then, are rational insofar as they adequately approximate this ideal.

The Developmental Theory of Social Evolution

As I indicated at the outset of this chapter, the theory of communicative action or formal pragmatics is inadequate in itself to sufficiently ground the normative claims of a critical social theory. When we consider the sociohistorical conditions of consciousness, we need to explain not just how communication free from coercion is possible, but also how forms of communication are conditioned by the sociohistorical context. The theory of communicative action is based on a formal analysis of the pragmatics of communication. It purports to uncover the "know-how" that every competent speaker utilizes in communicative practices, and it grounds a conception of communicative rationality. But what is (communicatively) rational is determined solely by the redemption of validity claims. When a speaker makes a validity claim, and that claim is challenged by an interlocutor, then the dialogue moves to the level of discourse, in which the contested validity claim is supported and challenged with reasons. The question then becomes, what count as good (or acceptable) reasons? What does it mean for an argument to be reasonable? Good reasons cannot be transcendentally grounded. Rather, according to the theory of communicative action, good reasons are thought to be good only when they are acceptable to the participants in a rational discourse. It is at this point that the sociohistorical conditions of consciousness become apparent. For only by reference to the given sociohistorical context can good reasons be identified. That is, the standards that determine good reasons will be a direct consequence of the sociohistorical milieu of the interlocutors.

The historical variability of good reasons, of course, has significant implications for a critical social theory that is interested in generating a critique of existing social conditions. The theory of communicative action informs us what the formal conditions of a rational claim are, but it does not say anything about the sorts of contents (that is, reasons) that are acceptable in rational argumentation in a given context. Some reasons are unacceptable, not because they violate the formal conditions of discourse, but because they are simply implausible in the given discursive situation. One might ask, Why should the standards of good reasons peculiar to modern forms of consciousness be taken as the normative standard for us moderns? What makes good reasons in the modern era superior (if indeed they are) to good reasons of the premodern era? Answering precisely these sorts of questions is the aim of Habermas's theory of social evolution.

Since the aim in this chapter is to show how the theory of social evolution is an essential part of Habermas's conception of a critical theory of society, it will be useful to present a brief overview of its development and mature formulation. Beginning with an examination of the details of his reconstruction of historical materialism, I will attempt to clarify the key differences between it and the orthodox conception of historical materialism.[27] I will then provide a sketch of the general contours and primary themes of the mature formulation of Habermas's theory of social evolution.

Habermas' s Reconstruction of Historical Materialism

Habermas originally presented his theory of social evolution as a reconstruction of historical materialism, where reconstruction involves "taking a theory apart and putting it back together again in a new form in order to attain more fully the goal it has set for itself" (CES, 95). The idea motivating such a theoretical reconstruction is that the original theory is not exhausted, but its further development has been misguided—by reconstructing the original theory one can reclaim its original aims with more adequate theoretical means. Habermas thus reconstructs what he calls the "orthodox" conception of historical materialism by revising several of its central concepts and claims so that it can more adequately explain the phenomena and pathologies of contemporary society. While my interest, as well as Habermas's, is not in exegetically interpreting Marx's texts, it should be noted that Habermas does claim that his reconstruction is implicit in the writings of the young Marx. Nevertheless, Habermas expands on and differs from Marx in the following concepts and theses: the concept of social labor, the idea of a history of the species, the base/superstructure thesis, the thesis of the dialectic of forces and relations of production, and the concept of the mode of production.

Whereas Marx claimed that what uniquely distinguishes the human form of life from the animal is material reproduction through social labor, Habermas argues that this key innovation in the development of Homo sapiens needs to be supplemented by recognizing the anthropological innovation in communication, namely language use.[28] So the characteristic features of the human form of life, for Habermas, are both (1) material reproduction through social labor, and (2) the use of language to mediate social roles.

According to Habermas, the distinguishing feature of the human species for Marx is that it uniquely raises itself above nature by virtue of the fact that human beings produce their own means of material subsistence. In other words, human society materially reproduces itself—developing the means to clothe, house, and feed itself—by engaging in social cooperation in the struggle to conquer the forces of nature. This model of human reproduction implicitly utilizes a conception of action that is instrumental. Habermas defines this as follows: "Instrumental action is governed by technical rules based on empirical knowledge. In every case they imply empirical predictions about observable events, physical or social."[29] Successful material reproduction requires the observation of apparently natural regularities, combined with the details of the particular circumstances that are present, thus producing predictions regarding future behavior of the circumstances of the present situation. Instrumental action can be distinguished from strategic action, which is simply socially coordinated instrumental action. Accordingly, if labor is the means by which the species reproduces itself, then social development, or progress, is determined by the level of technical efficiency of the skills and techniques utilized for material reproduction (the forces of production). This is usually understood by orthodox Marxists to mean more comprehensive and efficient technical and organizational knowledge through which the species manipulates, controls, and dominates nature.

The theoretical significance of the concept of social labor for Marx is its capacity to distinguish the specifically human form of reproduction from animal reproduction, where reproduction is the process that a thing goes through in order to ensure its continued survival. Marx postulated that the key anthropological innovation that gave rise to the human species was the development of social labor. Prior to this innovation, the continued survival of prehuman primates depended exclusively upon natural processes, for example, sufficient material abundance, instincts, natural competition, and the like. The innovation and employment of social labor in the service of ensuring the reproduction of the species specifically distinguished hominids from primates. Hominids now used tools and economic forms of organization to stabilize and reproduced the material means of existence. In contrast, Habermas argues that this conception is inadequate to distinguish the distinctly human form of material reproduction from prehuman forms. Specifically, while material reproduction of the species through social labor adequately distinguishes humans from primates, it does not adequately distinguish humans from hominids, since evidence suggests that hominids had developed an economy to secure material reproduction, as did humans (CES, 134). This evidence suggests that hominids made use of weapons and tools, cooperated through a division of labor, and distributed goods within the collective—all features of an economic form of material reproduction (CES, 134). Thus, a form of material reproduction that is identified by its possessing characteristic features of an economy does not adequately distinguish the human form of life from the hominid. Habermas argues that the significant evolutionary achievement that distinguishes the human form of reproduction from hominid reproduction is the development of a social structure that allows for the adoption of multiple social roles by individuals, and for the adoption of a single social role by several individuals. This was first accomplished with the development from the linear social hierarchy to the familial social structure: "Not hominids, but humans were the first to break up the social structure that arose with the vertebrates—the one-dimensional rank ordering in which every animal was transitively assigned one and only one status" (CES, 135). Only with the development of the family did human social structure obtain the capacity for multiple social roles, since the family allowed for the social mediation between the spheres of biological reproduction and material reproduction. For example, "Only a family system based on marriage and regulated descent permitted the adult male member to link—via the father role—a status in the male system of the hunting band with a status in the female and child system . . . ," and only the family system allowed the female to link her status in the hunting band with her status in the family, via the mother role (CES, 135).

Habermas thus distinguishes between three stages of development (rather than the two primate and hominid postulated by Marx) that resulted in the evolution of Homo sapiens. The first is the *primate stage,* in which purely natural mechanisms drive evolutionary developments. The second is the *hominid stage,* in which a mixture of natural and cultural mechanisms drive evolution. At this pre-human stage, evolution is constituted by a combination of natural evolutionary mechanisms (such as growth in brain size) and an environment that is no longer solely natural, but is in part determined by the pragmatic accomplishments of individuals. The third is the *sociocultural stage* of development. At this characteristically human stage of development, natural mechanisms, such as growth in brain size, are no longer a factor in evolutionary developments. All developments at this stage derive solely from sociocultural innovations. The relevant consequence of the development of the familial social structure exhibited by the sociocultural stage of development is that the familial relationship is structured according to a system of symbolically mediated social norms, and the system of social norms is in turn mediated by language use. Thus, according to Habermas, an individual's capacity to adopt multiple social roles presupposes the capacity for language use, and it does so in three ways. Firstly, adopting social roles requires the participants both to be capable of assuming the perspective of other participants, and to exchange the perspective of the participant with that of the observer. This capacity to exchange perspectives with other participants and to attain a third person perspective is necessary in order to construct a symbolically mediated system of reciprocal expectations that forms the basis of the system of social norms (and hence of social action). Secondly, language allows the generation of a temporal horizon of mutual expectations that extends beyond the immediate consequences of action and is required for the constitution of social roles. For example, a marriage promise is a set of mutual expectations that extends into the future beyond any immediate consequences of the situation. And thirdly, language mediates mechanisms of sanction that control (in part) the action motives of participants (CES, 136–137). Habermas concludes from this that "[w]e can assume that the developments that led to the specifically human form of reproducing life—and thus to the initial state of social evolution—first took place in the structures of both labor and language" (CES, 137). That is, what distinguishes the reproduction of the human species from nature is not simply labor, as orthodox Marxists argue, but the irreducible innovations of both labor and language.

Now that we have distinguished human history from natural history, or history from nature, we need a clearer understanding of what constitutes human history. The key to understanding the history of the species for Marx is the mode of production, which characterizes distinct social formations that in their historical ordering exhibit the direction of social evolution (CES, 138). The mode of production is constituted by the forces of production and the relations of production, where the forces and relations of production do not vary independently of one another. The productive forces include such things as the instruments of production, the raw materials, and the labor power (strength, skill, knowledge, inventiveness, etc.).[30] And the productive relations include ownership of the means of production and the economic distribution of wealth.[31] The orthodox version of historical materialism distinguishes five modes of production that delineate universal stages of evolution of the species: the primitive, the ancient, the feudal, the capitalist, and the socialist. Furthermore, Habermas notes, dogmatic versions of orthodox Marxism (that is, "vulgar Marxism") impute unilinearity, necessity, continuity and irreversibility to these evolutionary stages.

Habermas points to three general problems with this approach to the history of the species. First, historical materialism does not need to assume that the subject that undergoes evolution is the species as a whole. Second, the claim that the species evolves unilinearily, necessarily, continuously, and irreversibly opens orthodox historical materialism to the same problems of objectivism that are a consequence of eighteenth-century philosophies of history, and that Habermas wants to avoid. These philosophies of history result from the intersection of a universal history and developmental theory. They claimed to explain the universal course and development of world history. Of course, these were a priori claims, and did not cohere well with the actual historical evidence. History is far too contingent an affair for philosophers to explain monologically from their armchairs. The third problem with a history of the species is that continuing historical research suggests that the concept of the mode of production inadequately resolves the discrete stages of historical development.

Regarding the first problem, Habermas argues that historical materialism need not assume a species-subject, or macrosubject, that is the bearer of evolution. The proposition that there is a unified macrosubject, that is, a collective subject, that evolves in history appears indefensible. The immense body of cross-cultural evidence that has been collected militates against any assertion of a macrosubject of history. One simply cannot plausibly speak of a collective "subject" in the usual sense of a unitary subject of action. To avoid this difficulty, Habermas takes an action-theoretic perspective by suggesting that the subjects that evolve are specific, concrete societies, and the subjects integrated into them (CES, 140). He further argues that "[e]ven if social evolution should point in the direction of unified individuals consciously influencing the course of their own evolution, there would not arise any large-scale subjects, but at most self-established, higher-level, intersubjective commonalities" (CES, 140). Elsewhere, Habermas argues that whereas traditional philosophies of history (paradigmatically represented by Hegel) assumed a unified macrosubject that makes history in an increasingly rational manner, a critical theory of social evolution recognizes that only since roughly the Enlightenment has cross-cultural interchange generated a sort of global unity (see TP, 249–252). Furthermore, an increased capacity for rationalization has come to exist only historically, and so cannot be assumed to be a property of human evolution in general: "Especially the materialistic philosophy of history should comprehend its presuppositions in terms of the context of the epoch in which it emerged historically. It should incorporate critically into its self-consciousness the fact that the two categories—the unity of the world, and that history can be made—have only acquired their truth in history itself at a specific phase" (CES, 251). Consequently, a theory of social evolution that takes societies and their socialized individuals as its subject needs to analyze the structural developments of the identities of these social groups and the socialized egos of which they are composed.

The second problem, that orthodox interpretations impute to social evolution an indefensible unilinearity, necessity, continuity, and irreversibility, can be avoided by distinguishing between the *dynamics* of the mechanisms of evolution, and the *pattern* (or logic) of the structures through which the development of individual societies universally (but not necessarily) progresses. Central to this conception is the notion of a developmental-logical ordering of these highly abstract levels of learning, which are highly abstract structural conditions that determine the horizon of possible problem solutions within each level. These developmental levels of learning are discrete wholes that qualitatively differ from each other, and they form hierarchically complex sequences, in which development necessitates an ordered progression through each stage (not excluding regressions, stagnations, and so forth). Note that progression is not a necessary occurrence, only that if progression occurs, it will be ordered according to the developmental sequence.

In "Toward a Reconstruction of Historical Materialism," Habermas provides an example of a learning sequence in the dimension of social integration (see Table 1). Habermas repeatedly warns his reader that these proposals for a theory of social evolution are programmatic, so accordingly, this example should also be considered programmatic and tentative (CES, 157–158).

On this conception of social evolution, then, the subjects of evolution are particular societies, rather than the species considered as a macrosubject, and the stages of evolution are multilinear, reversible, contingent, and discontinuous.

The third problem is that the concept of the mode of production has insufficient resolution to distinguish significant stages of historical development. Habermas argues that ongoing historical and anthropological research has suggested that the concept of the mode of production is an inadequate category to describe universal stages of development because of its lack of explanatory power with regard to this recent evidence (for example, the need to add an ad hoc sixth type of social formation based on the Asiatic mode of production). One move would be to adopt some sort of cultural relativist position and drop the claim that these modes of production discern universal stages of development. Habermas rejects this move on the grounds that a less radical revision of the category of the stages of development might prove more fruitful for a critical social theory (since reducing the scope of its claims to particular cultures would effectively block the critical effect of Marxism). Taking this alternative path, he suggests replacing the category of mode of production with a more general and abstract category that can more adequately discern universal stages of development. Habermas refers to this new category as "principle of organization." It is worth quoting Habermas at length regarding this concept:

Table 1. Developmental Levels of Social Integration

	Type of Society	General Structures of Action	Structures of Worldviews (insofar as they are determinant for morality and law)	Structures of Institutionalized Law and of Binding Moral Representations
Level of Social Integration	Neolithic Societies	conventionally structured systems of action	mythological worldview still immediately enmeshed with the system of action	legal regulation of conflict from preconventional points of view
	Early Civilizations	conventionally structured systems of action	mythological worldviews, set off from the system of action, which take on legitimating functions for the occupants of positions of authority	conflict regulation from the point of view of a conventional morality tied to the figure of the ruler who administers or represents justice
	Developed Civilizations	conventionally structured systems of action	break with mythological thought, development of rationalized worldviews	conflict regulation from the point of view of a conventional morality detached from the reference person of the ruler
	The Modern Age	postconventionally structered domains of action—differentiation of a universalistically regulated domain of strategic action (capitalist enterprise, bourgeois civil law), approaches to political will formation grounded in principles (formal democracy)	universalistically developed doctrines of legitimation	conflict regulation from the point of view of a strict separation of legality and morality; general, formal, and rationalized law; private morality guided by principles

Source: Adapted from CES, 157–158.

> By principle of organization I understand innovations that become possible through developmental logically reconstructible stages of learning, and which institutionalize new levels of societal learning. The organizational principle of a society circumscribes ranges of possibility. It determines in particular within which structures changes in the system of institutions are possible; to what extent the available capacities of productive forces are socially utilized and the development of new productive forces can be stimulated; to what extent system complexity and adaptive achievements can be heightened. A principle of organization consists of regulations so abstract that in the social formation which it determines a number of functionally equivalent modes of production are possible. Accordingly, the economic structure of society would have to be examined at two analytic levels: firstly in terms of the modes of production that have been concretely combined in it; and then in terms of that social formation to which the dominant mode of production belongs. A postulate of this sort is easier to put forward than to satisfy. I can only try to elucidate the research program and to make it plausible. (CES, 153–154)

The advantage of the concept of the principle of organization is that it possesses sufficient abstractness to resolve (in the sense of adequately delineate) the universal stages that characterize the developmental logic of social evolution.

The base/superstructure model of society that is central to historical materialism states that both the forces and the relations of production together form the economic structure, or base, of society, and that the base has explanatory primacy with regard to all other subsystems that constitute the superstructure of society, such as its social, political, and legal institutions. This model has been famously interpreted in a variety of ways by Marxists.[32] Engels interpreted this model to mean that the base sets structural limits of variation upon the superstructure. Neo-Hegelian Marxists (for example, Lukács and Korsch) interpreted the superstructure as a manifestation of the economic base. "Orthodox" Marxists generally interpret the link between the base and superstructure causally; that is, the relations of production are causally determined by the forces of production, and the ideations of the superstructure are causally dependent upon the base.

Habermas, however, interprets Marx's statements about the base and superstructure of society not as an ontological claim about societal structure and the interdependency of its parts, but merely as a claim about the leading role that the economic system assumes in social evolution: "Marx introduced the concept of *base* in order to delimit a domain of problems to which an explanation of evolutionary innovations must make reference. The theorem states that evolutionary innovations only solve those problems that arise in the basic domain of society" (CES, 144). According to Habermas, the base/superstructure model asserts only that social evolutionary explanations must make reference to system problems that initially arise within the material base of society (CES, 144; TCA II, 167–168). For the transition between feudalism and capitalism, the base was coextensive with the economy; but the base should not be equated with the economy in all societies, since only in capitalism does the economy coincide with the base. Since the relations of production, according to Habermas, are defined functionally (as regulating access to the means of production), the institutional core that regulates access to means of production may be kinship, as in primitive societies; political, as in premodern societies; or economic, as in modern societies. And the specific institutional form of the relations of production specifies the form of social integration, which Habermas understands, following Durkheim, as "securing the unity of a social life-world through values and norms" (CES, 144). Thus, the system problems that arise in the base, the functional contradictions between the forces and relations of production, are directly related to the form of social integration of a society, which constitutes the core of that society's self-understanding. The overcoming of these system problems can only be achieved by an evolutionary development in the practical/moral dimension. Consequently, social evolution is not causally dependent solely upon the development of the forces of production. Indeed, Habermas maintains that in the transition to capitalism development of the forces of production followed the development of the normative structures, that is, the form of social integration. For Marx, the motor of history is found in the endogenously developing productive forces. For Habermas, however, the motor of history is bipolar; it requires both the endogenous development of productive forces (which generates problematic contradictions), and development in the normative structures of consciousness (which generates a new level of learning in which the problematic contradictions can be overcome).

According to Habermas, in orthodox historical materialism a crisis occurs in the social system when systemic problems can no longer be solved with the resources available in the dominant form of social integration (the superstructure of orthodox Marxism). In other words, the social system lacks the capacity to adapt to new challenges. Systemic problems arise in the following way. A universal, endogenous learning mechanism that drives the development of the productive forces is the result of constant natural pressures and challenges to the reproduction of material existence (for example, population growth, natural disasters, famine, and the like). This development of the forces of production leads to a disequilibrium between the forces and relations of production, resulting in a crisis that necessitates a concomitant alteration of the relations of production to restore equilibrium. Now, on the orthodox interpretation of Marx, the relations of production will automatically develop or evolve in such a way that equilibrium is restored, since there exists a functional relation between the forces and the relations of production.

Alternatively, Habermas argues that when crises arise such that when the productive forces develop to such an extent that they conflict with the relations of production, the relations of production do not necessarily evolve. To solve system problems that arise with the development of productive forces, new forms of social integration need to be introduced, but this can only be done through an evolutionary development of moral-practical knowledge (as distinguished from technical knowledge) as it is embodied in worldviews. The development of productive forces is the contingent event that destabilizes the social system, but only through moral-practical learning can individuals, and the society they constitute, evolve in such a way that equilibrium is restored. As Habermas states, "The development of productive forces can then be understood as a problem-generating mechanism that *triggers but does not bring about* the overthrow of relations of production and an evolutionary renewal of the mode of production" (CES, 146). To be sure, in the late European Middle Ages, a surplus cognitive-technical potential of knowledge had accumulated; but this knowledge potential could not be implemented until developments at the level of social integration occurred. Only when the political order of feudalism was replaced by the first modern states could this cognitive potential be utilized: "[T]he great endogenous, evolutionary advances that led to the first civilizations or to the rise of European capitalism were not conditioned but followed by significant development of productive forces" (CES, 146). The development of the cognitive-technical potential is the mechanism that generates the disequilibrium between the forces and the relations of production. But, unlike the orthodox version of historical materialism, the development of the forces of production do not necessarily cause the relations of production to develop concomitantly. The development of the forces of production should be understood as generating a social disequilibrium, while the development of the normative structures of social integration are necessary to restore equilibrium. The appearance of system problems that trigger evolutionary developments is contingently determined by disturbances in the reproduction of a society. System problems derive from the failure of a system to functionally incorporate evolutionary advances in a particular segment of the system. The development of the relations of production are in no way guaranteed, and Habermas sees new social movements as playing a central role in bringing about their development.

Whether a society is capable of evolving to the next level, which provides an expanded horizon of problem solutions allowing functional adaptation, is also contingently determined by the availability of new levels of learning in the society. Societies learn only in a derivative sense, since only individuals can be properly said to learn. But Habermas asserts that since individuals and their societies are reciprocally constituted, to speak of societal learning means the capacity of particular individuals to draw upon the latently stored cultural resources of their society to generate innovative worldviews that can stabilize a systemic crisis. To clarify, first, the cognitive abilities of individuals develop to higher levels in response to individual challenges; thus certain individuals gain new adaptive insights to system challenges. Second, these developed cognitive capacities are transposed into advanced worldviews that possess greater explanatory, and hence adaptive, power. And finally, the cognitive potential of these worldviews is institutionalized to solve particular problems, thus constituting an evolutionary development of society (CES, 121–123). Habermas concludes, "The analysis of developmental dynamics is 'materialist' insofar as it makes reference to crisis-producing systems problems in the domain of production and reproduction; and it remains 'historically' oriented insofar as it has to seek the causes of evolutionary changes in the whole range of those contingent circumstances under which (a) new structures are acquired in the individual consciousness and transposed into structures of world views; (b) system problems arise, which overload the steering capacity of a society; (c) the institutional embodiment of new rationality structures can be tried and stabilized; and (d) the new latitude for the mobilization of resources can be utilized" (CES, 123).

Here, it is useful to note that Habermas's theory of social evolution is in fact materialist. It is materialist since the catalytic mechanism that challenges a given social formation, that is, mode of production, to evolve (learn) is found in the development of the productive forces. But the development of the productive forces is not functionally adapted to by the relations of production, as in the technological determinist interpretation. The circumstances may be present for learning to occur, but whether it actually does occur in specific individuals is strictly a contingent matter.

Finally, it is important to understand that Habermas does not conceive of the history of human societies to be unambiguously progressive. He fully recognizes that as crises are resolved by advancement to a new structural level of learning, new problem situations arise, and he suggests that the new problems that arise at this higher level of learning may well be greater in intensity than those overcome (CES, 163–164). Thus, progress is ambiguous. On the one hand, evolutionary advances to higher levels of learning result in increases in the learning potential of a society. But on the other hand, evolutionary advances also usher in new problem situations; and not only do new problems arise, but the intensity of the problems increases.

Before going on to discuss the theory of modernity, it will be useful to recapitulate Habermas's reconstruction of historical materialism. Perhaps the most fundamental revision Habermas makes to orthodox historical materialism is the claim that human society evolves in not one but two irreducible dimensions. Social evolution occurs not only fundamentally in the sphere of technical and scientific knowledge, as orthodox Marxists claim, but also, according to its own internal logic, in the sphere of practical and moral insight. This thesis is grounded in the proposition that what distinguishes the human species from all other animal species is both the development of the economic form of social reproduction and the development of the capacity of an individual to adopt multiple social roles that are symbolically mediated in language use, which was facilitated by the innovation of the family social substructure.[33] Another important revision Habermas suggests for historical materialism is in the scope of the subject of evolution. In contrast to previous philosophies of history, including Marx's theory of social evolution, Habermas does not take the human species as a whole to be the bearer of evolution. Rather, he restricts the scope of the bearer of evolution to concrete societies and the individuals who compose them. The consequence is that societies will exhibit different histories, which do not follow the same sequence of evolution. He does, however, argue that we should distinguish the *process* of social change from the *pattern*. We can reconstruct these patterns of social change as universal and highly abstract levels of learning that are observable in both the cognitive-technical and moral-practical dimensions of social change. These developmental logics at the societal level roughly parallel (though with important differences) developmental logics discovered by psychologists at the individual level. Habermas argues that when societies evolve, they develop in sequence through these domains of logical possibilities. If a given society evolves it will unavoidably advance along the reconstructed logic of development. How each society progresses through each level, and whether it does, depends upon contingencies that cannot be theoretically determined. Only historical narratives can describe, in retrospect, the specific path of development of each individual society.

In light of these reconstructions, modifications must also be made in our understanding of the relationship between the forces of production, the relations of production, and the superstructural elements of society. Specifically, the base/superstructure model of understanding the structure of society is not interpreted ontologically. Habermas argues that the base/superstructure model indicates only the leading element in the evolution of society; it indicates only the leading role that the base has in explanations of social change. System problems first arise in the economic sphere (the base) and development then must occur in the superstructure in order for the system problems to be stabilized or overcome. Moreover, within the economic sphere the forces of production functionally explain the relations of production. So the forces of production are the leading element in evolution, but, on Habermas's interpretation, they do not in themselves bring about evolutionary developments. Evolutionary developments occur only when (and if) the superstructure of society develops in such a way that systemic problems can be solved. Social evolution, though, does not result in unqualified progress in the emancipation from domination. While advancement to new learning levels solves previous system problems, development also opens up the possibility of new problems, including problems that exhibit an increase in intensity. Habermas thus understands progress dialectically, as containing both progressive and regressive moments.

Overview of the Mature Theory

Since his reconstruction of historical materialism Habermas has gradually dropped references to historical materialism whenever possible. In my view, this is evidence of a gradual liberalization of his thought since the early seventies, culminating in *Between Facts and Norms*. Even by the time of *The Theory of Communicative Action* he was referring to this theory primarily as one of social evolution rather than a reconstruction of historical materialism. The term "social evolution" implies that the reproduction of human society is conceived to be a directional process. As was suggested earlier in my discussion of the paradoxes of modernity, the normative criterion of evolution, or development, for Habermas's conception of social evolution, is rationalization. Following Max Weber, Habermas understands rationalization as the expansion and amplification of the rational ordering of action. Habermas differs from Weber's account of social rationalization most significantly by conceiving of it as occurring independently in both the cognitive-technical and the moral-practical domains. The learning processes in each of these dimensions is independent insofar as they each develop according to an independent logic. This "bidimensional learning process" is entailed by Habermas's distinction between the two dimensions in which societies reproduce themselves: the material and the sociocultural.[34] Accordingly, he conceives of the meaning of rationalization in each of these dimensions differently. Specifically, in the domain of cognitive-technical knowledge, rationalization means the increase of instrumental control of nature. In the domain of moral-practical insight, rationalization means the expansion and institutionalization of communicative rationality in the ordering of social action structures. For example, the transition from feudalism to capitalism in Europe required both an advance from conventional moral and legal justifications to postconventional ones, which resulted in the establishment of the modern state and the development of the productive forces, most importantly technological advances and the institution of wage labor.

Thus, Habermas conceives of the evolution of society as a learning process that occurs in two dimensions: the cognitive-technical and the moral-practical.[35] These "[e]volutionary learning processes are understood as the implementation of a learning potential" (TCA I, 314). The cognitive-technical dimension corresponds to action that is regulated by instrumental rationality, and the moral-practical dimension corresponds to action that is regulated by communicative rationality: "As learning processes take place not only in the dimension of objectivating thought but also in the dimension of moral-practical insight, the rationalization of action is deposited not only in forces of production, but also—mediated through the dynamics of social movements—in forms of social integration. Rationality structures are embodied not only in amplifications of purposive-rational action—that is, in technologies, strategies, organizations, and qualifications—but also in mediations of communicative action—in the mechanisms for regulating conflict, in world views, and in identity formations" (CES, 120). Individuals and marginalized groups first acquire innovative insights, and these insights are then transferred into a society's collective stock of knowledge, typically in the form of worldviews (TCA I, 313–314). Societies learn when the cognitive potential contained in moral-practical insight is institutionalized in order to solve systemic problems and challenges. The development of a new level of social integration opens up the possibility for implementation of advances in technical-organizational knowledge: "[t]hus learning processes in the area of moral-practical consciousness function as a pacemaker in social evolution" (TCA I, 313).

The explication of the elements of the theory of social evolution that I have given so far is as yet insufficient to explain the phenomenon of social evolution itself. Social evolution is not sufficiently explained by reference to development in either of the two dimensions independently of the other, but by an explanation of the dialectical relation between the two levels of social life. Structures of consciousness in the cognitive-technical dimension, which coincides with the material conditions of social life, develop endogenously, and not in response to external factors, while in the moral-practical dimension, development of the structures of consciousness is impelled by certain challenges generated by the cognitive technical dimension. Moral-practical learning does not occur, however, as a functional response to these system problems; it follows its own logic. It is only "nudged" by the evolutionary challenges presented by the base.

Up to this point, however, Habermas's theory of social evolution appears to be merely another version of a philosophy of history. And if this were all, it would fall to the same difficulties that have plagued all philosophies of history from the belief in immutable progress of the eighteenth century, to the theories of social evolution of the nineteenth century (including at times, according to Habermas, Marx). Philosophies of history typically fail to convince because they rely on an untenable transcendental justification. Each, in order to justify its view of the whole of human history, must claim a viewpoint that is beyond that history. But since at least Marx, it is no longer plausible to maintain a claim to such a perspective. Habermas avoids this problem by drawing an important distinction between the *logic of development* and the *dynamics of history* (CES, 98, 140). The logic of development determines the conditions of possible problem-solving capacity of a society at each stage (and in each sphere—the cognitive-technical and moral-practical). If development is to occur in some action structure, then it will invariably follow the reconstructed logic of development. The actuality of development, whether it is to occur or not, is determined strictly by contingent conditions. The empirical and historical circumstances that a society faces at any given time (and at any particular stage of development) provide the mechanisms of evolution. Given certain conditions a society will have a certain propensity for problem solving that may or may not lead to a greater learning capacity and hence to development.

Habermas asserts that we can reconstruct patterns of structures of consciousness that are constituted by a hierarchical set of internally related stages. Each developmental stage forms a coherent whole and is qualitatively distinct from the others. The stages form an invariant and hierarchically ordered sequence, such that each of the stages must be passed through in an invariant order (if development even occurs), and each higher stage is conceived to be a development over the previous one. Since Habermas borrows the concept of developmental logic from developmental psychology, it may be useful here to briefly illustrate it with an example from psychology. Drawing on the work of Piaget and Kohlberg, Habermas asserts that the development of the individual ego in relation to its environment follows a developmental logical pattern (CES, 100–102). He labels the stages as the *symbiotic,* the *egocentric,* the *sociocentric-objectivistic,* and the *universalistic.* In the symbiotic stage the ego is not able to distinguish clearly between subject and object. The ego cannot distinguish between itself, its body, and its environment. Subjectivity at this stage is not clearly differentiated. In the egocentric stage the ego achieves subjectivity through the capacity to broadly distinguish the internal self and the external environment. The ego perceives external objects as such, but does not yet perceive itself objectively. That is, the ego cannot yet see itself from an external standpoint. Thought and action are accomplished through a body-bound perspective. At the sociocentric-objectivistic stage of development the ego learns to differentiate the external environment into a physical domain of manipulable objects and a social domain of subjects and their understandable utterances. Further, at this stage the ego learns to see itself as an objective subject in the social domain. It can take an external perspective in relation to itself. Thought and action are conventional in that they dogmatically follow generalized social expectations. At the universalistic stage of development the ego becomes reflective, thus freeing itself from the dogmatism of the previous stage. The quasi-natural norms of thought and action of the previous stage are interrogated for their validity and no longer merely accepted as valid. In the development of the ego, the ego—if it indeed develops—must pass through the stages in the order specified. No stage can be skipped. However, stagnations and regressions are possible, but only traced through the invariant ordering of the hierarchy. I have presented this sketch, not for consideration of the validity of the contents, but to illustrate the concept of a developmental logic, which will be further analyzed below.

By distinguishing the logic of development from the dynamics of history, Habermas asserts that he retains a weak universalism for the normative implications of his theory of modernity, while avoiding the unjustifiable transcendentalism of traditional philosophies of history: "The universalist position does not have to deny pluralism and the incompatibility of historical versions of 'civilized humanity;' but it regards this multiplicity of forms of life as limited to *cultural contents,* and it asserts that every culture must share certain *formal properties* of the modern understanding of the world, if it is at all to attain a certain degree of 'conscious awareness' or 'sublimation.' Thus the universalist assumption refers to a few necessary structural properties of modern forms of life as such" (TCA I, 180). Thus, Habermas's theory of social evolution does not purport to explain the totality of historical development. Rather, it provides a theoretical structure that explains formal stages of development of forms of consciousness. Further, it does not attempt to predict actual historical paths of concrete societies—it only reconstructs the internal logic that explains the previous development of social action structures.

The Theory of Modernity

While neither Habermas's theory of communicative action nor his theory of social evolution constitutes in itself a critical theory of society, each performs an essential role in his general conception of a critical social theory. In this section I intend to make clear just how these two theories combine to result in a well-grounded critical social theory. On the one hand, the theory of communicative action provides the theoretical means by which we can understand the basic modes of societal reproduction. In particular, it gives us an account of communicative action, which relies on the complementary concept of the lifeworld. Most importantly, the notion of communicative action explains the means by which the symbolic reproduction of society occurs. Thus, society can be understood to reproduce itself both materially and symbolically. On the other hand, explaining the rationality of this process of societal reproduction (in both the material and symbolic dimensions) requires the theoretical underpinnings of the theory of social evolution. The central thesis of Habermas's theory of social evolution is that the historical change of normative structures (that is, those structures of consciousness that determine the horizons of the symbolic content of a culture) follows a developmental logic, and this developmental logic of normative structures cashes out the claim that societal development is a rationalization process. Thus, by combining the theories of communicative action and social evolution a theory of modernity is generated that is intended to explain the specific rationalization processes of modernity.

Habermas's theory of social evolution obtains its critical power through the immanent comparison of the de facto institutionalization of moral-practical knowledge and the learning potential available to a given culture at a particular level of development of structures of communicative action. In other words, critical theory asks, Do the existing institutions that govern the social relations of a particular society possess unnecessary forms of domination, and if so, what cultural resources are available to that society to eliminate that domination? Has that society utilized the learning potential available to it at its particular stage of development? The function of the theory of social evolution in this conception of critique is twofold. First, for critical theory considered under that aspect of a theory of society, the theory of social evolution explains how societies collectively learn, that is, evolve. And second, for critical theory considered under the aspect of critique, the theory of social evolution illuminates the space between existing social institutions and the progressive potential inherent at the current learning level.

Habermas's explicit intention in *The Theory of Communicative Action* is to present the general contours of a critical theory of society, and at the heart of this project he advances a thesis that is intended to overcome one of the most pervasive problems faced by modern social theory, that of the methodological perspective adequate to social phenomena. Should the social theorist take up an internal aspect and analyze society with respect to the intentional orientations and attitudes of its members, or should the social theorist adopt the external perspective of an observer and analyze society with respect to observable regularities, whether or not these follow from the intentional acts of the members? In other words, should social theory be done on the model of action theory or on the model of systems theory? Habermas devotes a significant amount of space to this problem by discussing the primary figures of the sociological tradition, such as Weber, Mead, Durkheim, and Parsons. For reasons of brevity I cannot summarize his determinate critiques of each of these major social thinkers, but I will discuss his proposed solution as it relates to his conception of a critical social theory. Briefly, his solution is that social theory needs to accommodate both aspects in order to provide an adequate theoretical explanation of society.[36] Neither of these perspectives can adequately explain the totality of social phenomena. Society can be adequately conceptualized only if we give an account of both the lifeworld of the socialized individuals from the internal perspective of those individuals and the system of actions of those same individuals from the external perspective of an observer. Only in this way can social theory give an adequate account of both the action orientations of members of society and the unintended action consequences that further serve to integrate society. Thus, Habermas proposes "that we conceive of societies *simultaneously* as systems and lifeworlds" (TCA II, 118).

The idea of a rationalization of the lifeworld is fundamentally that the structures of interaction based in communicative action and that constitute the lifeworld develop such that the rationality potential inherent in communicative action is progressively released. The focus is on the variations of forms of lifeworld structures, and not on the variations in content. Furthermore, for the moment, the contingent events that trigger lifeworld structural changes are bracketed in this analysis.

Following Mead and Durkheim, Habermas sketches the rationalization of the lifeworld under three aspects: structural differentiation of the lifeworld, separation of form and content, and growing reflexivity of symbolic reproduction (TCA II, 145–146). The lifeworld becomes increasingly differentiated with respect to the three previously identified structural components of the lifeworld: culture, society, and personality (see TCA II, 146). Culture and society become differentiated when social institutions gain independence from worldviews. Personality becomes differentiated from society through a greater independence for the development of interpersonal relations, such that interpersonal relations are no longer strictly regulated by social institutions. Culture becomes differentiated from personality when the individual is no longer a strictly socialized being; that is, the individual continues the cultural tradition with an increasingly critical attitude. These differentiations represent a release of rationality potential because they structurally embody the three different validity claims raised in each and every utterance. The consequence is that intersubjective agreement becomes less dependent upon a given normative consensus anchored in tradition, and it relies increasingly on the communicative accomplishments of the individuals. In other words, these differentiations embody an increase of personal autonomy.

In addition to the structural differentiation of the lifeworld, the rationalization of the lifeworld manifests itself in an increasing degree of separation of form and content (see TCA II, 146). In the dimension of culture, the meaning-securing tradition separates into formal concepts such as abstract basic values, argumentative procedures, and so on, and concrete contents. For instance, in the modern era, scientific procedures for the accumulation and testing of valid knowledge are distinguished from the contents of that knowledge. In the dimension of society, abstract principles and procedures separate from concrete contexts. So in the modern era there is a differentiation of law and morality from concrete prescriptions concerning the good life. And in the dimension of personality, the process of socialization no longer is accomplished through an undifferentiated accommodation to a cultural tradition. Rather, in the modern era socialization is first accomplished primarily through the acquisition of formal competencies, and the contents of socialization become devalued in this process.

Finally, rationalization of the lifeworld manifests itself in increasing reflexivity of the reproduction of the lifeworld. As culture, society and personality are differentiated from each other, they manifest themselves in cultural value spheres that develop their own specific modes of reproduction. Furthermore, the reproduction of the lifeworld in each of these dimensions becomes increasingly reflexive.

It is important to realize that Habermas is not writing a Whiggish history of the lifeworld in which it becomes increasingly rationalized without any negative consequences manifesting themselves. He explicitly acknowledges that the *rationalization* of the lifeworld does not guarantee that the *reproduction* of the lifeworld will occur free of disturbances (TCA II, 147). Habermas maintains that "[i]t is only the level at which disturbances can appear that shifts with the degree of rationalization" (TCA II, 147). This formulation of the thesis is perhaps a bit misleading. The level at which these disturbances appear remains the level of the lifeworld, but in the course of the rationalization of the lifeworld a second level of society becomes differentiated: that of the system.

There are several ways of characterizing the distinction between lifeworld and system, depending upon one's theoretical perspective. In terms of the integration of individuals in a society—how they are bound together—the distinction can be made between social integration (lifeworld) and system integration (system). Social integration refers to the type of integration of individuals which occurs through meaningful communicative actions. In contrast, system integration refers to the form of integration which occurs through nonsymbolic media, such as money and power. Another way to characterize the lifeworld/system distinction is ontologically, as that between the public sphere and families on the one hand (lifeworld) and the economy and society on the other hand (system). A third way to characterize the distinction is methodologically, as the distinction between understanding (lifeworld) and explanation (system). From this methodological perspective, society can be viewed and analyzed from either the inside, from the first-person perspective of the participants, or from the outside, from the third-person perspective of a disinterested observer. Neither perspective in itself sufficiently represents all features of society, but together they form a complementary pair.

Furthermore, the first and the last characterizations of this distinction are connected. Only by alternatively adopting the first- and the third-person perspectives can the social theorists adequately both understand and explain the forms of societal integration. Lifeworld and system provide distinct methodological perspectives on societal integration for the social theorist. From the lifeworld perspective, societal integration is explained by mechanisms of consensus formation, whereas from the system perspective, societal integration is explained by the strategic coordination of interest positions. Corresponding to each of these perspectives, then, is an aspect of societal integration: from the lifeworld perspective society is integrated *socially,* and from the system perspective society is integrated *systemically*. However, Habermas emphasizes that social and system integration are initially introduced as "two *aspects* of societal integration which must be considered *analytically* distinct."[37] Only in the course of the rationalization of the lifeworld as sketched out above do spheres of social action that are integrated primarily either socially or systemically differentiate out of the sociocultural lifeworld. Thus, in modern societies mechanisms of system integration differentiate out from mechanisms of social integration to form spheres of action that are primarily integrated according to money and power relations: "[T]he objective conditions under which the systems-theoretical objectification of the lifeworld becomes necessary have themselves only arisen in the course of social evolution" (TCA II, 153). Thus, what needs explanation is just this historical differentiation of social and system integration.

We saw above that in the course of rationalization the lifeworld structures of culture, society, and personality become differentiated. A particularly interesting consequence of the differentiation of culture and society is an increase in what Parsons called "value generalization." Value generalization refers to "the tendency for value orientations that are institutionally required of actors to become more and more general and formal in the course of social evolution" (TCA II, 179). This increase in value generalization results in two further tendencies relevant to critical social theory. First, value generalization is a necessary condition of the rationality potential contained in communicative action (TCA II, 180). And second, "freeing communicative action from particular value orientations also forces the separation of action oriented to success from action oriented to mutual understanding" (TCA II, 180). That is, with value generalization space is opened up for the development of subsystems of action integrated by purposive-rational action. Of course the structural capacity for the development of these purposive-rational subsystems (necessary conditions) does not address the sufficient conditions of their development. But as the lifeworld becomes rationalized in general, and value generalization progresses in particular, the burdens of societal integration rest with an increasing degree on the successful achievements of consensus. In nondifferentiated lifeworlds societal integration is less risky due to the strong binding effects of mythical worldviews. However, in civilized and modern societies, where societal integration is achieved increasingly through the achievement of mutual understanding, the risk for dissension is much greater. Thus, subsystems can achieve societal integration while reducing the risk of dissension. In this way the subsystems of political administration and capitalist economy develop to fulfill the function of societal integration with a lower degree of risk than can the lifeworld. In order to lessen the risk of dissension, these subsystems must function through delinguistified media of interaction. On Habermas's model, then, the subsystems of political administration and the economy function through the exchange of power and money, rather than through speech acts, and power and money are exchanged in purposive-rational systems of action. Habermas summarizes this process as follows:

> Everyday communicative practice is, as we have seen, embedded in a lifeworld context defined by cultural tradition, legitimate orders, and socialized individuals. Interpretive performances draw upon and advance consensus. The rationality potential of mutual understanding in language is actualized to the extent that

> motive and value generalization progress and the zones of what is unproblematic shrink. The growing pressure for rationality that a problematic lifeworld exerts upon the mechanism of mutual understanding increases the need for achieved consensus, and this increases the expenditure of interpretive energies and the risk of dissensus. It is these demands and dangers that can be headed off by media of communication. The way these media function differs according to whether they focus consensus formation in language through specializing in certain aspects of validity and hierarchizing processes of agreement, or whether they uncouple action coordination from consensus formation in language altogether, and neutralize it with respect to the alternatives of agreement or failed agreement. (TCA II, 183)

Recall that the motivation for a critical social theory is to explain the paradox of modernity, which is that modernizing rationalization processes do not usher in greater control over social reproduction, rather, they form an "iron cage," as Weber describes it. Habermas's theoretical framework as discussed so far fails as critical social theory if it cannot explain the paradox of modernity. Habermas's thesis of the "colonization of the lifeworld" is intended to provide just such an explanation.

As the subsystems of political administration and capitalist economy differentiate out of the lifeworld, they enter into contradiction with those lifeworld structures from which they originated. These subsystems are integrated systemically (coordinated primarily by mechanisms of strategic action), which is a radically different type of societal integration than that of the lifeworld, which is integrated socially (coordinated primarily by mechanisms of communicative action). This uncoupling of the system from the lifeworld functions in the first instance to relieve the lifeworld of some of the risk of dissension, and it thus increases the stability of societal integration. However, since the action-coordinating mechanisms of system integration are significantly different from those of social integration, a tension develops such that one form of societal integration tends to expand into all areas of the lifeworld. Now Habermas notes that we cannot infer from this fact of the uncoupling of the system from the lifeworld whether the structures of social integration will expand to limit the structures of systemic integration of the media-steered subsystems, or whether the structures of systemic integration will expand to limit the structures of social integration (see TCA II, 185). But he goes on to argue that since this particular conception of a critical social theory gives genetic primacy to the lifeworld, that is, the explanation of the uncoupling of the system is derived from the explanation of the rationalization of the lifeworld, we have the means by which to determine a destructive increase in complexity of the system. In other words, the same dynamic that led to the rationalization of the lifeworld, which in turn led to the differentiation out of the system, also leads to a further rationalization of the system, that is, an increase in complexity. But since the analysis gives genetic primacy to the lifeworld, we have the means to interpret a destructive increase in complexity. It becomes destructive, and hence pathological, when it encroaches upon the natural rationalization processes of the lifeworld itself. Thus, given Habermas's theoretical framework, we can see how the imperatives of system integration will tend to expand and encroach upon the domains of social integration (TCA II, 186).

The thesis of the colonization of the lifeworld, then, is the concrete critical substance of critical social theory as conceived by Habermas. It explains with the backing of an extensive theoretical structure the ways in which modern forms of consciousness have become reified. When systemic imperatives coordinated through strategic action colonize domains that can only be integrated socially (that is through communicative action), social relations (in these domains) become reified. The symbolically mediated structures of cultural reproduction, social integration, and socialization, can be legitimately coordinated only through communicative action. So when these structures of symbolic reproduction are colonized by the imperatives of system integration, they are prevented from reproducing in a legitimate way these meaning-generating structures of consciousness.

Summary

In this chapter I have outlined the contours of Habermas's critical social theory as it is formulated in *The Theory of Communicative Action*. Part of the aim here is to show that as for Marx, Horkheimer, Adorno, and so forth, Habermas's critical theory is a theory of modern society with a practical intent. In this respect Habermas does fall within the tradition of the Frankfurt School, for his conception of critical theory explicitly incorporates an historical dimension. It seeks to understand present social conditions in sociohistorical terms, and it is self-reflective on its own origins in those conditions. And while Habermas's linguistic turn in critical theory is important, his critical theory should not be reduced to formal pragmatics. Formal pragmatics alone cannot constitute a critical theory; it requires the historical or diachronic dimension that is part of the very concept of a critical theory. While it is understandable that much of the attention has been directed at Habermas's formal pragmatics, for it does represent a significant contribution to the idea of a critical theory, it is crucial not to confuse this aspect of the critical theory with the entire theory itself.

The temptation to reduce his critical theory to the theory of formal pragmatics is further motivated by Habermas's relative silence on the theory of social evolution since the publication of *The Theory of Communicative Action*. Here, those critics who maintain that Habermas does not belong to the tradition of the Frankfurt School have a point. It is the case that since the mid 1980s Habermas has turned his attention to what can be characterized as more liberal concerns, writing on the foundations of moral philosophy, normative political philosophy, and the philosophy of law. One explanation of his silence is simply that he has turned his attention to other problems. But even in these works he has not renounced or contradicted his earlier work. One can see in the essays of *Moral Consciousness and Communicative Action* and in *Between Facts and Norms: Contributions to a Discourse Theory of Democracy* a careful attention to the modern historical context out of which his theorizing derives. Thus, even in his more recent work, Habermas continues to rely on the critical-theoretical insights of *The Theory of Communicative Action*.

Even so, it is quite understandable why commentators have not taken up the theory of social evolution. This is a complex theory, ranging over a considerable amount of theoretical and historical terrain, and it was presented in a rather unsystematic way by Habermas, even in *The Theory of Communicative Action*. Thus, in the next chapter I will analyze the main elements of this theory in order to hone its conceptual clarity and general coherence.

Chapter 3

The Developmental Theory of Social Evolution

As I have shown in the previous chapter, the theory of social evolution plays a complementary role to the formal-pragmatic analysis of language use in Habermas's conception of critical theory. It complements the formal-pragmatic aspect by providing an explanation of the historical, or diachronic, development of structures of consciousness. It postulates universal logics of development for these structures, which delimit the horizon of possible determinate historical forms. Thus, we can identify the rational structures underlying any given society, while at the same time explaining the possibility of value and cultural pluralism.

It is my objective in the present chapter to systematically explicate and clarify Habermas's theory of social evolution.[1] Before we can critically examine its fruitfulness as a research program, we first need to clarify the basic concepts and logical structure of the theory itself—only when we are in possession of a theory that is sufficiently specific and hence capable of falsification can we proceed to judge its theoretical merits.

General Considerations

Habermas assembled the central elements of the theory of social evolution primarily during the 1970s when he was codirector with C. F. von Weizsäcker of the Max Planck Institute for the Study of the Conditions of Life in the Scientific-Technical World.[2] There he was able to draw upon substantial interdisciplinary research out of which the theory of social evolution is derived, and which the theory is intended to explain. He developed it in a series of early essays proposing a reconstruction of historical materialism, but he never systematized the theory as a whole.[3] Unfortunately, Habermas has not returned to the topic of social evolution since these early programmatic essays. In each of the collections of critical essays concerning Habermas's work that include replies by Habermas, when issues regarding the theory of social evolution arise, Habermas declines to take up and expand upon this topic.[4] He indicates, however, that he declines not because he has had second thoughts, but because of the difficulty and complexity of the issues involved. In each case he defers specifically to the complexity and difficulty of the task.[5] It is my intention here to contribute to the clarification and systematization of this important and necessary element of Habermas's critical social theory.

Conceptual and Theoretical Distinctions

An adequate understanding of any theory requires a proper understanding of its constitutive concepts and terms. This is especially important regarding a theory of social evolution because of the general disagreement and lack of clarity concerning the basic concepts of *social evolution, development,* and *progress*. I will attempt in this section to clarify the definitions of, and distinctions between, the central concepts that characterize Habermas's theory of social evolution.

In a 1946 report on the theory and practice of historiography to the Social Science Research Council, Charles Beard and Sydney Hook explicitly attempted to clarify various historical concepts.[6] In this report, Hook (who was primarily responsible for the section containing the definitions) defines change as "any difference in position, form, quality," where difference is determined relative to some criterion.[7] Hence, historical change refers to "differences in the behavior of human beings as members of a social group or differences in the behavior and organization of things and institutions which condition changes in human behavior."[8] This definition of historical change, however, is limited to a third-person observer's perspective, and thus it does not account for fundamental changes in the structures of consciousness of the historical agents. It would be useful, then, to expand Beard and Hook's definition of social change to include (1) the qualitative changes in the behavior of social agents as members of a group, or (2) changes in the organization of social structures that condition social action, or (3) changes in fundamental attitudes or orientations of social agents with respect to their environments. This sense of social change does not imply any notion of directionality, or value judgment; it is strictly a descriptive term.

The concept of social evolution also has various senses, the ambiguity arising in part from the origins of the concept. Tom Bottomore asserts that "[t]he notion of social evolution was taken directly from the theories of biological evolution. . . ."[9] But Robert Nisbet argues that "it is one of the more curious misconceptions of much modern writing in the history of social thought that nineteenth-century social evolutionism was simply an adaptation of the ideas of biological evolutionism, chiefly those of Charles Darwin, to the study of social institutions."[10] Nisbet gives two reasons in support of this claim: first, the principle works of social evolution either appeared before Darwin's *Origin of the Species* (for example Comte, Hegel, Marx, and Spencer[11]), or made reference to work that predated Darwin; and second, the differences in theory and method between theories of biological and social evolution are substantial and far outweigh any similarities that obtain.[12] My interest here is not in this controversy over origins, but in adequately clarifying the concept of social evolution as it relates to Habermas's theory. According to Hook, the concept of development should be distinguished from the concept of evolution. On his understanding, evolutionary social change is development (that is, directed social change) that is gradual, to be distinguished from revolutionary social change, which is abrupt. Setting aside for the moment Hook's inadequate understanding of development, we can understand social evolution as social change that exhibits a direction (according to some criterion) and that is primarily continuous and gradual and not significantly discontinuous or abrupt. We should be careful to distinguish this sense of social evolution (directional social change) from development (teleological social change). Social evolution need not determine the direction of change according to a teleological criterion, as does development. The directional criterion of social evolution can refer to accumulation without referring to a telos or end.[13] I also want to emphasize that a theory of social evolution may be based on a developmental model of social change (in either sense), or it may be based on some other model. Social evolution and social development are not coextensive. They may coincide in one theory but they need not necessarily do so.[14]

The concepts of social change and social evolution just defined should be further distinguished from the concept of development. Hook defines development as "any change which has a continuous *direction* and which culminates in a phase that is qualitatively *new*."[15] Any series of events or structures that exhibit directional and qualitative change should be characterized as developmental. The criterion of directionality is rarely explicitly specified, but it usually involves some form of accumulation. So cognitive-technical knowledge is said to develop in this sense in part because of the accumulation of scientific knowledge about the world. In contrast to this sense of development as directional social change, Bottomore has defined the original use of development as "a gradual unfolding; a fuller working out, of the details of anything; the growth of what is in the germ."[16] In this Hegelian sense of the term, the development of society can be understood to refer to the teleological unfolding of the potentials originally inherent within it. An important characteristic of this sense of development is that it determines the limits of possible change. That is, a developmental theory of social change explicates the horizon of possible forms change can assume, and this horizon is internally determined according to the telos.[17] For present purposes, then, the concept of development will refer to teleological social change metaphorically understood as the gradual unfolding of an inherent potential.

Furthermore, the concept of progress should be distinguished from both concepts of development and evolution (in the senses I have adopted). Progress differs from both development and evolution since it explicitly associates a normative moment to descriptions of social change. Hook adequately defines progress as directional historical change that is "favorably evaluated from the standpoint of a human interest, end, or ideal."[18] Progress implies a normative claim with respect to the directional criterion or criteria of social change. Either evolutionary development or revolutionary development can be characterized as progressive (or regressive); there is no intrinsic connection between the concepts of evolution and progress, or development and progress. The concepts of evolution and development are strictly descriptive terms, but the concept of progress is an evaluative or normative term.

In summary, the definitions of these concepts that will be adopted for the purposes of this study are as follows. "Social change" refers to qualitative changes in the behavior of social agents as members of a group, or changes in the organization of social structures that condition social action, or changes in fundamental attitudes of social agents with respect to their environments. "Development" refers to teleological social change metaphorically understood as the gradual unfolding of an inherent potential. "Social evolution" refers to social change that exhibits a direction (according to some criterion) and that is continuous and gradual and not discontinuous or abrupt. "Progress" refers to any directional social change that is favorably evaluated according to a criterion of value.

Theories of social evolution have a special need for the clarification of concepts, since often the basic concepts are not disaggregated. Given that Habermas's theory of social evolution is complex and draws on a variety of theoretical traditions, it has a special need for relatively unambiguous basic concepts. Habermas himself, however, contributes to misunderstandings with inconsistent use of some of the key concepts of his theory. His explicit writings on social evolution, for instance, remain ambiguous as to whether or not he understands it in a teleological sense. A central feature of his theory of social evolution is its assertion of a developmental logic of normative structures, which implies some sort of teleological unfolding of these structures. But he is critical of philosophies of history that purport to see in history an immanent teleology. Furthermore, he fails to distinguish adequately the concepts of development and social evolution. For example, in the context of a discussion of the origins of the idea of rationalization, he describes "the developmental theories *[Entwicklungstheorien]* of the nineteenth century" as theories that "interpreted advances in civilization in a Darwinian manner, as the development of quasi-organic systems *[sie deuten die Fortschritte der Zivilisation darwinistisch als Entwicklung organischer Systeme]*" (TCA I, 151). First, here he refers to the nineteenth-century theories of social evolution as "developmental theories." According to the distinctions presented above, these two concepts should not be conflated. Second, he assumes that theories of social evolution are modeled on theories of natural evolution. As we have seen above, this is at the least a problematic assumption. And third, Darwin's theory of natural selection is not a teleological model of change that can be understood according to the metaphor of the growth of an organic system. While it can be argued that nineteenth-century theories of social evolution were teleological models of social change, they assuredly were not Darwinian in the strict sense.[19] These theories collapsed the concept of progress into the concept of evolution. But biological evolution does not conflate these two concepts; the criterion of evolution in biological models is sufficient fitness to ensure survival.

Regarding the concept of social evolution, Habermas says that "[w]hen we speak of evolution *[Evolution]*, we do in fact mean cumulative processes *[kumula-*

tive Vorgänge] that exhibit a direction *[Richtung]*" (CES, 141). What he seems to mean by this is that the property of accumulation is part of what determines the directionality of change. He goes on to discuss the advantages and disadvantages of the directional criterion of neoevolutionism of increasing complexity (see CES, 141–142). So the directional criterion in this case would be complexity that accumulates. What is not clear is why the property of directionality needs to incorporate accumulation. Could not directionality be specified without reference to the accumulation of some feature? For example, in theories of history that posit a cyclical historical process we could specify a direction (in the weak sense of not being random), but there would not seem to be any accumulation of any directional properties. Here, Habermas seems to be thinking of the concept of developmental logic, but using development as directional, cumulative social change—*without* a telos. This leads us back to the question of what Habermas means by development.

While at this point these conceptual distinctions may seem to serve no end, they serve the purpose of clarifying the historical characteristics of Habermas's theory of social evolution. It is an important question as to whether Habermas's theory of social evolution, despite its name, should be characterized as an evolutionary theory or a developmental theory (or a hybrid combination of both). Habermas calls it a theory of social evolution, but its central concept is that of developmental logic. Given the definitions that I have adopted in this study, evolutionary theories and developmental theories will entail significantly different interpretations regarding the ends of history, and this will have critical implications regarding the normative import of the theory of social evolution. For, on one hand, if the theory is to be characterized as teleological, then the normative orientation is unambiguous, but difficult to defend.[20] On the other hand, however, if the theory does not specify a telos, and derives the criterion of directionality according to some internal properties of social change, then the normative orientation is perhaps less focused, but (perhaps) easier to defend.

Any social theory that seeks to provide a comprehensive and adequate account of society must provide an account of the reproduction of society, that is, of the self-maintenance of society over time. An adequate account of the reproduction of society must explain at least three features. First, it needs to explain just how a society maintains its existence in the diachronic, or historical, dimension. Second, it also needs to explain social change; that is, it needs to explain the historical maintenance of identity through changing structures of social relations. Third, it needs to explain the progressive, regressive, or even stagnant nature of that social change. It may be the case, however, that we can only describe social change without imputing any normativity to that change. As I discuss above, whether we can specify the progressive or regressive character of social change cannot be determined a priori. Nevertheless, if we adopt a sociocritical perspective with an interest in emancipation and happiness, then we have a fundamental interest in describing and explaining the progressive (or regressive) character of social change. The inherent goals of critical social theory provide sufficient motivation for at least attempting to provide a well-grounded account of progressive social change.

Habermas's theory of social evolution intends to explain the reproduction of society, consisting of the elements of the maintenance of society, social change, and the directional character of social change. Habermas has labeled his theory one of "social evolution" *[soziale Evolution]*, which, as he understands it, refers to the directional change of the structures that constitute society as a whole. There are three claims that are embedded in this definition: (1) that the theory of social evolution explains social change in society as a whole; (2) that the object of the theory of social evolution is the intersubjective structures that constitute society; and (3) that the theory of social evolution describes and explains the directionality of the changes of those structures. So, first, the theory of social evolution intends to explain the evolution of society as a whole, and not merely some element or aspect of it. This includes such elements of society as material production, culture, and social relations (for example, civil society, institutions, and practices). The scope of the theory of social evolution is more comprehensive than theories that explain directional change in only the cultural or the social domains. Thus, when Brian J. Whitton critiques Habermas's theory of social evolution, he focuses exclusively on the development of normative structures, and he ignores the relations of these normative structures to the material reproduction of society.[21] Consequently, Whitton misunderstands the scope of Habermas's theory, and his critique falls short of its intended goal.

Second, Habermas's theory of social evolution takes as its explanatory object the structures of intersubjectivity that constitute society: "[S]ocial evolution can be discerned in those structures that are replaced by more comprehensive structures in accord with a pattern [that is, a developmental logic] that is to be rationally reconstructed" (CES, 140). These structures are abstract structures of consciousness that delimit the horizon of possible concrete forms of consciousness, they "describe the logical space in which more comprehensive structural formations can take shape. . . ." (CES, 140). In addition to limiting the range of concrete forms of consciousness, these structures also embody the knowledge potential of a given society at a given level of development. And, as will be clarified below, Habermas argues that social evolution is best explained by reference to the structures of consciousness in both the cognitive-technical knowledge and moral-practical insight.

Third, Habermas's theory of social evolution describes and explains the directionality of social change in terms of cumulative processes that are directionally specific (CES, 141). "Cumulative processes" refers to the accumulation of both cognitive-technical knowledge and moral-practical insight, and when conjoined with an adequate theory of rationality can be understood as rationalization processes. In what sense do these types of knowledge accumulate? Clearly this presents a problem for any postempirical philosophy of science that wants to be consistent with Kuhn's analysis of incommensurable paradigm shifts. To address this problem, Habermas again appeals to an analogy with cognitive developmental psychology. According to Piaget, as children mature through the stages of cognitive development they pass through various stages of learning. Each successive stage is said to reorder the know-how of the previous stage. So at one stage the same tasks can be accomplished as at the previous one, but under a transformed conceptual scheme. Moreover, this transformed conceptual scheme opens up the possibility of mastering new tasks, that is, accumulating new knowledge.

Epistemological Assumptions

Habermas conceives of both elements of his critical social theory, the theory of social evolution and the theory of communicative action, as reconstructive sciences. According to Habermas, reconstructive sciences seek to explain the universal structures of our pretheoretical knowledge: "Starting primarily from the intuitive knowledge of competent subjects—competent in terms of judgment, action, and language—and secondarily from systematic knowledge handed down by culture, the reconstructive sciences explain the presumably universal bases of rational experience and judgment, as well as of action and linguistic communication" (MCCA, 15–16). Reconstructive sciences apply the methods of formal analysis, understood as "the methodological attitude we adopt in the rational reconstruction of concepts, criteria, rules, and schemata" (CES, 8).[22] The procedures of rational reconstruction, according to which reconstructive sciences operate, "are not characteristic of sciences that develop nomological hypotheses about domains of observable events; rather, these procedures are characteristic of *sciences that systematically reconstruct the intuitive knowledge of competent subjects*" (CES, 9). While I cannot pursue here a comprehensive critical examination of the concept of a reconstructive science, it is sufficiently important to warrant further clarification. My discussion will generally follow Habermas's own attempt to elucidate the concept in "What Is Universal Pragmatics?" (CES, esp. 8–25).[23]

Habermas begins his clarification by contrasting the characteristics of reconstructive sciences with those of the empirical-analytic sciences. Empirical-analytic sciences are primarily concerned with observation of perceptible reality, whereas reconstructive sciences are primarily concerned with understanding *[Verstehen]* (communicative experience), which is concerned with the meaning of utterances (CES, 9). Here, the object of understanding is symbolically prestructured reality. Moreover, the process of observation is accomplished by an observer who is in principle alone, but in the process of understanding the individual adopts the attitude of a participant in communication. Habermas associates the pragmatic accomplishments of these two types of sciences with the functions of description and explication: "By using a sentence that reports an observation, I can describe the observed aspect of reality. By using a sentence that renders an interpretation of the meaning of a symbolic formation, I can explicate the meaning of such an utterance" (CES, 10). An important characteristic of both descriptions and explications that Habermas points out is that they can operate at different levels (or as Habermas says, they "have different ranges"). They can either describe or explicate surface phenomena, or they can "push through" to describe or explicate the determining structures that underlie the surface phenomena.

The concept of explication, however, remains ambiguous for our purposes. It is desirable, Habermas asserts, to distinguish between two levels of explication of meaning (see CES, 11–12). On the first level, explication is the process of understanding the semantic content of some act of communication (for example, a written sentence, action, gesture, work of art, tool, theory, commodity, or transmitted document), and, to begin with, this process of understanding proceeds by associating the meaning of the ambiguous content with the meaning of familiar acts of communication: "[T]he *understanding of content* pursues connections that link the surface structures of the incomprehensible formation with the surface structures of other, familiar formations. Thus, linguistic expressions [for example] can be explicated through paraphrase in the same language or through translation into expressions of another language; in both cases, competent speakers draw on intuitively known meaning relations that obtain within the lexicon of one language or between those of two languages" (CES, 11–12). If we describe this process as "horizontal explication," then the second level of explication can be termed "vertical explication." In this case, the interpreter attempts to understand a meaningful expression by looking to the generative structures of that expression, that is, those rules the speaker herself used (CES, 12). This deep structure is the pretheoretical know-how of competent knowing and acting subjects.

While I agree with the validity of this distinction, I think Habermas's discussion of vertical explication is a bit misleading. He introduces this second level of explication as an alternative approach to explication that seemingly comes into play only when horizontal explication fails: "If [the interpreter] cannot attain his end in this way [horizontal explication], the interpreter may find it necessary to alter his attitude" (CES, 12). It is not clear why this is limited to a secondary approach to explication. It seems to be a different sort of explication, with a different end. Horizontal explication seeks to grasp the meaning of an expression, but vertical explication seeks to uncover the generative rules of that expression. Horizontal explication really performs a different function than vertical explication, so introducing them as different approaches to explicating meaning is somewhat misleading. I am not arguing that Habermas's distinctions are confused, only that his presentation is rather misleading. Vertical explication is qualitatively different from horizontal explication, and, I think, this is what Habermas unsuccessfully tries to articulate here. While vertical explication can contribute in important ways to understanding the semantic content of a symbolic expression, it cannot of itself explicate that meaning. So vertical explication is not just an alternative method of understanding meaning in relation to horizontal explication; it possesses a qualitatively different function. And, as Habermas subsequently explains, the function of vertical explication is to make explicit our pretheoretical knowledge; that is, it transforms our know-how into "know-that" (see CES, 12–13).

Returning to the general characterization of reconstructive sciences, Habermas notes a distinction between the way empirical-analytic and reconstructive sciences relate to everyday knowledge. Where empirical-analytic knowledge typically refutes and replaces our common sense knowledge of the world, rational reconstructions merely make explicit our pretheoretical knowledge; they do not falsify that everyday knowledge: "At most, the report of a speaker's intuition [in a reconstruction] can prove to be false, but not the intuition itself" (CES, 16). This emphasizes the claim that reconstructive sciences simply transform know-how, which we already rely on intuitively, into "know-that."

Finally, reconstructive sciences admit only an essentialist epistemological interpretation.[24] Where the correspondence between description and object domain in empirical-analytic sciences admits of various epistemological interpretations, such as realist, conventionalist, or instrumentalist, rational reconstructions must be interpreted as explicating essential features of the object domain: "[I]f they are true, they have to correspond precisely to the rules that are operatively effective in the object domain—that is to the rules that actually determine the production of surface structures" (CES, 16).

Furthermore, Habermas emphasizes that rational reconstructions possess only hypothetical status. In this sense they are just like any other knowledge claims. They are simply knowledge claims about basic competencies of the knowing and acting subject, as they are formed in history. Thus, there is nothing a priori about them: "There is always the possibility that they rest on a false choice of examples, that they are obscuring and distorting correct intuitions, or, even more frequently, that they are overgeneralizing individual cases. For these reasons, they require further corroboration" (MCCA, 32). Thus, reconstructive sciences are empirical and not transcendental sciences.[25]

This claim of hypothetical status is not just one of a theoretical nature. It also indicates Habermas's fundamental approach to social theory. His understanding of his own project is that of a research program, and this indicates his general attitude about the fallibility of his concepts: "Recasting his thought as a research program is not something Habermas did simply because he wished to return to the founding spirit of the Frankfurt School. Rather, it constitutes a fundamental acceptance of the tentativeness and fallibility of his basic concepts. Once they are interpreted as part of the core of a research program, they can no longer be advanced with the self-confidence of orthodox Marxism or the tradition of German Idealism. And in this sense Habermas is explicitly distancing himself from the lingering foundationalism that characterized a work such as *Knowledge and Human Interests*."[26]

A useful example of the type of formal analysis of the reconstructive type is Chomsky's research program, which is a reconstructive science of grammatical structures. Whereas Chomsky is concerned with the universal deep structures of grammar, Habermas's formal pragmatics is concerned with the universal deep structures of the use of language in communication. In this connection it is worth noting that Habermas rejects as ahistorical and too strong Chomsky's assumption that the universal grammatical structures that are rationally reconstructed by his theory are innate dispositions of the mind. A reconstructive science does not need to make a claim as to the location of the structures it reconstructs: "Within the reconstructivist conceptual strategy, the more plausible assumption that grammatical theory represents the linguistic competence of the adult speaker is sufficient. This competence in turn is the result of a learning process that may—like cognitive development in the case of Piaget's cognitivist approach—follow a rationally reconstructible pattern" (CES, 20). Providing good reasons for the development and existence of universal competencies is sufficient for reconstructive sciences.

In conclusion, I want to summarize the important features of reconstructive sciences. The object domain of the reconstructive sciences is the symbolically prestructured reality of social life. The aim is not the clarification of surface meanings (which is the task of hermeneutics), but the reconstruction of the deep structures that generate those surface meanings. The scope of these reconstructions is not limited to individual or group performances, but is universal; that is, they reconstruct competencies that are such for all mature adult members of society. The function of reconstructive sciences is an essentialist one making explicit the pretheoretical knowledge always already in actual use in our social lives. The reconstruction of universal competencies operates in two dimensions: a horizontal dimension that reconstructs the competencies presently in effect, and a vertical dimension that reconstructs the development of these competencies. Reconstructions in each dimension have internal relations to the reconstructions of the other dimensions, but they are distinct enterprises with their own unique problems. Although they possess different perspectives on the reconstruction of universal competencies, reconstructions of developmental logics presuppose the reconstructions of horizontal structure (formal pragmatics). And lastly, the rational reconstruction of universal competencies is an empirical science since it is dependent on a posteriori knowledge.

Principal Elements

Having clarified some basic concepts and epistemological assumptions, we now have a basis for examining the details of the theory itself. The key to Habermas's theory is to understand several important distinctions. These distinctions concern the different dimensions of social existence in which developmental change can occur, the difference between labor and social interaction—and the relation between these, and the distinction between the pattern or logic of development and the concrete empirical conditions of social change. It is to these aspects of the theory that I now turn.

The Dimensions of Development

The central distinction Habermas makes concerning the reproduction of society is between interaction and labor. Human society, Habermas argues, reproduces itself along these two interrelated dimensions. Despite the reciprocal influences each exerts upon the other, however, neither dimension can be reduced to the other. To be sure, distinguishing between labor and interaction in an irreducible way is a significant deviation from the tradition of orthodox historical materialism, where societal reproduction is explained by only one of these dimensions, that of social labor, and the other dimension, interaction, is explanatorily reducible to labor. In contrast to this tradition, Habermas emphasizes the fundamental importance of interaction to the reproduction of human society, as well as the importance of rationalized interaction to emancipation. As McCarthy emphasizes, "The point of insisting on the 'heterogeneity' or 'irreducibility' of work and interaction is to avoid just that conflation of *techne* and *praxis*, of technical progress and the rational conduct of life, that . . . [is] at the roots of the technocratic ideology. Rationalization is not emancipation."[27] Moreover, Habermas postulates that the determining structures of both labor and interaction each develop according to their own internal logics. Since labor and interaction are mutually irreducible, any adequate theory of society which also explains social change needs to account for the logic of development in each of these dimensions, as well as the ways in which these two modes of action are dynamically related to each other. In what follows I will begin with a discussion of how the labor/interaction distinction derives from the theory of communicative action. After explicating the nature of the distinction, I will discuss how these two irreducible modes of engagement in the world are related to each other.

In Habermas's theory of social evolution, labor and interaction are the two basic modes of societal reproduction. What this means is that through both labor and interaction humans engage their environment in order to produce and appropriate, or reproduce, their existence. Thus the labor/interaction distinction is fundamentally grounded in the typology of action Habermas develops in *The Theory of Communicative Action*.[28] Recall that in action theory Habermas makes the fundamental distinction between two action orientations. Although all actions possess a general teleological (or purposive) structure such that agents act to achieve some goal based upon an interpretation of the situation, actions can be distinguished according to their dominant orientation. From the first-person perspective, actions can be oriented either towards success (instrumental and strategic actions) or towards mutual understanding (communicative actions). In contrast to the theory of communicative action, in which the distinction between *strategic* and *communicative* actions was most important, the theory of social evolution emphasizes the distinction between *purposive-rational* and *communicative* actions. Whereas the theory of communicative action was primarily concerned to justify an action typology that distinguishes between social actions primarily oriented towards success and those primarily oriented towards reaching understanding, the theory of social evolution more generally is concerned to explain the reproduction of human society, and this requires an understanding of the ways in which humans engage with the world. Now, Habermas's theory of communicative action distinguishes between instrumental and communicative action types. In instrumental action agents are primarily interested in successfully controlling and manipulating some object in conformity to their will, while in communicative action multiple interlocutors are primarily oriented towards coming to an understanding with each other about some thing, thus coordinating the actions of individual actors.

Returning to the level of social reproduction, we can see that instrumental action is associated with the material reproduction of social life, and communicative action is associated with the symbolic reproduction of social life. In order for societies to flourish and hence for their members to survive, they must reproduce at the minimum the enabling conditions of society as such. This entails that both the material and social conditions of society must (at the minimum) be reproduced over time. The material conditions can be met by the satisfaction of the physical needs of individuals, for example the appropriation and production of food, clothing, and shelter. The symbolic conditions of society are embodied in the lifeworld and its structures. Communicative actions draw upon the symbolic resources of the lifeworld for their content, and conversely the lifeworld is reproduced in the performance of communicative actions. Through communicative action, cultural knowledge is reproduced, stored and utilized; institutions of social cohesion are generated and reproduced; and individual personalities are differentiated and socialized. Thus, together communicative actions and lifeworld structures generate and reproduce the structures of culture, society and personality.

The categories of labor and interaction, which are present in Habermas's essays throughout the 1970s, should not be conflated with the categories of system and lifeworld, which are elaborated in *The Theory of Communicative Action*. While "labor" and "interaction" refer to the basic ways that humans interact with their environment, and thus to the dimensions in which society is reproduced, "system" and "lifeworld" refer to the two mutually irreducible heuristic perspectives that are necessary to obtain an adequate and comprehensive understanding of society. Tom Rockmore commits this error when he asserts that in *The Theory of Communicative Action* Habermas has simply renamed the categories of labor and interaction as "system" and "lifeworld."[29] This claim is based on a misunderstanding of some key concepts and their relation to each other in *The Theory of Communicative Action*. As we have seen immediately above, Habermas clarifies and sharpens the notions of labor and interaction through a formal-pragmatic analysis of action types, resulting in the distinction of the concept of communicative action. And the action typology developed there does ground the idea that society reproduces itself in two irreducible dimensions. But the concepts of system and lifeworld are not identical with the concepts of labor and interaction; they do not even perform similar functions in Habermas's critical social theory. The concepts of system and lifeworld are first, intended to indicate the two aspects by which society can be conceived. That is, we can conceive of society as either a system (from an external, observational perspective) or a lifeworld (from an internal, participatory perspective), and further, neither aspect sufficiently grasps all social phenomena. Second, as societies make the transition from traditional forms to modern forms the lifeworld becomes differentiated, eventually resulting in the emergence of systemic subsystems of society (the economy and state administration) from the structures of the lifeworld. In a response to critics, Habermas explicitly addresses this misinterpretation:

> There can . . . be no talk of my having wished to confine functionalism [the methodological approach of systems theory] to the observation of phenomena of

> material reproduction. And it is equally misleading to suppose the processes of symbolic and material reproduction can only be grasped in terms of one respective aspect [either system or lifeworld]. An approximate description can be given of all phenomena using *each* of the two aspects—although there is a difference in depth of field. It is always possible to approach from its own perspective the manner in which a lifeworld reproduces the material conditions for its existence; yet whether these processes have become so opaque and complex as to be inadmissibly foreshortened by being examined from this perspective and can thus be *better* explained under the aspect of system depends on the degree of differentiation within a society. Conversely, systems analysis will also always embrace those contributions which cultural tradition, social integration and socialization make to stabilizing boundaries in an over-complex environment; in doing so, however, it must treat the internal limitations that symbolic structures impose on the steering capacity of a system as contingent data without being able to explain them adequately, for example, with the aid of a developmental logic. (R, 253)

As this statement makes clear, Habermas does not simply rename the categories of labor and interaction as system and lifeworld in *The Theory of Communicative Action*. While there are theoretical relations between the two sets of concepts, they are far from identical with each other.

The fundamental thesis underlying Habermas's theory of social evolution, that the reproduction of human society occurs in the two irreducible, but interrelated, dimensions of labor and interaction, stands or falls with the validity of the distinction between actions oriented to success and actions oriented to reaching understanding. The discussion of the theory of communicative action in the previous chapter should have made at least a prima facie case for the plausibility of this distinction.[30]

Now that we have seen how Habermas's labor/interaction distinction is grounded in the theory of communicative action, it is necessary to clarify how this distinction manifests itself in the evolution of society. First, recall that Habermas understands the individual ego and society to be reciprocally constituted, such that persons are individuated from each other in the very process of socialization. In other words, the autonomous ego does not preexist its entering into society with other autonomous egos; rather, only by interacting with other egos do numerically distinct egos develop their own respective identities: "[T]he reproduction of society *[die Reproduktion der Gesellschaft]* and the socialization *[Sozialisation]* of its members are two aspects of the same process; they are dependent on the same structures" (CES, 99).

Social evolution, according to Habermas, is a directional process of social change that occurs in two dimensions, those of labor and interaction. In the dimension of labor, the structures of cognitive-technical consciousness develop according to their own logic, and in the dimension of interaction, the structures of moral-pragmatic consciousness develop according to their own logic. Each dimension does influence the development of the other, but only in an empirical sense. The developmental logic in each dimension is wholly independent of the other: "The species learns not only in the dimension of technically useful knowledge decisive for the development of productive forces but also in the dimension of moral-practical consciousness decisive for structures of interaction. The rules of communicative action do develop in reaction to changes in the domain of instrumental and strategic action; but in doing so they follow *their own logic*" (CES, 148). In other words, these two dimensions are not functionally related; instead, developments in each dimension—when, and if, they do occur—possess their own unique pattern. In the dimension of labor, the structures of consciousness of instrumental action determine the horizon of possible actions.[31] And in the dimension of interaction, the structures of consciousness of communicative action determine the horizon which determines the range of possible interactions. Following Weber, Habermas conceives of these developmental logics of structures of consciousness as embodying a process of rationalization. Thus, Habermas conceives of social evolution as a rationalization process that occurs in two dimensions, the dimension of cognitive-technical knowledge and the dimension of moral-practical insight: "I am convinced that normative structures do not simply follow the path of development of reproductive processes and do not simply respond to the pattern of system problems, but that they have instead an *internal history*. In earlier investigations I have tried to argue that holistic concepts such as productive activity and *Praxis* have to be resolved into the basic concepts of communicative action and purposive rational action in order to avoid confusing the two rationalization processes that determine social evolution; the rationalization of action takes effect not only on productive forces but also, and independently, on normative structures" (CES, 117).

Before going on to discuss Habermas's conception of rationalization, I first want to emphasize that though Habermas conceives of the evolution of society as occurring in both the cognitive-technical and the moral-practical dimensions, he has focused his efforts primarily upon reconstructing the development of moral-practical structures of consciousness. There are two reasons for this unbalanced emphasis. First, Habermas believes that the developmental logics of structures of moral-practical consciousness have been the object of much less investigation than those of cognitive-technical structures of consciousness (such as in the history of science). Second, Habermas conceives of developments in moral-practical consciousness to be the "pace-maker" of evolution. Following Marx, he recognizes that the development of the productive forces constitutes the primary dynamic force of history, but unlike the technological interpretation of historical materialism,[32] Habermas does not understand the relation between the cognitive-technical and moral-practical dimensions as a functional relation; developments in the moral practical dimension cannot be functionally explained by reference to the cognitive-technical dimension.[33] Developments in the productive forces generate certain problems or crises that can only be solved or overcome by evolutionary learning processes in the dimension of moral-practical rationality: "The development of productive forces can be understood as a problem-generating mechanism that *triggers but does not bring about* the overthrow of relations of production and an evolutionary renewal of the mode of production" (CES, 146). In other words, the development of productive forces is a necessary, but not sufficient, condition of social evolutionary change. The idea is that when a crisis arises, the solution is not found in an overthrow of the existing relations of production such that they no longer fetter the forces of production; the form of the necessary—necessary to overcome the crisis—relations of production is not determined by the forces of production. Evolutionary crises are overcome only when moral-practical learning occurs, and since this is a type of learning, it possesses its own logic. Thus, in Habermas's model the key to understanding social evolution is found in the domain of moral-practical consciousness. Habermas's unbalanced emphasis, however, has resulted in misinterpretations of his theory of social evolution. As I mentioned briefly above, Whitton criticizes Habermas's theory as being idealist, in the sense that it pays insufficient attention to the role of material interests in social evolution. But he conflates the theory of social evolution with the development of just the normative structures. The result of this misinterpretation is that Whitton is guilty of committing the straw man fallacy; the theory he criticizes simply is not Habermas's. It is important to remember, then, that while Habermas has focused primarily on the development of normative structures of consciousness, the scope of the theory of social evolution also includes an explanation of the development of the productive forces and their dialectical relationship to the normative structures.

Rationalization

In the previous section I explicated the sociological use (in the theory of social evolution) of the distinction between the two fundamental action types of purposive and communicative action. These two action types are associated with corresponding action structures that are primarily determined by cognitive-technical structures of consciousness (that is, labor) and moral-practical structures of consciousness (that is, interaction); that is, they are oriented towards either success or mutual understanding. The theory of social evolution explains how these structures of consciousness change over time. In his work during the 1970s, especially in *Zur Rekonstruktion des Historischen Materialismus* (1976), Habermas sketched out the general outlines of a theory of social evolution. In *The Theory of Communicative Action* (first published in German in 1981) Habermas applies this conception of social evolution to an analysis of the transition in the West (especially Europe) from traditional to modern forms of society. This process of modernization is "the process through which a traditional or pretechnological society passes as it is transformed into a society characterized by machine technology, rational and secular attitudes, and highly differentiated social structures."[34] Habermas, following Weber, understands the process of modernization as a manifestation of the process of rationalization, where rationalization is understood as the expansion of rational structures of action into ever more areas of life (see TCA I, 157–242).[35]

In the introductory essay to *Zur Rekonstruktion des Historischen Materialismus*, translated as "Historical Materialism and the Development of Normative Structures" in *Communication and the Evolution of Society* (95-129), Habermas explains what he means by rationalization. As a consequence of the distinction between labor and interaction (that is, instrumental and communicative action) he understands the process of rationalization in a more differentiated way than did Weber. In accordance with the distinction between instrumental/strategic action and communicative action, and their corresponding forms of rationality (instrumental and communicative rationality), he specifies the criteria of rationalization differently in each of these dimensions. In the dimension of labor, which is characterized by the primacy of instrumental/strategic action and the accumulation of objectivating, cognitive/technical knowledge, rationalization consists in the optimization of the degree of success. The characteristic feature of instrumental and strategic action is that it is oriented towards success: maximizing the degree of success of instrumental/strategic actions results in the increase in power, and hence domination, over objectivized nature. In contrast to the rationalization of structures of instrumental action, rationalization in the dimension of interaction, which is characterized by the primacy of communicative action and accumulates as moral-practical insight in normative structures, consists of the realization of the rational potential of communicative action. Realization of the rational potential of communicative action means that norms of action are justified solely on the basis of the unforced force of the better argument, that is, norms that result from a process of rational agreement:

> *Rationalization* here means extirpating those relations of force that are inconspicuously set in the very structures of communication and that prevent conscious settlement of conflicts, and consensual regulation of conflicts, by means of intrapsychic as well as interpersonal communicative barriers. Rationalization means overcoming such systematically distorted communication in which the action-supporting consensus concerning the reciprocally raised validity claims—especially the consensus concerning the truthfulness of intentional expressions and the rightness of underlying norms—can be sustained in appearance only, that is, counterfactually. The stages of law and morality, of ego demarcations and worldviews, of individual and collective identity formations, are stages in this process. Their progress cannot be measured against the choice of correct strategies, but rather against the intersubjectivity of understanding achieved without force, that is, against the expansion of the domain of consensual action together with the re-establishment of undistorted communication. (CES, 119–120)

In other words, communicative rationalization means expanding the deployment of forms of communicative action—in which uncoerced and undistorted understandings are achieved—in those spheres of social life that are properly linguistically mediated, such as in the coordination of social action, the socialization of individuals, and the transmission of cultural knowledge.

In *The Theory of Communicative Action* Habermas considerably expands this analysis through a critique of Weber's understanding of modernity and the theory of rationalization that underlies it. In this critique Habermas concedes that Weber is correct to observe that the modernization of Western society resulting from sociocultural rationalization leads to a loss of freedom and meaning.[36] Weber fails, however, to grasp the structural possibilities that were also opened up with the process of rationalization. Western modernization is only adequately conceived when we understand the actual processes of rationalization that occurred within the structurally possible processes of rationalization. In this way we can then understand the pathological consequences of an undeveloped rationalization process. According to Habermas, Weber primarily makes two errors that lead to his misunderstanding of modernity.[37] First, Weber conceives of reason only in the limited aspect of purposive rationality. Second, Weber's limited conception of reason leads him to conflate rational society with capitalism. Habermas goes on to argue that only an expanded conception of reason that takes into account communicative rationality is adequate to understand modernity.

According to Habermas, modern structures of consciousness are "decentered," meaning that we moderns have developed the capacity to adopt various attitudes towards elements of experience.[38] We can adopt either a subjective attitude in an egocentric standpoint, a norm-conformative attitude in a sociocentric standpoint, or an objectivating attitude in a universalistic standpoint. When these are combined with the three formal worlds that constitute experience, the objective, social, and subjective worlds, we derive the three "rationalization complexes" of science, morality, and art that are associated with Weber's cultural value spheres. Accordingly, the rationalization complex of cognitive-instrumental rationality is derived from the adoption of an objectivating attitude towards the objective and social worlds. The complex of moral-practical rationality is derived from the adoption of the norm-conformative attitude towards the social and subjective worlds. And the complex of aesthetic-practical rationality is derived from the adoption of the expressive attitude towards the social and subjective worlds. These complexes are rationalizable because each thematizes a validity claim (cognitive-technical rationality thematizes the claim to truth, moral-practical rationality thematizes the claim to rightness, and aesthetic-practical rationality thematizes the claim to truthfulness), each complex produces knowledge that is cumulative, and the continuity of the knowledge generated by each complex is grounded in a reflective learning process that is institutionalized in a specialized form of argumentation (TCA I, 239).[39]

Habermas, following Weber, asserts that these rationalization complexes have made their historical appearance with the transition to modernity, especially in Europe, in the form of value spheres. These value spheres have appeared at two levels. At the level of ideas, scientific theories, universalistic moral and legal theories, and autonomous art have become differentiated from each other, and at the level of cultural action systems, professional discourses have become institutionalized in each sphere. The specialized discourses of science, morality, and art are each structured by a different rationalization complex. Thus, the scientific enterprise institutionalizes cognitive-technical rationality, positive law and universalistic moralities institutionalize moral-practical rationality, and the artistic enterprise institutionalizes aesthetic-practical rationality.

The significance of this model of rationalization is located in its normative implications. This model states that based on the three value spheres and their respective rationalization complexes that historically have been differentiated in the process of modernization, a normal process of rationalization can be specified. This normal process of rationalization, then, serves as the normative criterion according to which actual processes of rationalization in modernity can be said to have occurred; although to the extent that rationalization has occurred, it coexists with deformed rationalization processes. To be sure, the normative moment presupposes the theory of communicative action, for without the normative claim of consensus being the telos of speech and the distinction between the three validity claims, Habermas's theory of rationalization would be somewhat speculative.

To sum up, rationalization should be understood as an expansion of reason that is historically realized as a differentiation process in which rationalization complexes associated with the validity claims to truth, rightness, and truthfulness are distinguished from each other. Thus, rationalization entails the differentiation of Reason into three dimensions of rationality. The theory of social evolution, then, can be said to theorize the historical forms of rationality.

The Dynamic between Interaction and Labor

In the previous two sections, I have explicated the rationalization of structures in the dimensions of cognitive-instrumental knowledge and moral-practical insight. In this section I will examine how these two dimensions of rationalization are related to each other. Recall that the theory of social evolution explains societal reproduction in both the material (cognitive-technical) and the sociocultural (moral-practical) dimensions. One of the key debates that has shaped speculative philosophies of history (including theories of social evolution, broadly conceived) concerns the material priority of either interests grounded in material existence or ideas grounded in symbolic structures. This debate, of course, is the familiar one between materialism and idealism, where materialism entails the claim of material priority of interests, and idealism entails the claim of material priority of ideas. Despite misinterpretations to the contrary, Habermas insists that his theory of social evolution is, in a sense, both materialist and idealist, or better, it is neither simply materialist nor idealist. It is materialist in the sense that it locates the problem-generating dynamic of history in the material domain, and it is idealist in the sense that it allocates an autonomous developmental logic to the normative structures of consciousness. Thus, Habermas's theory of social evolution is neither materialist nor idealist in the above senses, for it does not explain evolutionary advances by reductive reference to material interests, nor does it explain these same advances solely by reference to a history of a disembodied mind.

The interaction of these two dimensions of rationalization constitutes the evolutionary process, and the process of social evolution is understood by Habermas "as a two-stage activity of problem solving by macro-systems" (HE, 31).[40] Thus, as the development of cognitive-technical knowledge generates crises for the reproduction of society (for example, the incongruity between the development of empirical science in the sixteenth century and the theological worldviews that justified social, moral, and political views), a need for development, that is, learning, in the dimension of moral-practical insight arises. Whether or not moral-practical learning occurs is an empirical matter, upon which rests the successful reproduction of the society. In order to explain this complex evolutionary process, Habermas draws on two competing theoretical traditions: action theory and systems theory. As already noted, Habermas maintains that since neither theoretical model is adequate in itself to explain societal reproduction, they must be combined in a systematic way (see TCA II).

According to systems theory, society is viewed as a functionally integrated system, in which each subsystem is functionally regulated with every other subsystem.[41] The functional correspondence of each part to every other is referred to as system integration. The system is distinguished from, but in direct contact with, a hypercomplex environment. The environment in general can be further distinguished into outer nature, inner nature, and other social systems, the first two of which are adapted to by means of material reproduction and socialization. The goal of the system is to reduce the complexity of its environment in order to ensure a continued healthy survival, that is, the social system must functionally adapt in order to reduce the complexity of the environment so as to ensure the system's continued survival and continuous identity.[42] Functional adaptation is accomplished through systemic differentiation, leading to an increase in complexity. Systemic differentiation is constituted by an increase in the internal structural complexity of the system. This differentiation generates the capacity to assume a greater number of states, thus allowing it to successfully master challenges. A system is said to have a greater degree of autonomy when it possesses a greater "steering capacity," which is a society's capacity to functionally adapt to an altered environment.

The first stage of social evolution is accomplished by the functional adaptation of a society to its systemic problems. Within a given level of development a society possesses, by virtue of the differentiation of its structure, a specific capacity for adaptation. When a society encounters a challenge, whether from an external or internal source, it has a finite set of sociocultural resources upon which it can draw in order to meet the challenge. Functional adaptation to system challenges as described above follows the standard model of systems theory. Thus the first stage of social evolution on Habermas's model, what I will call intralevel change, follows the general lines of systems theory. But adequately explaining *interlevel* change requires more than a functional explanation.

Habermas argues that the systems-theoretic model of social evolution is limited by its inability to adequately and clearly determine a system's historical boundaries. In other words, systems theory runs into explanatory problems when a society faces challenges that are significant enough to threaten the very identity of that society. In functionally adapting in response to systemic problems, a society may either alter its boundary with the environment, or its internal structure. But simultaneously altering both in response to system problems can lead to difficulties in determining the continuity (or discontinuity) of the identity of the society: "[W]hen systems maintain themselves through altering both boundaries and structural continuity *[Bestand]*, their identity becomes blurred. The same system modification can be conceived of equally well as a learning process and change or as a dissolution process and collapse of the system. It cannot be unambiguously determined whether a new system has been formed or the old system has merely regenerated itself" (LC, 3). So when a society experiences structural change from state A to state B (in order to reduce the complexity of its environment), one of the things we want to know is whether the society at state B is the same society as at state A, or whether the structural changes have altered that identity of the society to such an extent that we can no longer understand the society at state A as the same society as at state B. As McCarthy puts the problem for systems theory, "Did France survive the French Revolution? Did the United States survive its Civil War? Did Germany survive the First World War?"[43] Because systems theory adopts only an external perspective with respect to social explanations it cannot clearly demarcate and establish the constituent elements of the identities of societies.

Furthermore, complexity is not an adequate criterion to identify the qualitative types of changes entailed by evolution and development (CES, 173). Systems theory can only describe the directionality of social change in terms of increasing complexity; it thus cannot specify when an evolutionary threshold has been overcome, or when a developmental level has been reached. Moreover, an increase in complexity (even in biological organisms) is not always a progressive change; it "often proves to be an evolutionary dead end" (CES, 174).

Habermas seeks to overcome these difficulties by systematically combining an internal action-theoretic perspective with the external systems-theoretic perspective. The identity of societies is normatively secured, that is, it is determined from the internal perspective. Only the members of a society can themselves determine their common identity, and only from an internal perspective can we determine which structures are essential to the identity of a society: "[O]nly when members of a society experience structural alterations as critical for continued existence and feel their social identity threatened can we speak of crises" (LC, 3). Crises are persistent system problems that threaten social integration. Systemic problems, or challenges, become crises when the social system is challenged by its environment in such a way that the system lacks the capacity to functionally adapt. Habermas notes that the concept of a crisis has a normative moment, for failure to adapt to an external challenge radically limits the self-determination of the system: "To conceive of a process as a crisis is tacitly to give it a normative meaning—the resolution of the crisis effects a liberation of the subject caught up in it" (LC, 1). If unresolved, crises can lead to failure in the reproduction processes of the system, and thus to a loss of its identity as a functional system.

The theoretical disadvantages of the criterion of increasing complexity as a measure of evolutionary status can be overcome by adopting an internal perspective with respect to the developmental process: "A reliable evolutionary classification is possible only if we know the inner logic of a series of morphological changes or of an expansion of reaction potential" (CES, 174). Only when we know the developmental logic of a society, namely the development of the structures of consciousness that constitute the horizon of the learning potential in the domains of cognitive-technical knowledge and moral-practical insight, can we classify the adequacy of determinate social formations.

Now, societies can be categorized according to the type of social formation they exhibit. According to Habermas, however, social formations are themselves abstractly determined by their principle of organization. Principles of organization are constituted by 'abstract regulations' (or rules *[Regelungen]*; see CES, 153) that delimit the range of possible structural changes available to a particular society (CES, 153–154; LC, 7–8). In forming the horizon of possible structural changes of a society, a principle of organization determines the range of institutionally allowable adaptations in the cognitive-technical, moral-practical, and aesthetic-practical dimensions: "By principles of organization I understand innovations that become possible through developmental-logically reconstructable stages of learning, and which institutionalize new levels of societal learning. The organizational principle of a society circumscribes ranges of possibility. It determines in particular: within which structures changes in the system of institutions are possible; to what extent the available capacities of productive forces are socially utilized and the development of new productive forces can be stimulated; to what extent system complexity and adaptive achievements can be heightened" (CES, 153). The principle of organization constitutes the horizon of consciousness determined at a given learning level, that is, at a given stage of evolutionary development. Recall that this is not deduced a priori, but reconstructed only after the fact; thus it does not say anything about the future course of development.

The principle of organization of a society determines the dominant form of social integration that constitutes the society's institutional core. The abstract rules of a principle of organization in a sense mediate between a given developmental-logical level of learning and the institutionalized form of social integration. The principle of organization determines the horizon of possible forms of social integration available at a given level of learning:

> Habermas construes organizational principles of society as sociostructural innovations that institutionalize developmental-logical levels of learning; they establish the structural conditions for technical and practical learning processes at particular stages of development. Principles of organization circumscribe ranges of possibility within which institutional systems vary, productive forces can be developed and utilized, and system complexity and steering capacity can be increased. The concrete

> embodiments of these abstract principles are the "institutional nuclei" that function as relations of production and determine the dominant form of social integration (for example, kinship relations in primitive societies, the political order in traditional societies, the economic system in liberal capitalist societies).[44]

In Chapter Three of *Legitimation Crisis* Habermas provides an illustration of what he means by a principle of organization. He distinguishes between four types of social formation: primitive *[vorhochkulterelle]*, traditional, capitalist, and post-capitalist.[45] The organizational principle of primitive societies is constituted by the primary roles of age and sex, and these are institutionalized in the kinship system. The kinship system functions to integrate the society at both the social and the systemic levels. The organizational principle of traditional societies is politically organized class domination, which is institutionalized in the state and economic systems. In traditional social formations, social and system integration become functionally differentiated. The organizational principle of (liberal) capitalist societies is depoliticized class domination; that is, it is institutionalized not through political legitimations, but in the relationship of wage labor and capital. In liberal capitalist social formations, social and systemic integrative functions are differentiated, but system integration in the form of the economic system begins to usurp tasks of social integration.

Since the adaptive capacity of a society is determined by the principle of organization, the only way system crises can be resolved is through a development of the principle of organization. The principle of organization uniquely determines the level of development of a society, and the level of development is understood to be its learning level. Thus, it is clearer to speak of the learning level of a society. Therefore new principles of organization come about through evolutionary achievements. On Habermas's theory of social evolution, we can properly speak of social evolution only when a new principle of organization has been institutionalized. This institutionalization of a new form of social integration constitutes the second stage of the process of social evolution.

According to Habermas, then, the entire process of social evolution, that is, development from one stage to the next higher stage, occurs in the following way. A social system (society) maintains its existence and identity through a reduction of the complexity of its environment. When the environment generates challenges (system problems), the social system solves the problems (adapts) by increasing its internal differentiation in order to increase the number of states it can assume. System crises are system problems that are persistent and threaten the identity of the system. The existence of a system crisis implies the incapacity to solve the systemic problem through internal differentiation. A solution to the crisis can come about *only if* the society is able to draw upon latent cultural resources to generate a new level of social integration. If the necessary cultural resources are latently available, and they are institutionalized in a new form of social integration, only then can we speak of a development to a new stage (social evolution). And it is only at this new stage of development that further increases in system complexity (differentiation) become possible.

This sketch of the dynamics of the process of social evolution should help clarify in what sense Habermas means that "the development of . . . normative structures is the pacemaker of social evolution" (CES, 120). Following this assertion he goes on to clarify its meaning himself: "[F]or new principles of social organization mean new forms of social integration; and the latter, in turn, first make it possible to implement available productive forces or to generate new ones, as well as making possible a heightening of social complexity" (CES, 120). So while the problems that generate crises originate in the domain of material reproduction, evolutionary steps only occur when (and if) developments occur in the domain of symbolic reproduction.

Developmental Logic and Empirical Mechanisms

In constructing his theory of social evolution Habermas is concerned to avoid the difficulties surrounding the objectivism of traditional philosophies of history. Two suppositions in particular, Habermas argues, have persistently plagued philosophies of history. The first is that of a species-subject that undergoes evolution. The second is that structure and content are analytically inseparable such that we can only speak of a unilinear evolutionary path. Habermas contends that a theory of social evolution can forgo these two problematic assumptions. The assumptions that he proposes to replace these with are intended to improve the explanatory power of the theory of social evolution considered as a theory of social change. The proposed assumptions are a) that only concrete societies understood as integrated structures of communicating subjects undergo evolution; and b) that an adequate understanding of social change necessitates the theoretical distinction between social structures and content. The idea motivating the second assumption is that the combination of a genetic-structural level of analysis with an empirical-historical level of analysis will produce both the generality necessary for the identification of universal structures of evolution and the particularity necessary to adequately account for the multiplicity of concrete historical forms.

Habermas rejects the claim typically made by speculative philosophies of history that the species considered as a macrosubject undergoes evolutionary change. The claim they make is that the evolution of the human species, qua species, is both necessary and occurs in a single, unified macrosubject. As I have indicated, Habermas rejects this claim as monological and too strong. While we cannot speak about the species evolving as some macrosubject, we can speak of societies evolving. Societies understood as structures of intersubjective relationships can be said to evolve in the sense that the intersubjective structures that constitute societies evolve: "The bearers of evolution are . . . societies and the acting subjects integrated into them; social evolution can be discerned in those structures that are replaced by more comprehensive structures in accord with a pattern that is to be rationally reconstructed"

(CES, 140). The idea here is that if we adopt an intersubjective paradigm for conceiving of society, then the objects that evolve are the forms of social integration and the structures of consciousness of socialized individuals.

Recall that for Habermas, societies and individual egos are reciprocally constituted, so on this conception both societies and individual egos are altered in the course of evolution. Habermas is not just pointing to the fact that individuals or groups of individuals do not consciously make their own history in any true sense: "Even if social evolution should point in the direction of unified individuals consciously influencing the course of their own evolution, there would not arise any large-scale subjects, but at most self-established, higher-level, intersubjective commonalities" (CES, 140; see also HE, 42). So what actually evolves in social evolution are social structures and the (structures of consciousness of) individuals socialized into them. The evolutionary process is not generated by an acting subject, an agent, but by the intersubjectively mediated process of social reproduction. In the course of reproducing the common stock of knowledge (culture), reproducing the normative institutions that govern social interaction (society), and socializing individuals into the society (personality), societies change, and Habermas suggests that this change can be characterized, on the whole, as a learning process.

The considerable amount of cross-cultural empirical research during this century has undermined the tenability of speculative philosophies of history. Constructing a theory of social evolution that is universal yet can adequately account for the plurality of forms of life is a most difficult and conceptually problematic theoretical task. To address this problem, Habermas argues that an adequate theory of social evolution must distinguish between structure and content. The proposition is that there is on the one hand a set of universal developmental-logically ordered structures of consciousness, and on the other, uniquely determined histories of concrete societies. Since concrete histories are empirically conditioned, and empirical historical conditions are always unique, concrete histories possess unique contents.

Significantly, while the developmental logic of these structures is universal, there is no necessity in any determinate society's evolutionary change; that is, identifying a developmental logic of societal development does not imply anything about the probability of the occurrence of any such development:

> The systematically reconstructable patterns of development of normative structures are . . . of particular interest. These structural patterns depict a *developmental logic* inherent in cultural traditions and institutional change. This logic says nothing about the *mechanisms* of development; it says something only about the range of variations within which cultural values, moral representations, norms, and the like—at a given level of social organization—can be changed and can find different historical expression. In its developmental *dynamics*, the change of normative structures remains dependent on evolutionary challenges posed by unresolved, economically conditioned, system problems and on learning processes that are a response to them. (CES, 98)

This distinction is both a theoretical and a methodological one. It has the theoretical advantages of combining a universalist assumption with an account of a plurality of histories. Furthermore, in distinguishing the universal structures of development from the actual content of concrete histories, Habermas has constructed a theory of social evolution and not a philosophy of history. A philosophy of history would necessarily conflate structure and content in its propositions about the meaning of history. For similar reasons, Habermas's theory of social evolution is also not a theory of history. Theories of social evolution do not claim to explain the laws of history or evolution of the species (considered as a macrosubject of history). The theory of social evolution claims to explain only the directionality and the conditions of change of the intersubjective structures that constitute societies. The key thesis is that if and when societies evolve they do so according to the retrospectively identified developmental-logical structures. This thesis does not restrict the multiplicity of possible concrete contents of those social formations. Methodologically, the distinction separates the tasks involved in identifying the developmental logics of structures of consciousness, and in specifying in concrete instances the empirical factors involved in the contingent development of those structures. Thus, Habermas separates the functions of social theory, which identify universalizable features of societies, from history writing, which identifies the empirical conditions of concrete instances of social change (see HE). To be sure, this is not an uncontroversial claim. Many critics would argue that separating scheme from content is an untenable Enlightenment assumption and one that fatally wounds the theory. They would argue that what we identify as the pattern of development is intrinsically related to the determinate empirical historical circumstances of that development, and conversely, what count as relevant empirical mechanisms is determined intrinsically by our historical self-understandings. But Habermas argues convincingly in "History and Evolution" that the theories of historical social theory and the narratives of historiography complement each other. They should not be seen as contradictory methodologies, but as methodologies that are grounded in different perspectives. Historical social theory—the category in which the theory of social evolution belongs—approaches social change from the external, third-person observer perspective, and historiography approaches the same phenomena from the internal, first-person actor perspective. Thus, the distinction is not an absolute one, but nonetheless it is legitimate.

The concept of a developmental logic of genetic structures is borrowed from developmental psychology. A developmental logic is the set of rules that characterizes the internal relations between qualitatively different, hierarchically related levels of learning. Generally, the developmental logic of social evolution specifies the rules for possible collective problemsolving that are latently stored in a culture. Individual levels of learning, or stages, are related such that higher stages in the hierarchical ordering subsume each lower stage. Developmental stages possess the following characteristics: (a) They are individual stages that are both qualitatively distinct from one another and possess elements that are structured so as to form a coherent whole; and (b) the individual stages of development form an invariant and hierarchically structured sequence, such that 1) no later stage can be achieved without first passing through each earlier one, and 2) each higher stage can be interpreted as a development over the previous stage that incorporates the elements of the previous stage (CES, 220n.9). The most significant feature of a developmental logic is that it can explain the directionality of social change. This directionality, however, is not arbitrary. It derives from the internal relations between subsequent stages, and is determined (in Habermas's theory) according to the criterion of expanded rationality. To be sure, this only explains the directionality of social change as a learning process; however, we can impute progressiveness to this change. In the next section, I will further examine learning processes, and I will examine in detail this important concept of developmental logic in the next chapter.

The primary advantage of distinguishing the logic from the dynamics of social evolution is located in the expanded explanatory power of the theory. Incorporating this distinction allows us to drop many of the unwarranted assumptions typical of speculative philosophies of history, and allows the construction of a theory of social evolution that is universal, yet not transcendental. An adequate theory of social evolution would avoid both the unwarranted speculations of transcendental philosophy and the general moral and political relativism of contextualism. Some of the assumptions of traditional philosophies of history that Habermas wants to avoid are (1) that history follows a unilinear development; (2) that history develops necessarily; (3) that history develops continuously; and (4) that history is irreversible. By distinguishing between the logic and the mechanisms of social change, the theory of social evolution can avoid these rather implausible assumptions. I will now consider in detail how this distinction allows Habermas to avoid these assumptions.

The development of anthropological inquiry in this century has brought to light the deep differences that exist between cultures, and this has led to a devaluing of traditional theories of social evolution that posit a single path of evolutionary development. Instead, it is thought that each culture possesses its own unique historical form; that is, it follows a unique historical path. By distinguishing the logic from the mechanisms of change Habermas's conception of social evolution can rationally (that is, universally) explain social change while also giving an account of multilinear social change. This allows Habermas to distinguish between the deep structures of consciousness that are universal and the content of particular worldviews that are culturally determined: "Many paths can lead to the same level of development" (CES, 141). Concrete societies may possess unique and widely divergent cultural contents. This is explained by the unique empirical determinants that may form any one society's history. Nevertheless, this is consistent with the claim that if and when any particular society evolves it does so according to a set of deep structures that fundamentally condition the content of that culture. The key here is to specify these deep structures abstractly enough to account for the wide scope of divergent cultures, while not being so abstract as to be theoretically empty.

The distinction between the logic and mechanisms of evolution further allows Habermas to reconstruct the sequence of structures along with their internal relations to each other independently of an explanation regarding the concrete historical path of any particular society. Thus, while Habermas can claim universality for the rationally reconstructed pattern of development, he need not (and does not) claim any sort of necessity for the actual historical path of any concrete society. According to the theory of social evolution, if and when a society evolves it will evolve according to the reconstructed pattern of universal structures (which, it should be noted, are determined only retrospectively). But the theory says nothing regarding whether a society will evolve at any given time. The actual historical development of any particular society is a contingent matter resting on empirical conditions. The developmental-logical structures determine the logical conditions that circumscribe any change while providing no explanation of empirical change: "Such structures describe the logical space in which more comprehensive structural formations can take shape; whether new structural formations arise at all, and if so, when, depends on *contingent* boundary conditions and on learning processes that can be investigated empirically" (CES, 140).

Moreover, this distinction allows the theory to explain discontinuous as well as continuous social change. If the developmental-logical structure of social evolution is conceived as a hierarchical sequence of stages of development, then, strictly speaking, evolutionary achievements occur only when a society progresses from one stage to the next higher one. Social change, however, also occurs within a given stage. Since each learning level is constituted by a particular structure of consciousness, changes within stages (intrastage changes) appear as continuous. These sorts of changes seek to stabilize given crises with only the conceptual resources available at that stage. But when these resources are insufficient to stabilize the social order, the members of the society become motivated to seek out a solution to the crisis. Their motivation originates in their interest in maintaining the group's stability and identity. But crises can only be solved, on this model, by altering the underlying structure of consciousness that constitutes the current learning level. Again, whether a society develops to a higher level that has the resources to stabilize the present crisis is an empirical matter. The development from one level to another is perceived as discontinuous because a new form of consciousness is instituted. Nevertheless, the notion of a developmental logic of structures of consciousness ensures that there is an internal relation between stages that appear as discontinuous, and thus, though discontinuous, this interlevel change is evolutionary, not revolutionary.

According to Habermas, the distinction between the logic and mechanisms of evolution provides the capacity to explain regressions and stagnations in historical development: "*[R]etrogressions* in evolution are possible and in many cases empirically corroborated; of course, a society will not fall back behind a level of development, once it is established, without accompanying phenomena of forced regression; this can be seen, for example, in the case of Fascist Germany" (CES, 141). So clearly Habermas concedes that processes of social change are not always progressive, although they tend to be more progressive than regressive. An adequate theory of social evolution would tell a story about the overall development of societies while also explaining local stagnations and regressions. By distinguishing on the level of theory between an abstract pattern of the development of structures of consciousness and the actual empirical processes of history, Habermas can explain the progressions and regressions of the empirical histories of concrete societies by reference to the developmental logic of structures of consciousness. By "explain" I do not mean that the developmental logic of these structures explains the dynamics of their development; that is, the developmental logic does not say anything about how or why these structures develop in concrete societal histories. The developmental logic is only a description of the pattern of development and its internal structure, where the logic of this pattern entails a hierarchical ordering of developmental stages in which higher stages possess a greater value than lower ones.

On Habermas's model, stagnations at a particular stage of development are explained in the following way. The empirical conditions necessary for an evolutionary achievement that leads to a new learning level simply may not obtain. If any one individual does not learn how to see things differently in the way necessary to solve the particular empirical problem at hand, then that insight cannot be transferred to the cultural stock of knowledge in the form of a worldview, and it cannot then be institutionalized in a new form of social integration. Or if an individual or group does learn in the necessary way, then that insight might not be successfully transposed into a worldview. Or if the new insight is transposed into a worldview, it may never be successfully institutionalized in a new form of social integration. Every one of these contingent conditions must be met for an evolutionary achievement to occur. In the absence of any one of these conditions, development stagnates.

In the case of stagnation, a society would persist in a crisis state until either the contingent conditions are met or until the society's identity disintegrates. It would seem, however, that a society cannot persist in a crisis state indefinitely. Since the development of cognitive-technical knowledge proceeds endogenously, that is, motivated by an internal dynamic, and since developments in the material reproduction of society generate crises, the instability of the crisis will continue to expand. This is not to say that crises cannot be repressed and held in check for extended periods of time. Advanced capitalism has successfully stabilized itself in the face of crisis for a considerable time. The implication of Habermas's claim seems to be, though, that this state of forced stability cannot be maintained. At some point, either the society must collapse or it must learn.

If a society faces certain empirical conditions that weaken the social bonds of that society (a crisis), changes are required to restore stability. Here stability is understood in the sense that the level of interpersonal integration is sufficient to ensure social stability. Since evolutionary leaps from one stage of development to another are difficult and only occur under extreme conditions (that is, when the society's identity is threatened with collapse), a society will first explore the cultural resources available to it at the given level of development. In other words, a society will first try to solve structural problems by making adjustments that are within the given level of development of consciousness. Thus, a society may possess sufficient cultural resources to solve all problems that arise. When crises arise, the society is able to tap those resources to make adjustments within the given level of development. In this case the conditions simply do not occur that would motivate an evolutionary leap to a new level of development.

The question now arises, What does it mean to say that a society regresses? Habermas seems to understand regression such that a society may regress to a previous learning level, that is devolve, but it can do so only according to the ordered sequence of developmental stages: "It is not the evolutionary processes that are *irreversible* but the structural sequences that a society must run through *if* and *to the extent* it is involved in evolution" (CES, 141). In other words, a society might traverse in either direction the ordered sequence of learning levels, but it cannot skip levels. To be sure regressions are highly improbable, and when they do occur, they are accompanied by pathological side effects. Habermas cites Fascist Germany as an example of regression that exhibits these "phenomena of forced regression." Presumably, he interprets the rise of fascism to be a reaction to the socioeconomic problems of the 1930s. In turning to fascism, Germany regressed to pre-Enlightenment notions of a natural order of beings such that some human beings were considered higher and more perfect than others. This is a regression insofar as it devalues the sorts of reasons that are counted as acceptable. In the example, the sorts of reasons regarding the treatment of other human beings that have possessed social currency since the Enlightenment were no longer considered sound reasons. It is not the case that particular reasons are devalued. In regressions entire categories of reasons are devalued. A learning level is abandoned and the prior level is resurrected. Fascism abandons the postconventional stage of moral consciousness for a prior stage (conventional) in which a natural hierarchy of beings is presupposed. It is unclear what the "phenomena of forced regression" are in this case. I assume that these are psychological phenomena, since this seems to be the only location in which these phenomena would manifest themselves. At the least, this example oversimplifies the historical process, for it could be argued that the majority of the German people did not fully adopt the fascist consciousness, but rather were lured into the Nazi party by a combination of expert oratory, ideological mystification, and economic troubles. In any case, my intent here is not to determine the empirical adequacy of Habermas's thesis, but simply to clarify the meaning of the concept of regression within the theory.

The distinction between the logic and the mechanisms of social evolution in the theory of social evolution is a necessary element in that theory, and thus it is a defining feature. Given this defining role, it is worth considering further the plausibility of this distinction. As discussed above, there are conceptual advantages for making the distinction between developmental logic and developmental mechanisms, but conceptual advantages are empty if they do not also exhibit theoretical advantages in the form of greater explanatory power. Thus, we might ask, Does the distinction between the developmental logic and developmental mechanisms cohere with the current state of social research? To be sure, this is a difficult question that admits of no ready answer, and certainly a satisfactory determination is beyond the scope of this study. Nevertheless, we can consider whether this distinction has any significant prima facie empirical difficulties.[46] Perhaps the most difficult element to corroborate empirically is the assertion that the reconstructed developmental logics of structures of consciousness are universally valid.

There is no a priori argument for the universality of developmental stages, and Habermas does not intimate that there is one. He presents this claim to universality as a thesis (embedded in a comprehensive theory of social evolution) that needs to be corroborated empirically, and that must prove its validity through its explanatory power and pragmatic usefulness. Recall that the logic of stages of development reconstructs the highly abstract, deep structures of consciousness. One developmental-logical stage can underlie numerous societies with widely differing sociocultural contents. So diversity of cultural contents does not refute or even militate against the thesis of a universal developmental logic of structures of consciousness. To qualify as contravening evidence, the fact of diversity of cultures would need to be shown to be based in incommensurable structures of consciousness. That is, cultures that appear prima facie radically different would need to be shown to be determined by incommensurable structures of the fundamental ways that the members of each of the cultures interacted with their external and internal environments. Habermas has made the contrary argument that there is a core rational element present in any linguistically integrated society that has a lifeworld constituted by propositionally differentiated speech (see TCA I, 102–41). The giving of reasons in support of a validity claim is the communicative-rational element found in all linguistically based cultures. For an interpreter to understand the meaning of a speech act in a given culture, the interpreter must adopt the internal perspective of the participant, and in doing so, must also assess the soundness of the reasons given. Thus, any act of understanding involves a rational judgment as to the statement's validity. Habermas has made a prima facie case that the structures of consciousness that are developmental-logically ordered are universal features of human history, but I will return to a further examination of this issue at the end of chapter 4.

While empirical corroboration is an important step, it may well turn out that the thesis of the distinction between the logic and the mechanisms of social evolution is underdetermined. That is, the empirical evidence, on the whole, is merely consistent with the thesis, in which case the validity of the thesis rests with its explanatory power and its pragmatic usefulness. As discussed above, the distinction (and the theory of social evolution in which it is embedded) appears to possess a greater degree of explanatory power with respect to history than at least traditional philosophies of history.

Social Evolution as a Learning Process

As discussed above, the primary dynamic mechanism of social evolution is learning. In this section I will explicate what this means, and what its function is in the theory of social evolution.

Habermas's theory of social evolution distinguishes between the logic of development and the empirical mechanisms of development. There are the broadly conceived conditions of social evolution that can be empirically determined, and there is the developmental logic of social evolution that can be reconstructed. There are two types of necessary conditions for social evolution to occur: empirical conditions that determine the initial state; and the dynamic mechanism that is the motivating force of development. In Habermas's theory of social evolution, the necessary empirical conditions for social evolution are determined by systemic problems that constitute challenges to the reproduction of society, and the dynamic mechanism (also a logically necessary condition) of social evolution is located in the universal capacity to learn that cannot but be utilized. It is significant that the dynamic force of history is not in just the capacity we have for learning, but in this capacity that we cannot avoid using: "It is my conjecture that the fundamental mechanism for social evolution in general is to be found in an automatic inability not to learn. Not learning, but *not-learning* is the phenomenon that calls for explanation at the socio-cultural stage of development. Therein lies, if you will, the rationality of man. Only against this background does the overpowering irrationality of the history of the species become visible" (LC, 15). Thus, the evolution of societies is propelled by a learning process, and this learning process is an unavoidable condition of the reproduction of societies.

What makes learning an unavoidable condition of social reproduction? Recall that for Habermas when validity claims are disputed, if the interlocutors still want to coordinate their action by means of an understanding (and thus they want to avoid the use of force), then they must move to the level of discourse where contested validity claims are thematized, and reasons are given pro and con with respect to the various interpretations. It is in and through discourse (as opposed to communicative action as such) that learning processes can occur: "Evolution . . . takes place in the form of directional learning processes that work through discursively redeemable validity claims" (LC, 14). This should not be a surprise given Habermas's emphasis on the linguistic basis of social life. The constitutive conditions of communicative action underlie Habermas's conception of learning. It is a necessary condition of communicative action with its raising of validity claims, and if necessary their redemption in discourse, that the speaker/hearer has the capacity to adopt first-, second-, and, most importantly, third-person perspectives. Without this capacity the reaching of an understanding that is motivated by nothing more than the unforced force of a better argument would not be possible. So in engaging in discourse (in Habermas's sense), we unavoidably engage in discursive learning processes. And it is worth repeating that only through processes of communicative action is the lifeworld reproduced, and only through processes of communicative action are individuals simultaneously individualized and socialized into their lifeworlds. The very basis of social life requires our engagement in the learning processes that propel the evolution of societies.

The empirical learning process that is the mechanism of social evolution should be distinguished from the levels of learning that characterize stages of social development. Learning levels are structural descriptions of developmental-logical stages; they determine the "rules for possible problem solving." They circumscribe the degree that learning is possible at the given stage of development, and thus represent formal restrictions on learning processes. At higher stages of development, greater capacities for learning are achieved. Learning levels are structural descriptions of stages of development, and learning processes are the empirical mechanisms of development (see CES, 121).

Since learning is intrinsic to communicative action, one needs to begin an explanation of learning first on the psychological level. But individual learning and collective learning are interdependent processes, so it is also necessary to explain how learning achievements in the individual find their way into social structures: "*Individually acquired learning abilities* and information must be latently available in world views before they can be used in a socially significant way, that is, before they can be transposed into *societal learning processes*" (CES, 121). In other words, we also need an account of collective learning processes. In the linguistically mediated reproduction of lifeworld structures certain innovations are introduced that are the result of individual learning achievements. Alternative worldviews are formed and stored in the collective culture, but they remain on the margins of the culture. The appearance of a societal crisis which is unresolvable within the given learning level necessitates radically different approaches to the integration of society. Social movements oriented by alternative worldviews give concrete social and practical meaning to these worldviews, and only if the alternative worldviews meet improbable conditions, such as being sufficiently innovative, and meeting the necessary conditions of social integration, may they be institutionalized into new normative structures. Only then can we say that the given society has advanced to a new stage of development. Assuming that the society stabilizes at the new level, the process begins again.

Chapter 4

The Idea of a Developmental Logic of History

In the previous chapter I analyzed and clarified the main elements of the theory of social evolution. The aim there was to provide a clear and coherent account of the theory as a whole. In this chapter, I will analyze and assess the core concept of the theory of social evolution: the idea of a developmental logic of social change.

The concept of developmental logic plays a central role in Habermas's theory of social evolution by explaining the rationalization of structures of consciousness, especially normative structures of consciousness, in the evolutionary development of societies. Moreover, the concept of developmental logic provides the critical theorist with the normative grounds to analyze the processes of social change that have given rise to contemporary social structures, and this sociohistorical analysis of the present is intended to specify the deep structures that determine particular social formations. It is thus able to locate the rationality potentials that are latent within given societies, and it locates those developments that can be considered deformed in the sense that they are irrational. An adequate understanding of Habermas's theory of social evolution, therefore, requires a clear account of what is meant by the idea of a developmental logic of normative structures, and of the function this concept of developmental logic plays within the general theory.

There have been three general reactions to Habermas's developmental theory of social evolution. The first type of reaction arose in the period between the publication of *Communication and the Evolution of Society* (1979), and *The Theory of Communicative Action* (1984, 1987). In commenting on Habermas's conception of critical theory, which at that time was presented as a reconstruction of historical materialism, these commentators often addressed directly some of the apparent problems in Habermas's sketch of the theory of social evolution.[1] These commentators typically acknowledged the central role played by the theory of social evolution in Habermas's critical theory. This is not surprising given the fact that during this period, Habermas's attempts to clarify the normative foundations of critical theory remained explicitly within the framework and categories of historical materialism. The second and third types of reaction arose after the publication of *The Theory of Communicative Action*. On the one hand, some commentators simply reduced Habermas's critical theory to the theory of communicative action itself, or to the theory of discourse ethics based on this theory.[2] This, to be sure, was motivated in part by Habermas's presentation in *The Theory of Communicative Action*, which placed the theory of social evolution in the background, while developing the formal pragmatics of language-use and restricting diachronic considerations to a theory of modernity. These commentators effectively ignored the diachronic dimension of his critical social theory by focusing exclusively on the theories of communicative action and discourse ethics. A third set of reactions recognize the centrality of the theory of social evolution to Habermas's conception of critical theory, but for various reasons do not pursue an assessment of the theory itself. Some, such as Stephen White, maintain that the theory of social evolution is simply too sketchy at this stage to admit of adequate assessment, while others consider it only superficially and consequently dismiss it as prima facie implausible.[3] Yet others do acknowledge, whether explicitly or implicitly, the significance of the theory of social evolution in Habermas's system, but they present only partial critiques of limited aspects of it.[4] Despite these often insightful critiques, relatively little attention has been paid exclusively to the theory itself. While the criticism that the theory of social evolution is too underdeveloped to be properly assessed is valid—hence this study—only Michael Schmid has attempted to clarify and systematize it.

The general consequence of these reactions, in conjunction with the fact that Habermas has since focused on other topics, is that the current debates concerning Habermas's work almost completely ignore the role of the theory of social evolution by focusing on the formal pragmatics of language use, or on the theory of discourse ethics. Moreover, the trajectory of Habermas's interests in the last decade and a half, in the direction of moral and political theory, has solidified the view that Habermas has effectively abandoned the theory of social evolution. This view, however, is quite mistaken. Although in *The Theory of Communicative Action* Habermas was not interested in developing further the theory of social evolution, he did apply its basic categories in a critique of modernity.[5] And in a 1983 essay, Habermas confirms that "genetic structuralism in developmental psychology . . . seems promising for the analysis of social evolution and the development of world views, moral belief systems, and legal systems" (MCCA, 23). Thus, the view that Habermas has abandoned the theory of social evolution and consequently also the developmental logic thesis is unfounded.[6] Of those critics (such as Ingram, McCarthy, Strydom, Honneth, and Eder) who do take the theory of social evolution seriously enough to attempt a critique, most are critical of the assertion of a reconstructable developmental logic of normative structures that is homologous to the structures of ontogenesis.

When such critiques are examined, however, it becomes apparent that the critics have failed to do two things. First, they typically do not reconstruct with sufficient care Habermas's theory of social evolution, the relation between his theory of social evolution and his general critical social theory, and the role played by the concept of developmental logic in his theory of social evolution. Because they are based on misunderstandings of the theory, these critiques miss their mark. In the two previous chapters I have attempted to address this problem by clarifying and making plausible the theory of social evolution and its relation to critical theory. Second, when such critics do acknowledge the significance of the theory of social evolution and its relation to critical social theory, they often fail to analyze the developmental logic thesis with sufficient care. The result is that their critiques rely only on a somewhat superficial understanding of the developmental logic thesis, as well as the homology arguments given in its support. Therefore, it is of considerable importance to formulate an adequate understanding of Habermas's thesis concerning the developmental logic of normative structures.

The Concept of Developmental Logic

In order to understand the developmental theory of social evolution it is essential first to have a firm grasp of the concept of a development logic. In this section I will analyze the concept and assess its applicability to social theory. Since the concept is borrowed from Piaget, it will be useful to first look at the concept as it is used in developmental psychology. The first task, then, will be to explicate the concept as it is understood in the discipline of developmental psychology.[7] This will be followed by an analysis and assessment of the social-theoretic conception of developmental logic.

The Psychological-Theoretic Conception

This section is intended to provide only a sketch of Piaget's theory for the analysis of the psychological-theoretic conception of developmental logic. Since the intention is to provide a general map to orient our analysis, this introductory sketch is not intended to be comprehensive; this is especially true given the richness, complexity, and staggering volume of Piaget's work in developmental psychology.[8]

The overarching interest that fundamentally orients all of Piaget's work relates to questions of epistemology. Traditional epistemologies, he holds, are too static; that is, they do not possess a historical dimension. An adequate account of epistemology, that is, one that is "genetic," must link both structuralist and constructivist explanatory approaches. Such a genetic epistemology conceives of knowledge as predetermined neither in the subject nor in the properties of the object, but as involving "an aspect of novel elaboration."[9] Thus, genetic epistemology in this sense is naturalistic, but it is not positivist; it focuses on the activity of the subject, but it is not idealist; and it conceives of the object as a limiting condition of knowledge.[10] According to Piaget, knowledge is the result of a process of increasing differentiation between subject and object, where the differentiation is accomplished by means of the active construction of cognitive structures.

Piaget is especially concerned with "the theoretical and experimental investigation of the qualitative development of intellectual structures," where the intellectual structures are those intermediaries constructed by the subject to make sense of its environment.[11] Piaget's attention is focused specifically on the structures of cognitive development, where structure is to be distinguished from both function and content.[12] "Content" refers to the "raw uninterpreted data" of behavior. In contrast, "function" refers to the essential and invariant properties of intellectual activity as such: "Intellectual content will vary enormously from age to age in ontogenetic development, yet the general functional properties of the adaptational process remain the same."[13] Piaget identifies organization and adaptation as the two properties of intellectual functioning. Organization refers to the fact that all intellectual functioning is highly structured in the sense that it always involves the coordination between discrete actions, and the coordination of actions with multiple concepts and their meanings. Piaget views intellectual functioning in a holistic way, viewing intellectual organizations as totalities. The cognitive structures that organize our conscious experience are not composed of an ad hoc conglomeration of skills; rather, they form a coherent whole. Thus, my various cognitions about such things as conservation of matter, momentum, the permanence of objects, and so forth, all fit together to form a coherent whole, regardless of the stage of development I am at. The second of the invariant intellectual functions, adaptation, involves two processes: assimilation and accommodation. Very briefly, assimilation is the process by which the organism integrates the environment into the organism's previously established categories, and accommodation is the process by which the organism adapts its categories to the environment.[14] Adaptation refers to the balanced assimilation and accommodation of the environment by the organism. Note that organization and adaptation are complementary. Cognitive organization presupposes prior actions (adaptations) that organize a given intellectual structure, and adaptation presupposes an intellectual structure (organization) that is either accommodated to the environment, or assimilates that same environment (or both).

Cognitive structures (which are Piaget's primary interest) mediate between the invariant functions and the variable contents: "They are the organizational properties of intelligence."[15] Moreover, they are the consequence of intellectual functioning, and they are inferred by abstracting from the overt behavior of subjects. The change of these structures, that is, their development, is determined by the process of adaptation discussed above. Piaget conceives of this development of cognitive structures as occurring in stages. This feature of Piaget's work is perhaps the most relevant to the present study, because the conception of developmental stages of intellectual activity underlies the concept of developmental logic. Although we will analyze this concept further below, it would be worthwhile to mention here some of its key elements. First of all, the development of intellectual activity must be sufficiently heterogeneous to warrant a description of stages. In other words, the behavioral changes of ontogenesis must readily appear to divide into relatively discrete stages, or the attribution of developmental stages would be arbitrary.[16] Moreover, the stages of cognitive development are invariantly ordered, meaning that any individual must, insofar as development does occur, pass through the sequence of stages in an invariant order. For example, given posited stages 1, 2, and 3, stage 2 cannot be reached without first going through stage 1, and stage 3 cannot be reached without first passing through both stages 1 and 2 (and only in that order). Another feature of developmental stages is their hierarchical ordering. Higher stages in the sequence are said to be more developed precisely because they incorporate each lower stage into themselves. Each qualitative stage must also form an integrated whole; that is, "[O]nce structural properties reach an equilibrium . . ., they characteristically show a high degree of interdependence, as though they formed part [of the] processes within a strong total system."[17] This property Piaget refers to as the *structure d'ensemble*. To be sure, stages do not appear in a state of full equilibrium; they also pass through transitional periods of "preparation" and "achievement." Nevertheless, once equilibrium is reached, an integrated whole can be discerned. The notion of periods of disequilibrium is not ad hoc, however, since "the concept of intellectual development as a movement from structural disequilibrium to structural equilibrium, repeating itself at ever higher levels of functioning, is a central concept for Piaget."[18] Piaget's interest in the deep structures of intellectual development further requires an account of behavioral variations. In other words, a genetic-structuralist theory of development will need to explain how observed variations in behavior are possible (Piaget deals with this with the concept of *décalage*).

The result of this theory of genetic epistemology as applied to ontogenesis is an empirically grounded description of the stages of cognitive development. According to Piaget, the developing child advances through four basic levels of cognitive activity, the sensorimotor, preoperational, concrete-operational, and formal-operational. At each level the child's intellectual capacities are fundamentally organized by the structural properties of the given level, and each level is further differentiated into stages of preparation and stabilization.

In the initial stage of the sensorimotor level there is virtually no subjective distinction between the subject and the object. The infant is not conscious of itself, and it does not differentiate between data received from internal sources and that received from external sources.[19] The actions of the child are radically egocentric, since all action is centered on the infant; that is, it is direct and unmediated by complex intellectual activity, and the egocentrism of its actions is completely unconscious.[20] Moreover, the actions of the infant involve no distinctions between the subjective and the objective. At the age of approximately eighteen to twenty-four months the infant makes a transition to a new stage of the sensorimotor level. At this stage basic semiotic functions and representative intelligence appear.[21] Individual actions begin to be coordinated by the subject into schemas, and this coordination of actions leads to an initial differentiation of subject and object, that is, of the thing performing the actions and that which is acted upon. Thus, with this initial subjective differentiation of subject and object, and the achievement of a rudimentary degree of self-awareness, a process of decentering occurs: the radical egocentrism of the initial stage is replaced by a more general egocentrism of action schemas. These schemas are simply regular behavioral reactions to certain stimuli, for example, the infant's sucking anything placed in or near its mouth, kicking anything within reach, grasping things within reach, and so on. From this point on, subject and object become increasingly differentiated. This process has two aspects: an increasingly complex coordination of subjective actions; and an increasingly sophisticated understanding by the subject of the causal relations between objects.

At approximately three to four years of age the child enters the preoperational level of cognitive activity. Action schemas combined with basic semiotic skills allow the child to construct representative schemas that are then utilized more effectively to coordinate actions.[22] Moreover, these action schemas become interiorized in the form of representations or concepts, and action itself is first subjectively viewed as a mediator between the subject and object. The process of decentering is extended to concepts at the next stage of development, which is achieved at roughly five to six years of age. This decentering of concepts or conceptualized actions is connected to the discovery of certain objective relationships to things that are interiorized in the form of relations of dependent variables, or functions.[23] These "constituent functions," as Piaget calls them, are only semilogical. That is, they remain closely connected to action schemas, and are not reversible as are operations. While at this stage the child discovers these constituent functions and can reliably differentiate between individual and class, there is as yet no conception of conservation and no capacity for inferential thought.

The level of concrete operations is achieved between the ages of approximately seven and eight. The key characteristic of this level of development is the achievement of the reversibility of operations. The child no longer makes corrections to action schemas after the fact, but now errors are anticipated. Anticipation and retrospection are fused with action schemas. This fusion of anticipation and retrospection implies a closure of the system of thought on itself, and this implies that the internal relationships of the system acquire a necessity. At this level the concepts of transitivity and conservation make their appearance, but the form/content distinction is not yet made.[24]

At the age of nine to ten years, concrete operations are stabilized. The child's conception of space is elaborated, and the conceptualization of causation increases. As concrete operations are elaborated, however, certain "lacunae" appear, and these lead to the development of the next level of cognitive structures.

The final level of formal operations is achieved at approximately eleven to twelve years of age. The key property of this level is that operations are freed from their time dependence; they become hypothetical. Knowledge at this level can be said to transcend reality, since it dispenses with the concrete as an intermediary.[25] The consequence is the development of propositional logic and of operations applied to operations, or as Piaget says, "sets of all subsets."[26]

Formal Properties

While Piaget's theory consists of both functional (organization and adaptation) and formal (developmental logic) aspects, our interest in this chapter is confined to just its formal aspects (that is, developmental logic). The functional aspects of development are not relevant here because with reference to social theory the functional aspects would be analogous to other elements of the theory of social evolution, such as the distinction between cognitive-technical and moral-practical rationalization processes. It should be noted that the psychological-theoretic conception of developmental logic is not a matter of settled science. That is, the conclusions in the literature concerning the various aspects of this concept are varied, and there is no strong consensus within the discipline of developmental psychology as a whole about its proper understanding. Moreover, within the various analyses that can be found in the literature, the authors typically emphasize the underdetermination of the concept by the empirical data. Nevertheless, while there still may be much debate concerning the proper characterization of the concept of developmental logic, my purpose here will be to identify what I see as the points of convergence between some of the more important studies of the concept. Thus, the analysis below should not be understood as the last word on the psychological-theoretic conception. The analysis will, however, follow the contours of Piaget's theory of development, since this is a specific inspiration for Habermas's developmental logic thesis.

The formal aspects of Piaget's theory (in contrast to the functional) are embodied by the stage model of development. Roughly, this model describes cognitive development in terms of the acquisition of a sequence of hierarchically ordered stages, or levels, of cognitive capacities. In order to avoid confusing the two dimensions of this model, I will distinguish the vertical and the horizontal dimensions, although this is not typically done in the literature.[27] The horizontal dimension refers to those aspects that formally characterize stages as such. Certain properties such as structure and qualitativeness are characteristic of this dimension. In contrast, the vertical dimension refers to those aspects of the stage model that concern the structural relations between qualitatively distinct stages, though not what causes or impels development from one stage to another, but only the formal features of the developmental pattern of these relations between stages. One could even speak here of horizontal and vertical structures, although to avoid confusion, I will restrict the use of "structure" to the horizontal dimension. Analysis of the vertical dimension will be concerned with such features as the hierarchization of stages, and the sublation of lower stages into higher stages. Both dimensions are necessary to the stage model of development as conceived by Piaget, and thus it should be emphasized that the distinction I have drawn between them is only an analytic device. Each dimension of a developmental logic is intimately and inextricably related to the other, and so even though for purposes of analysis I will distinguish stage (horizontal dimension) from sequence (vertical dimension), neither dimension can be understood independently of the other.

Although the concept of stage is fundamental to Piagetian developmental psychology, there is no consensus as to its definition.[28] Nevertheless, one can give an approximate definition of stage as "a mode, pattern, or constellation of behaviors (or dispositions towards behavior) that seems to characterize some definable period in the child's life, be this period specified in terms of chronological age (with the resultant difficulty of taking individual differences in rate of development into account) or in terms of its position in a sequence."[29] It is apparent from the empirical data that the range of behaviors encompassed by a stage can be quite wide, but, for these behaviors to be grouped into a stage, they must be interrelated, either structurally or functionally.

There are two primary formal properties of stages that are crucial for genetic-structuralist (that is, Piagetian) models of development, and these are structure and qualitativeness.[30] Structure is that property that provides the internal holistic character of individual stages, and qualitativeness is that property that determines the substantive differences between stages. In their analysis of the concept of "stage," Adrien Pinard and Monique Laurendeau describe the property of structure as concerning "the actual organization of the intellectual behaviors characteristic of a particular level of functioning."[31] The key function of the notion of structure in a developmental logic, then, is to characterize that property of stages that determines their internal organization. Not just any characterization of the internal organization of stages is adequate, however, since in Piagetian developmental theory each stage possesses a holistic character. More specifically, the individual elements of a given stage are understood as interconnected in such a way as to be reciprocally dependent upon each other: "[T]he typical actions or operations of a given level are not simply juxtaposed one with another in an additive fashion, but are organically interconnected by ties of implication and reciprocal dependence that unite and group them into total structures—Piaget's *structures d'ensemble*."[32] The functional or organic interdependence of elements of a stage is thus the key to understanding its structuration.

In developmental psychology, at least, determining the scope of this notion of *structures d'ensemble* is a highly complex matter. Piaget's observations regarding the structuring of stages are typically at the interconcept level, meaning that the functional interdependence that is observed is between concepts within a given level of development.[33] But all of the structural elements of a given stage do not develop simultaneously. Concepts of a given stage go through a period of consolidation in which they are used more consistently and progressively applied to a greater range of objects. Thus, each stage includes what Pinard and Laurendeau call "achievement and preparation" substages.[34] In the achievement substage the concepts typical of the given level come into use and are successively applied to a greater number of problems and with greater success. During the preparation substage the concepts of the given stage are further consolidated, but preparation begins for development to the next higher stage, and the child encounters more and more problem situations which cannot be solved by the concepts of the current stage. Moreover, Piaget observes that often concepts, once attained with respect to one object, are not immediately generalizable across all objects of application; he refers to this phenomenon as *horizontal décalage*.[35] For example, the achievement of the concept of the conservation of substance does not occur simultaneously with the achievement of the concept of the conservation of weight and volume. These horizontal *décalages* of a single concept across objects of application, however, can be accounted for by the achievement/preparation character of stages. Once a given concept, say conservation, is achieved, it should not surprise us that the child does not immediately comprehend the entire scope of its application. The child learns within the limits of the given stage to which objects this new concept can and cannot be applied, and this process occurs over time. But the phenomenon of horizontal *décalage* can also apply to asynchronous developments of different but closely related concepts. Nevertheless, Pinard and Laurendeau conclude,

> These *décalages* between distinct concepts ought not to compromise the economy of stages: (1) in their hierarchal characteristics, so long as the order of succession of the levels peculiar to each of the concepts and the order of appearance of these concepts among themselves remain invariable (which is a distinct problem); (2) in their integrative characteristics, so long as the succession of behaviors peculiar to the different levels of these concepts takes each time the form of a restructuring or a progressive coordination in spite of the differences in their ages of acquisition; (3) in their structural characteristics, so long as the set of groupings relevant to each of these separate concepts is constructed in synchrony (this is also a problem in itself that will require subsequent discussion); (4) and finally, in their equilibration characteristics insofar as the evolution of these concepts could in each case be described in terms of successive levels of equilibrium and where both concepts might become accommodation hypotheses concerning the continuity of development and the transition between stages.[36]

Here they conclude that despite the difficulties involved in specifying the structuration of stages, we can continue to understand stages as hierarchically ordered sequences of qualitatively different, functionally structured levels of learning.

At a strictly theoretical level there are several key properties of the concept of structure that are essential to Piaget's (and Habermas's) understanding of a developmental logic.[37] Structuralism in general, according to Piaget, refers to the intellectual construction of structures that serve to order data. The idea is that through the projection of an ordering structure an incoherent body of data or experiences is transformed into an intelligible system. For Piaget, this amounts to the cognitive learning processes of the individual ego in its attempt to make sense of its experiences. According to Rotenstreich, construction here refers to "a method of projecting models or as a method whose tools qua hypotheses are structures."[38] The constructive character of structuralism is also interestingly related to the rationality inherent in structuralism. The rationality of structuralism is determined by the autonomy of the process of the projection (or construction) of the intelligible structures. The key characteristic of structuralism, then, is that it is a way in which intelligibility is imposed on data: "Thematically speaking, structuralism is opposed to the atomic tendency to reduce wholes to their elements. . . . But epistemologically, structuralism is an expression of an attempt or aspiration to realize the ideal of intelligibility. . . . Intelligibility is safeguarded by the fact that models qua structures are of hypothetical validity and are not data to be read or discerned. Rationality in this sense amounts therefore to the production of patterns or structures through intelligence, reason, or understanding. The only way to conceive of data and to explain them is by observing them and interpreting them as embraced in structures."[39] The intelligibility that is imposed on the data by structures, however, is an intelligibility that is circumscribed by the actual in the possible: "Structure is conceived as a set of *possible* states. The actual is interpreted or explained as an instance of the possible."[40]

The property of the qualitativeness of stages is also of fundamental importance to a genetic-structuralist theory of development. In such a theory, development is conceived as progressing through a sequentially ordered series of discrete stages, where the stages are qualitatively different from each other. So in Piaget's conception of cognitive development the child normally progresses from the sensorimotor stage to the preoperational stage, followed by development to the concrete operational stage and finally to the formal operational stage of development. Each stage is a discrete entity and each is qualitatively different from both the one preceding it and the one following it (as well as each of the others). If one denies that successive stages of development differ qualitatively, but asserts instead that they differ only quantitatively, then it is difficult to see in what way this might be a Piagetian model of development, since Piaget explicitly asserts the qualitative character of the differences between stages.

Now, as Flavell and Wohlwill have shown, there are two versions of this claim, a stronger one and a weaker one. On the strong version, it is asserted "that *all* cognitive-developmental changes are best construed as changes in kind rather than degree or amount."[41] And on the weak version, it is asserted only that "there exist *some* changes, of prima facie importance, which are undeniably 'quantitative' in any usual meaning of that term."[42] That there are *some* quantitative changes undeniably is the case in cognitive development. For example, given $A < B < C$, and reaching the conclusion that $A < C$ by means of a transitive inference is surely qualitatively different from reaching the same conclusion by other means (say directly comparing A and C), or the use of the concept of conservation is surely qualitatively different from achieving a similar looking solution by alternative means.[43] But while the successive stages of development are conceived of as differing qualitatively, it is admitted at the same time that there also exist quantitative differences, both within and between stages.[44] Flavell concludes that "whereas quantitative changes may be conspicuous attributes of passage from one stage to another, qualitative ones seem to be criterial attributes of this passage."[45] There seems, then, to be agreement among Piagetian developmental psychologists that the strong version of the qualitative thesis is false and the weak version is more likely true, and that perhaps both qualitative and quantitative changes are necessary conditions of cognitive development.

Sequence as it is used here refers to certain relations that obtain between stages. Since we are interested only in those relations that are relevant to the concept of developmental logic, we will examine only the logical or structural relations between stages. We are not concerned here with the empirical and dynamic relations that exist between stages, that is, with those factors that determine if and when a given stage is sublated by a higher stage and a development occurs. Just as there are two primary formal properties of stage—structure and qualitativeness—there are two formal properties of sequence—hierarchization and integration.[46] Hierarchization characterizes the invariant order that cognitive structures assume in the course of development. The premise of a hierarchy of developmental stages "simply states the necessity of a fixed order of succession of the different levels that constitute a developmental sequence. This condition does not thus characterize any particular stage, but the succession as such. It directly poses the problem of the transitivity of stages (the second stage must never precede the first, or the third the second, and so on)."[47] Of course, the transitivity of stages does not imply that sociocultural factors can have no effect in cognitive development; these factors can impede or accelerate cognitive development.

Although the property of hierarchization is a central concept in genetic-structuralist theories of cognitive development, it does not fully capture the idea of sequence. Sequence implies not only the transitivity of the ordering of levels of development, but also that the transitive ordering of stages represents a hierarchy of development, in the sense that later stages are higher, or more developed. The property of integration captures this developmental relation between stages. Integration characterizes the interrelations between qualitatively distinct and hierarchically ordered structures, or levels. Successive levels of development are said to be structural reorganizations of previous levels; as such they involve a revised structural representation of the same content. It must be made clear that integration here means that the contents of stage S_1 are structurally reorganized in stage S_2; in Hegelian terminology they are "sublated." This does not mean that S_1 should be expected to be found in S_2, as if the relationship were merely additive.[48] The integration of one stage by another involves a transformation of the one into the other, and entails "the two processes of *restructuring* and *coordination*."[49]

Pinard and Laurendeau note that the process of restructuring is particularly applicable to developments between major learning levels (in contrast to the stages that subdivide these learning levels).[50] Piaget, they note, refers to restructuring in just this sense, as applying to interlevel transformations, and he gives a theoretical account of this in the form of the concept of *vertical décalage*. This concept represents the observation that "the development of a given conceptual content (e.g. causality, space) is accomplished on several successive levels (sensorimotor, concrete-operational, and formal-operational) according to an analogical process in which this content, already structured at a level established by earlier kinds of actions or operations, is restructured at a higher level by a new kind of operation."[51] Notably, the restructuring of concepts at each successive learning level involves a progressively expanded differentiation of application. That is, as a given concept is restructured at each higher level it becomes increasingly differentiated, thus allowing it to be discriminately applied across a greater domain. This process not only enhances the clarity and coherence of the given concept, but it also makes the application of the concept more effective:

> Thus it is that before the advent of logico-arithmetic operations, at once distinct from spatio-temporal and practical operations, these three kinds of operations were at the sensorimotor level completely undifferentiated, the initial differentiation being produced between the practical and the reflective or cognitive domain (including logic and sublogic) at the preoperational level. Now these diverse and successive restructurings would not operate in a simple additive or subtractive fashion as if, for example, the logical were added to the sublogical, or as if reflective intelligence suppressed practical intelligence at a given moment; we must rather see in this a phenomenon of liberation (or of emergence) that transforms and enriches the domains *a* and *b*, for example, at first indistinguishable within the *ab* whole.[52]

As you may recall from the previous discussion of Piaget's genetic epistemology, the notion of differentiation plays a key role in his theory of how our conceptual and theoretical categories develop.

In contrast to restructuring, which is primarily an interlevel process, coordination is primarily an interstage process, that is, between stages within a given level.[53] As in restructuring, coordination specifies the relation between intralevel stages that involves the functional integration of increasingly differentiated conceptual schemas. So within a given learning level, the transformation from one stage to another involves not just differentiation of conceptual schemes, but also a coordination of these schemes within the general structural framework of the given level.

The analytic distinctions of structure, qualitativeness, hierarchization (transitivity), and integration explicated above are intended to clarify, in part, the sense in which a given developmental stage can be said to sublate another. Nevertheless, the characterization of this sublation remains conceptually unclear. In particular, what does it mean to say that a given level of development "emerges" from the previous one? To answer this question it will be useful to turn to an analysis by Flavell of the notion of a cognitive-developmental sequence.[54]

Flavell has analyzed specifically the concept of a cognitive-developmental sequence with the explicit intention of categorizing the modes in which one structure becomes developmentally transformed into another.[55] He notes first that simply defining the sequential emergence of different cognitive "items" is problematic, since cognitive items do not simply appear fully formed but develop over a given time frame.[56] What, then, is an adequate criterion for determining the existence of a cognitive sequence? Is it that we regularly observe cognitive item X_1 to begin its development before X_2?[57] Or when both items begin their development simultaneously, but X_2 ends its development after X_1? What about the case where X_1 begins its development before X_2 and ends its development after X_2? This case, Flavell comments, is the most common, but the overlapping, codevelopment portion is significantly longer than the beginning and ending portions of X_1's development. Flavell sidesteps this definitional problem by simply stipulating that "two items will be said to have been 'acquired in the sequence X_1-X_2', providing only that X_1 *began* its development before X_2 did: i.e., regardless both of the duration of any subsequent periods of codevelopment and of the temporal ordering of the terminal points of the two developments (i.e., synchronous, X_1-X_2, or X_2-X_1, with respect to the time of developmental completion)."[58]

This leaves open, however, the methodological question of how the investigator can measure or determine with sufficient precision the initial emergence or completion of development of a given cognitive item.[59] Flavell concludes that the most interesting cognitive sequences often will be the most difficult to empirically verify. For his purposes, Flavell chooses to set aside these interesting and challenging problems in order to concentrate on another aspect of understanding cognitive-developmental sequences, that of classifying the various relations between two cognitive items in a sequence. In other words, Flavell is interested in the different theoretical interpretations that can be given to a verified cognitive sequence. Just because a given cognitive sequence has been identified does not necessarily mean that an interesting interpretation of that sequence can be given. The sequences, then, that he wants to examine are those he refers to as "interesting," such a sequence being "one where we can at least imagine some sort of fairly direct, meaningful, and substantive (i.e., other than merely temporal-sequential) relationship between its constituent items."[60]

Flavell begins his analysis by proposing a classificatory schema of cognitive-developmental sequences. Specifically, he claims that "cognitive items composing 'interesting' developmental sequences can be related to one another in five principal ways: *addition*, *substitution*, *modification*, *inclusion*, and *mediation*.[61] This is intended to be a complete list: every case of cognitive-developmental change can be characterized as an instantiation of one or more of these categories. He does caution, however, that his proposed categories "have simply not proven to be the unitary, nonoverlapping, definitionally elegant affairs originally hoped for," and therefore the members of each category are members by virtue of their familial characteristics (in the Wittgensteinian sense).[62]

The category of *addition* refers to cognitive-developmental sequences in which two cognitive items develop at different times, and either one appears utilizable to achieve the same cognitive ends.[63] Moreover, both items, X_1 and X_2, remain "fully and permanently available as a cognitive pattern," and there is no regularity to their usage patterns. As an example, Flavell cites the development of spatial knowledge.[64] In infancy, our motor movements react behaviorally to our environment, thus developing a "sensorimotor map" of our surroundings. Not until much later are we able to represent our spatial environment symbolically. Nevertheless, once this symbolic capacity has developed, we do not lose the capacity to react behaviorally to the spatial features of our environment.

In contrast to addition, the category of *substitution* contains sequences in which one cognitive item (X_1) is replaced by another, clear and distinct item (X_2). X_1 and X_2 continue to be seen, as in addition, as equally viable potentially alternative cognitive tools for responding to a given situation. Whereas in addition the two cognitive items come to coexist in the cognitive inventory and are used alternately, in substitution, the second cognitive item replaces the first as a cognitive response to a given situation.[65] Flavell is careful to emphasize that while the two categories of addition and substitution often overlap, they have very different cognitive functions. Whereas addition sequences function primarily to expand and enlarge the inventory of cognitive responses, substitution sequences function primarily to replace more or less inadequate cognitive items with more adequate ones: "Like certain personality traits, some cognitive acquisitions are seen as distinctly 'changeworthy'—to be commended as first efforts, maybe, but decidedly unacceptable as permanent adaptations to the milieu. The substitution category, unlike the addition one, has essentially 'changeworthy' items as its X_1's."[66]

The category of *modification* is more complex and interesting than the others. This is because modification conceptualizes development in the true sense of the term; it refers to sequences in which one cognitive item develops into or becomes another item: "In the typical Addition or Substitution sequence, there is the definite sense that X_1 and X_2 really are two quite distinct and discontinuous entities: first 'one thing' (X_1) develops and later on 'another thing' (X_2) develops. In the typical Modification sequence, on the other hand, X_1 and X_2 give more an impression of merely being different forms or varieties of 'the same thing'. That is, X_2 strikes one rather as being some sort of improved, perfected, or matured version of X_1; some sort of transform, derivative, or variate of X_1; in brief, some sort of 'modification' of X_1 in the direction of cognitive maturity."[67] Flavell hastens to note that as with all of the other categories there is a certain degree of overlap between addition, substitution, and modification. Nevertheless, the distinct category of modification can be conceptually identified. A sequence in which the latter item appears only to develop after the earlier item is most likely an instance of either addition or substitution, but a sequence in which the latter item appears to develop from the earlier item can be categorized as a modification sequence.[68] Flavell analyzes modification into "three principal forms of development": *differentiation, generalization,* and *stabilization.*

Differentiation is, as Flavell notes, a key category of developmental change, and it is the most important of the three subcategories.[69] Differentiation is a functional adaptation of the individual to the environment that conditions the way the environment is responded to: "Differentiation is largely a matter of specialization and delimitation of function, with the newly acquired distinctions and discriminations that result from the differentiation process representing some sort of constraint or restriction, generally an adaptive one, on the way the individual responds.[70] Examples of differentiation in cognitive development abound. Flavell cites Piaget's observation of the development by differentiation of the infant's "sucking schema."[71] At first the infant behaviorally recognizes only "suckable objects," but this category is soon differentiated into "suckable and nourishing objects" (for example, a bottle) and "suckable and non-nourishing objects" (for example, the fingers)

The second subcategory of modification, generalization, involves the extension of the range of application of a cognitive item. In this case X_1 comes to be seen as too specific, and it is modified to include a greater range of applications, resulting in X_2. Whereas in addition a distinctly different cognitive item is added to the inventory, in generalization the same item is modified to expand its scope of application. Generalization is the complement to differentiation; rather than limiting the range of application of a cognitive item, as in differentiation, generalization expands it. An example of generalization is the development of measurement skills in the concrete-operational period.[71] At first, the child can measure objects (say their length) by direct reference to his own body, for instance, by holding his hands a certain distance apart. He generalizes this skill by utilizing an external, fixed standard of measurement. At this point, however, the fixed measure must be at least as long as the object being measured. Finally, use of a fixed measure is generalized to include the capacity to measure objects whose length exceeds the length of the measuring rod at hand.

The third and final subcategory is stabilization. Stabilization refers to the development towards "functional maturity" of a cognitive item, in which the item becomes solidified, consolidated, and stabilized within the cognitive inventory. As it develops the cognitive item "may become more consistently and reliably brought into play when appropriate (and *only* then), more quickly invoked, and more smoothly and efficiently deployed."[72] This subcategory, however, is not on an equal par with the other two, since it seems to be closely associated with and, at least in part, the by-product of the other two. Nevertheless, Flavell notes that there is a conceptual distinction between it and the other two, since whereas differentiation narrows the domain of application and generalization broadens it, "an item can be more or less stable (quickly and reliably evoked, efficiently executed, etc.) within that domain."[73]

One final comment on the category of modification should be made. Recall that addition expands the inventory of cognitive items by the addition of a distinctly new one, and substitution replaces inadequate cognitive items by a more adequate, distinctly new item. In both cases there is a discontinuity between the two items of the sequence. In contrast, the two items of a modification sequence are continuous with one another; that is, while the latter item is qualitatively distinct from the earlier one, it maintains something of the earlier one's identity. The point is that modification captures those sequences in which one and the same item develops into another one; it is a case of neither simple addition nor substitution.

The fourth category of developmental change, *inclusion*, describes sequences in which one item becomes a part of, in the sense of a "component, subroutine or 'module,'" of another new and distinct item.[74] Furthermore, if it is the case that X_2 cannot function without the inclusion of X_1, "the developmental sequence X_1-X_2 is classified as 'invariant,' 'universal,' 'necessary,' and the like."[75] Inclusion, however, does not require that one and the same X_1 be included in X_2 in all cases. Alternative X_1's can and will be recruited for inclusion in X_2. Presumably the only apparent requirement for an acceptable alternative for X_1 is that it satisfy the necessary functional conditions required by X_2. An interesting example of an inclusion developmental sequence cited by Flavell is role taking inferences.[76] The developed capacity for role taking is a necessary element in constructing an audience-sensitive message. In order to choose the best words, word order, phrases, sentences, and so forth, it is necessary for the speaker to imaginatively project herself into the role of the listener(s). Without the use of such role-taking inferences, the message would not be adapted to the audience, and hence would be less effective.

The final category of developmental sequences discussed by Flavell, *mediation,* describes that category of sequences in which one item serves as a bridge or mediator for the development of another item.[77] Flavell recognizes the similarities between this category and inclusion, but notes that there are important differences. Most notably, in cases of mediation, X_1 serves only to bring about X_2, and thus will not be utilized in each and every subsequent use of X_2, as is the case in inclusion sequences. Flavell describes the role of the mediating items (X_1's) as "constituting some sort of developmental route or path to X_2, as providing an occasion or opportunity for the emergence of X_2, as facilitating the genesis of X_2—or simply, as helping to mediate the growth of X_2."[78] And as with inclusion, the initial item in the sequence may be uniquely necessary to the development of X_2, or it may be substituted for by an alternative, but functionally equivalent, item. Flavell cites as an example the mediating role played by the emergence of a new cognitive skill (X_1) that characterizes the start of a new period or level of development.[79] These newly acquired basic cognitive skills are then applied in interpreting experience, problem solving, and general cognitive interaction with the environment (X_2).

What, then, can be said generally about Flavell's schema of the five types of cognitive-developmental sequences? First of all, the categories of addition and substitution possess the unique characteristic of enriching the inventory of cognitive items. Addition enriches the inventory by expanding it, by adding new items to the stock, and substitution enriches the inventory by replacing inadequate items with more adequate ones.[80] This "enriching function" of addition and substitution can be contrasted with the characteristic of being "future-oriented," which modification, inclusion and mediation each possess; they serve to "remind us that cognitive-developmental acquisitions are transitive, future-directed affairs."[81] The idea here is that each development prepares the ground for the next development; none is strictly an end in itself. This can be seen when one views these categories from the perspective of their continuity and discontinuity. Both addition and substitution are discontinuous sequences, such that the second item in the sequence does not have a causal-genetic relation to the first item. In these cases, there is a strict discontinuity in the developmental sequence. Indeed, one might wonder in what sense addition and substitution are developmental sequences at all (we will return to this below). Modification, inclusion, and mediation, on the other hand, each represent a causal-genetic continuity between the first and the second items in the sequence. Modification is the clearest case of continuity; the first cognitive item in the sequence is literally transformed into a qualitatively different item, such that the second can be said to have developed from the first. Inclusion is also a straightforward case of causal-genetic continuity. The first item in the sequence becomes incorporated into the second item, without which the second item would be undeveloped, or incomplete. Mediation, however, is a bit more complex case of continuity.[82] At first glance, the fact that the second item in the sequence requires the first to develop, but that the first is neither transformed into nor included in the second seems to suggest that the two items are discontinuous. And they are, but only formally. That is, the first item is not a substantive part of the second item of the sequence. In this sense, one can describe mediation as formally discontinuous. Nevertheless, there is also a causal-genetic continuity between the first and second items of the sequence, for the second item would not develop were it not for the mediating role of the first item.

Finally, Flavell does recognize that his classificatory schema, and perhaps any such schema, encounters certain problems and ambiguities.[83] On the one hand, some cognitive-developmental sequences do not seem to quite fit into any of the proposed categories. Flavell cites the acquisition of certain grammatical structures as a possible example of this sort of problem. On the other hand, other cognitive-developmental sequences appear to share features of several of the proposed categories. Here he cites the acquisition of measurement skills as a possible example of this sort of ambiguity. Whereas the progressive development of measurement skills can be seen as a clear example of modification by generalization, it can also be seen as an example of addition, where the use of alternative measuring devices is added to the cognitive inventory. Moreover, Flavell admits that the particular definitions of each of the proposed categories have various weaknesses. In other words, he is suggesting that this is a preliminary proposal for a schema of developmental-sequence categories, and that it is open to debate and refinement.

None of these problems, in my view, is sufficient to undermine the value of such a schema. In cases of developmental progressions that seem to fit none of the proposed categories, it may turn out to be the case that the taxonomy of categories needs to be expanded, or perhaps there is a methodological problem with the way the problematic progression is represented. In any case, this does not seem to be an insurmountable problem, and, indeed, can best be dealt with from within a schema of developmental-sequences. Insofar as some developmental progressions appear to share features of several categories, this, again, is not sufficient to undermine the validity of such a schema. There is no good reason to think that progressions can and should be neatly describable by only one category. Cognitive development is a highly complex affair, and it should not be surprising that developmental sequences can involve more than one type of relationship between two sequentially ordered items. None of these reasons, then, is sufficient to warrant the jettisoning of such a schema.

In summary, there are four essential properties falling under two categories of stage and sequence that characterize a developmental logic: structure, qualitativeness, hierarchization, and integration. Structure and qualitativeness together characterize what constitutes a stage, and hierarchization and integration characterize what constitutes a sequence of stages. Both elements, stage and sequence, are necessary for a complete description of the concept of developmental logic. Furthermore, the idea of a developmental sequence can be further analyzed into the categories of addition, substitution, modification (as differentiation, or as generalization), inclusion, and mediation. Addition sequences expand the inventory of cognitive items by simply adding a new item to the stock. Substitution sequences refine the given inventory of cognitive items by replacing inadequate items with more adequate ones. In modification sequences one and the same cognitive item is transformed, either by differentiation, generalization, or both, into a more developed form. In inclusion sequences a previously developed cognitive item is included as a "subroutine" in a more general item. And in mediation sequences one cognitive item mediates the development of another item.

The Social-Theoretic Conception

In Habermas's theory of social evolution the psychological-theoretic conception of developmental logic informs the social-theoretic thesis of a developmental logic of social orders. The foregoing analysis of the psychological-theoretic conception is intended to serve as a basis for a clarification and systematization of Habermas's developmental logic thesis. So what does it mean to say that normative social structures change according to a developmental logic? Specifically, what is developmental about this pattern of change? It is the task of this section to attempt to answer this question.

Developmental Stages. I will begin by considering the differing functions of the social-theoretic and the psychological-theoretic conceptions of developmental logic, and the unique demands made of the social-theoretic conception by the aims of critical theory. For instance, the developmental logic of social evolution describes a hierarchical ordering of learning levels of a society, just as the developmental logic of cognitive or moral development describes a hierarchical ordering of learning levels of the individual ego. However, since by definition societies are composed of a plurality of individuals, the social-theoretic conception of developmental logic needs to be more flexible to accommodate the range of individual cognitive and moral capacities found in any given society.

Recall that Flavell and Wohlwill define a (psychological-theoretic) stage as "a mode, pattern, or constellation of behaviors (or dispositions towards behavior) that seems to characterize some definable period in the child's life. . . ."[84] How do we interpret this idea of stage in social-theoretic terms? To begin, it is important to remember that Habermas assumes that there is an intrinsic relation between the structures of the individual ego and the structures of social interaction. In fact, the structures turn out to be the same, since the constitution of both the ego and society are dependent upon the same structures (CES, 99). These structures are communicative structures such that both the ego and society are constituted in and through communicative action and its underlying structures. Keeping this in mind, we can define a social-theoretic stage as *a mode, pattern, or constellation of dispositions towards behavior that seems to characterize some definable period in the history of a society.*

The social-theoretic definition of stage emphasizes the disposition towards some behavior rather than concrete behavior itself. This is because the theory of social evolution specifies only the stages of possibility of social formations. In other words, at any given level of development, the structure constituting the given stage determines the range of possibilities; that is, it constitutes the domain of variations that are possible at the given level of development. Which concrete form a society takes within the given level of development is determined only by contingent, historical factors. So a social-theoretic stage of development determines only the range of concrete social forms that are possible.

The two formal properties of the psychological-theoretic conception of stage—structure and qualitativeness—are features of the social-theoretic conception as well. The property of structure captures the internally organized, holistic aspect of the concept of stage. The internal organization is constituted by the interdependence of the individual elements of the structure, where the specific features of the interdependence itself constitute the structure. There are two forms this interdependence of elements of a structure can take: *formal* and *functional.* A structure that is constituted by the formal relations of interdependence between its elements is one in which the individual elements receive their significance by virtue of their specific relationship to each of the other elements. An example of a formally organized structure is Saussure's linguistics, in which a word's meaning is determined by being contrasted with the other words in the language. Another example is Habermas's formal-pragmatics, which is a structuralist analysis of the formal relations of communicative actions.

In contrast to formal structures, functional structures are constituted not only by the formal relationships of their members, but also by their functional relationships. In this case, the significance of each element is determined by its place in the structure, and by the effects it has on each other member. An example of this sort of functional interdependence is the operation of the economy. The economy of a society is constituted by the individual actions of its members, and each member's economic actions have meaning and significance in relation to the economy as a whole. Not only can particular aspects of a society be seen under the aspect of structure, but society as a whole also can be viewed as such. Niklas Luhmann is a leading exponent of systems theory, which explains society only under the aspect of its functional relationships (as we have seen in chapter 2, Habermas finds this theory one-sided).

Recall that a specific difficulty with psychological-theoretic definitions of structure is that the components of the child's cognitive inventory develop and change at different times and at different rates, so it is difficult to define and explain cognitive structuration when the elements are seemingly in a constant process of development. Dealing with this difficulty is the motivation behind Piaget's concept of horizontal *décalage,* which refers to the gradual solidification and generalization of a newly acquired concept. A similar phenomenon to horizontal *décalage* can be observed at the social level as well. Consider a new scientific, moral or political theory, and how such a new theory, if well grounded, can spread throughout a society, eventually becoming a fundamental paradigm on which social institutions are based. The phenomenon of horizontal *décalage* is less problematic for social theory than it is for psychological theory. This is because in processes of individual maturation the cognitive dissonance that results from the uneven development of various intellectual items poses a greater threat to the integrity of the self than does the uneven development of learning processes in society. For a society has a much greater cognitive flexibility to absorb the shocks of incongruent ideas that arise in learning processes.

Finally, just as cognitive structures are constructed through processes of cognitive learning, social structures are also the result of a constructive process of learning. Social structures, however, result from a process of collective learning. To be sure, collective learning depends in the last instance on the cognitive achievements of individuals, but it can be understood best in a nonreductive manner. That is, a theory of collective learning needs to explain just how individual learning achievements become transferred and integrated into a sociocultural system as a whole. For Habermas, this is not simply a process of more and more individuals independently learning something, until these individuals either are numerous enough or hold a sufficiently high social station to impose their ideas on others. The transference of individual learning achievements into a sociocultural system, according to Habermas, takes place through the actions of social movements.

Structure alone is insufficient to characterize the concept of stage, since this concept implies also a series of qualitatively discrete steps or stages. Thus, the second property of stage is qualitativeness. This property refers to the discontinuity between stages, where each stage can be represented as a discrete entity that is qualitatively different from both the stage preceding and the stage following. When understood in conjunction with the property of structure, the qualitativeness of stages will cash out as a series of discrete structures. That is, that which is qualitatively different between stages is their structure. Thus when Habermas speaks of a developmental logic of normative structures he has in mind a genetic structure of qualitatively different learning levels which determine the normative organization of the given society.

As with the psychological-theoretic conception, one can understand the qualitativeness of social-theoretic changes in both a strong and a weak sense. The strong version claims that all such changes are qualitatively distinct, while the weak version claims only that some social-theoretic changes are qualitatively distinct. As in the psychological-theoretic conception, the strong version seems false. No supposedly adequate theory of social change could assert with good reason that all sociocultural change was of a qualitative character. But simply to deny the warranted assertability of the strong version and affirm the weak version would ignore some important issues. Since the aim of this study is not to infer a theory of social change from an interpretation of history, but to conceptually clarify Habermas's theory of social evolution, understanding the notion of qualitativeness with respect to his theory is the goal.

How is the property of the qualitativeness of stages to be understood in relation to Habermas's theory of social evolution? Recall that there are two types of sociocultural change: change that occurs within a given learning level of a society (intralevel change), and change that occurs between learning levels (interlevel change). Intralevel change is conceived primarily on the model of functional adaptation. Given the potentials and constraints of the specific learning level, a society makes functional changes to adapt to socially significant problems. For example, the introduction of the New Deal welfare system in the United States in the 1930s was a functional reaction to the socially disintegrative effects of an advanced capitalist economy. This was a functional adjustment necessary to restore socioeconomic stability and secure the continued reproduction of the society. The deep structure of the given learning level is not altered in this type of change; only the functional relationships between elements of society are changed. Thus, the emergence of the welfare state did not reflect a fundamental change in worldview, moral consciousness, or national identity; it was an internal adjustment in reaction to a disruptive economic system.

In contrast, interlevel change is conceived as a fundamental reordering of the deep structure of the society in such a way that the motivating crisis is overcome. This is emphatically not conceived by Habermas as simply a functional adaptation; rather it is understood as a process of collective learning in which the newly achieved level of learning is a developmentally higher step. Thus, the qualitativeness of discrete stages applies only to interlevel changes, so that when Habermas's theory of social evolution speaks of a developmental logic of normative structures it is referring to the series of learning levels which are qualitatively distinct from one another. The obvious example of this kind of development (and the most relevant for a critical social theory) is the sociocultural change referred to as the Enlightenment. The Enlightenment stands at the threshold of the transition in the West from Medieval, premodern to modern structures of consciousness. This transition is marked by the disenchantment of the comprehensive metaphysical-theological worldviews (for example, Christianity), accompanied by the rise of modern empirical science; the development from a conventional morality and natural law backed by the metaphysical-theological worldviews to a postconventional form of moral consciousness in which moral norms (the right) are distinguished from questions of the good life (the good), and justifications that are backed by universal consent. In sum, the transition to modernity experienced by the West in the sixteenth and seventeenth centuries is understood by Habermas's theory of social evolution as an interlevel transition between learning levels that define the structures of consciousness.

This understanding of the theory of social evolution, however, is not unambiguously represented by Habermas's texts. The general impression given by his writings concerning the theory of social evolution is that the notion of a developmental logic is applicable only to interlevel changes, that is, to changes between learning levels. But this is not entirely consistent with the results of the homological arguments, especially the argument for the homology between the development of moral consciousness in the child and the evolution of moral norms and legal institutions. Kohlberg schematizes the development of moral consciousness into three levels (preconventional, conventional, postconventional), and six stages (two per level). The psychological-theoretic analysis of developmental logic discussed above clearly refers to changes between stages; thus qualitativeness is a property of stages. So it would seem that the notion of developmental logic refers to changes between both stages and learning levels. The homological argument concerning moral consciousness and law implies that the developmental logic of moral norms and legal structures in society is one between these narrower stages and not just one between learning levels. Therefore, one might conclude that there are at least some intralevel sociocultural changes that are susceptible to a developmental-logical analysis (in contrast to merely functional analysis). The ambiguity lies between Habermas's explicit statements concerning a developmental logic of normative structures, which imply that only learning levels are ordered according to a developmental logic, and his homological arguments, which imply that intralevel stages might also be ordered according to a developmental logic.[85]

The ambiguity, however, does not originate in Habermas's texts. It can be traced to the various psychological-theoretic analyses of the concept of developmental logic. In each of the developmental psychology sources I have relied on, there is little or no effort to distinguish stage from level, despite the fact that the distinction is a key element in Piaget's theory. These analyses concern themselves only with developmentally significant changes in cognitive items, whether they be changes between concepts, stages, or learning levels. Because Habermas appeals to homological arguments concerning similar structures between ontogenesis and sociocultural development, it would seem that this ambiguity is unavoidably transferred to the social-theoretic level. But the question then becomes, how does this ambiguity affect the theory of social evolution? I want to suggest that this ambiguity is insignificant for Habermas's theory, because his theory is primarily interested in deep structure social changes, that is, those changes that occur between learning levels. If it should be the case that there are changes within learning levels, between intralevel stages, say, that can be analyzed according to a developmental logic, then this would certainly refine the theory of social evolution, but it would not significantly undermine it. And if the converse were the case, that no intralevel changes are ordered according to a developmental logic, then, again, the theory would be unaffected in any significant way. This ambiguity, then, is more of a problem for neo-Piagetians than it is for Habermas's theory of social evolution.

Developmental Sequences. The concept of sequence was analyzed above into the formal properties of hierarchization and integration. These two properties characterize in a general way the notion of a sequence of stages in the developmental-logical sense. Hierarchization and integration clarify the two functional relations between two stages in sequence, thus distinguishing a sequence of stages from a simple series of stages. Whereas a series is constituted by an ordered grouping of stages with no structural relationships between its members, a sequence is constituted by an ordered grouping in which two particular structural relations (namely, hierarchization and integration) hold between its members. These two structural relations have been further analyzed (following Flavell) into five types of sequential relations: addition, substitution, modification, inclusion, and mediation. The aim of this section is to give this psychological-theoretic analysis of sequence a social-theoretic interpretation. In particular, how can the developmental-logical concept of sequence be meaningfully understood from the perspective of Habermas's theory of social evolution?

The property of hierarchization entails the invariant transitive ordering that developmental sequences exhibit. That is, given a developmental sequence ABC, A is developmentally prior to B, B to C, and, given the principle of transitivity, A to C. Hierarchization also entails the invariant ordering of the members of the developmental sequence, such that (given the above developmental sequence), C cannot be reached without first passing through both A and B, in that order. Habermas's theory of social evolution posits a developmental logic of normative structures, which can now be understood (in part) in terms of a hierarchy of normative structures. Since these normative structures refer only to the deep, linguistically based structures that condition sociocultural interaction, they can be understood as an invariant, transitively ordered sequence of structures that determine the range of possible concrete sociocultural forms. For example, prior to the Enlightenment, the dominant Western worldview was Judeo-Christian. This worldview can be characterized as metaphysical-religious because its fundamental explanatory principles refer to a metaphysical or a religious conception of the cosmos. Thus, theoretical explanations of natural phenomena and practical justifications of moral norms and ethical values were both backed by this worldview; that is, the types of reasons that were considered acceptable, or good, reasons in theoretical explanations and moral-ethical justifications were determined by the structure of the worldview. With the transition to modernity, marked by the disintegration of comprehensive worldviews, the premodern form of backing became devalued. That is, the types of reasons that were considered good or acceptable reasons in theoretical explanations and practical justifications changed. The modern structures of consciousness required theoretical explanations (that were considered acceptable) to be backed by accessible and reproducible empirical facts, and moral justifications were now backed by appeal to universal consensus.

The complement to the property of hierarchization is integration, which entails the functional relations between two members of a developmental sequence. The functional relation is transformative, such that, given developmental sequence AB, A is in some sense transformed or sublated into B as determined by the processes of restructuring and coordination. On the social-theoretic conception of developmental logic this entails that when normative structure A is sublated into normative structure B, the structure of A is reorganized. In the psychological-theoretic analysis, coordination is identified as a feature of integration that is complementary to restructuring. But as Pinard and Laurendeau note, restructuring is primarily a feature of inter*level* developmental sequences, and coordination is primarily a feature of inter*stage* (that is, intralevel) developmental sequences.[86] Given this distinction, and the fact that Habermas's theory of social evolution analyzes only interlevel sociocultural sequences as developmental (where intralevel sequences are analyzed as functional), only the restructuring feature of integration is relevant to the social-theoretic analysis of developmental logic. Therefore, from the social-theoretic perspective, the integrative character of a given sociocultural sequence entails (only) a restructuring of the normative structures. Since Habermas understands normative structures to be based in communicative structures, this restructuring involves a revision of fundamental communicative practices. Accordingly, the transition from traditional to modern societies involves a fundamental restructuring of sociocultural justificatory practices. Specifically practical questions of action become differentiated from theoretical questions of fact, and within each sphere justification becomes universalistic and reflexive.

To review, the social-theoretic conception of developmental logic is analyzed into the formal properties of hierarchization and integration. Hierarchization is further analyzed in terms of transitivity and invariance, and integration is understood as a transformative restructuring. This notion of transformative restructuring, however, remains somewhat unclear. It is here that Flavell's analysis of what he refers to as "interesting" developmental sequences is most valuable. The interesting developmental sequences he identifies are addition, substitution, modification, inclusion, and mediation. This condition of being sufficiently interesting, derived from the psychological-analysis of developmental logic, is valid for the social-theoretic analysis as well, because both the concept of social evolution and the developmental logic thesis entail a substantial relation in this sense between the members of a sequence.

But what are the interesting developmental sequences in sociocultural development? The first two categories of addition and substitution are the most suspect, and not only for social-theoretic reasons. Habermas's theory of social evolution explains social change according to (in part) a model of development. This conception of development entails that the structure of one item of a developmental sequence be transformed or sublated into the next item in the sequence (Hegel's *aufheben*). Addition and substitution, by Flavell's own admission, fail to meet this criterion. Recall that both of these categories represent discontinuous relations between the items of a sequence, that is, there is no direct causal-genetic relation between the items. Moreover, on the psychological-theoretic analysis of the concept of developmental logic as well it is difficult to see how these two categories meet this condition of being sufficiently interesting. Therefore, both addition and substitution fail to meet the condition of being an interesting developmental sequence.

This is not to say, of course, that the sequential relations of addition and substitution as described by Flavell play no role in development, whether at the cognitive or social level. Flavell makes a strong case that these types of relations between cognitive items exist in the course of individual cognitive maturation, but his own qualifications (that addition and substitution represent discontinuous relations) remove these categories from serious consideration as interesting developmental sequences. Again at the social level, new ideas, concepts, and theories are continuously added to the collective inventory of knowledge, and better ones often replace those that are less adequate. Nevertheless, they are not the sort of elements that are fundamental to developmental sociocultural structures. These are deep structures; they set the terms of possibility for concrete ideas, concepts and theories. Habermas's theory of social evolution is interested only in the developmental logic of these deep structures, and this entails a conception of developmental sequence in which one structure sublates another. The transformation of one structure into another entails a direct, causal-genetic relationship that is continuous, conditions that addition and substitution fail to satisfy.

The most interesting of Flavell's categories is modification because it is clearly closest in conception to the idea of transformation, or sublation. Modification is explicitly intended to capture those sequences in which "X_2 strikes one rather as being some sort of improved, perfected, or matured version of X_1; some sort of transform, derivative, or variate of X_1; in brief, some sort of 'modification' of X_1 in the direction of cognitive maturity."[87] Thus, modification type developmental sequences entail a strong causal-genetic continuity between the items. According to Flavell's analysis there are two modes of developmental modification: differentiation and generalization. The third subcategory, stabilization, he notes is somewhat secondary in that it is in part a consequence of the other two subcategories. For this reason, our social-theoretic analysis will concentrate on differentiation and generalization, and stabilization will be understood only as a consequence of the other two modes of modification.

Differentiation and generalization form a complementary pair. On the one hand, differentiation narrows the scope of a sociocultural structure, through specialization and delimitation of function. On the other hand, generalization broadens the scope of application of a sociocultural structure, to a wider range of objects. The importance of differentiation and generalization to the social-theoretic analysis of developmental logic is readily apparent, and these two modes of development are emphasized in Habermas's theory of social evolution, especially in his work concerning the transition to modernity (see TCA I). The adaptive capacity of any social structure would seem to rely significantly on processes of differentiation and generalization. A key developmental characteristic of the modern age is the differentiation between theoretical and practical reason, and also between questions of right and duty (morality) and questions of value and the good life (ethics). History abounds with such developmental differentiations that in turn further increase the adaptive capacity of a social structure owing to the greater variety of specialized functions and the wider range of interrelationships. Generalization of functions is equally significant to the adaptability of a social structure. When a given function is too limited the structure as a whole is limited in the range of its possible adaptive responses to challenges. With the process of generalization, however, a previously too narrowly delimited function is expanded to encompass a greater range of application, thus giving the social structure as a whole greater stability and adaptability. With the differentiation of questions of right from those of value, questions of right were opened to increasing generalization or universalization. In modernity then, moral norms become universalized such that their validity holds for all persons; this is in contrast to values, which are valid only for a circumscribed community that shares a substantive identity. The universalization of moral norms was only possible after morality, concerned with questions of the right, and ethics, concerned with questions of the good, became differentiated in the transition to modern structures of consciousness.

Despite his acknowledgment that the final two categories of inclusion and mediation are quite similar, Flavell maintains that they are distinct categories. Inclusion is Flavell's category for those developmental sequences in which the first item becomes a part of the second item. The second item cannot function without the inclusion of the first, but it is not the case that in each and every instantiation of X_2, the identical X_1 serves as the subroutine. Inclusion, as defined by Flavell, seems to say only that some items in developmental sequences require certain functionally characterized elements in order to develop. Although there clearly exists a causal-genetic continuity between the two items, the continuity is only functional, such that the first item in the sequence is a functional precondition of the second item. This interpretation of inclusion highlights its similarities to mediation. Mediation is Flavell's category for those developmental sequences in which a functionally mature X_1 mediates the development of X_2. In contrast to inclusion, once the first item serves to mediate the development of the second item in the sequence, X_1 is no longer instantiated in subsequent uses of X_2. Nevertheless, as in inclusion the first item is a functional precondition for the development and maturity of the second item. Thus, although there are differences, they are not sufficiently significant to warrant two distinct categories. I propose that the category of mediation be redefined to include instances of inclusion. Mediation developmental sequences would then be understood as cases in which X_2 cannot develop or mature without the prior development of a functionally specific X_1. Understanding mediation in this way clarifies what is meant by the property of transitive invariance exhibited by (interesting) developmental sequences. Suppose developmental sequence ABC; if A and B are related by mediation, and C is a modification of B, then A is a precondition of C. In other words, C cannot develop unless A develops prior to B. The ordering of the sequence is thus both transitive and invariant.

The Developmental Logic Thesis

We now have a better understanding of the meaning of the concept of developmental logic. Since we need to assess the arguments for formulating a theory of social evolution on the basis of such a concept, our next task is to examine the arguments given in support of what I call the "developmental logic thesis." Habermas claims that we can properly understand rationalization processes only if we distinguish the autonomous developmental logic of normative structures from the development of productive forces:

> I am convinced that normative structures do not simply follow the path of development of [material] reproductive processes and do not simply respond to the pattern of system problems, but that they have instead an *internal history.* In earlier investigations I have tried to argue that holistic concepts such as productive activity and *Praxis* have to be resolved into the basic concepts of communicative action and purposive rational action in order to avoid confusing the two rationalization processes that determine social evolution; the rationalization of action takes effect not only on productive forces but also, and independently, on normative structures (CES, 117).

Thus, the developmental logic thesis states that there is a reconstructable pattern of development (that is, developmental logic) of normative structures, the logic of which is independent of the logic of the rationalization of the productive forces. Habermas takes a developmental approach to theorizing social evolution because he sees several significant weaknesses to functionalist explanations of social change. Before we can examine whether or not the developmental logic thesis is an adequate solution to the functionalist problems, we must first clarify and analyze the arguments supporting the developmental logic thesis.

The Homological Arguments

Habermas introduces and develops the developmental logic thesis in *Zur Rekonstruktion des Historischen Materialismus* (1976). Of course, he did not originate the idea that the course of human history reproduces the course of individual human maturation, but he does sketch it here with enough care to make it more plausible than previous formulations. Habermas's notion of a developmental logic of normative structures presupposes a key proposition: "[t]he structures of linguistically established intersubjectivity—which can be examined prototypically in connection with elementary speech actions—are conditions of both social and personality systems" (CES, 98). The communicative structures themselves constitute the forms of both society and personality. The basic idea guiding Habermas's thought here is that individual egos become differentiated and individuated through processes of socialization and social interaction. One is not first an individual, subsequently becoming socialized (for example, as conceived by social contract theorists such as Hobbes and Locke); nor is one solely an effect of the social. We become individualized and socialized simultaneously in the same social processes. Thus, Habermas recognizes that the same structures will condition both systems: "If one examines social institutions and the action competencies of socialized individuals for general characteristics, one encounters the same structures of consciousness" (CES, 98–99).

When thinking about social change and in particular how social structures change, it is not surprising, then, that Habermas has looked to psychological theories of cognitive development. For various theoretical reasons Habermas is especially interested in the ways that social consensus and action coordination are maintained and reestablished after a disturbance.[88] For this reason he pays particular attention to the domain of law and morality as mechanisms that serve to reestablish a social consensus by means other than the use of force. In this domain he claims that the same structures of development, or developmental logic, occur in both the individual moral consciousness and societal moral and legal institutions: "Cognitive developmental psychology has shown that in ontogenesis there are different stages of moral consciousness, stages that can be described in particular as preconventional, [conventional,] and postconventional patterns of problemsolving. The same patterns turn up again in the social evolution of moral and legal representations" (CES, 99, translation altered). Habermas maintains that we should not be surprised that we discover these homologous structures, since both personality and social systems are constituted by linguistic structures "if we consider that linguistically established intersubjectivity of understanding marks that innovation in the history of the species which first made possible the level of socio-cultural learning. At this level the reproduction of society and the socialization of its members are two aspects of the same process; they are dependent on the same structures" (CES, 99).

Here it is important to note that Habermas distinguishes between natural and social evolution. The processes of natural evolution were primarily responsible for the development of the human species prior to the development of language. Once these natural processes led to the acquisition and expansion of capacities of symbolically mediated interaction and role-taking capacities, the processes of sociocultural evolution became dominant in the further development of the species.[89] At this sociocultural stage of the reproduction of societies the species develops not as a macrosubject, but only in and through structures of symbolically mediated communicative actions. Thus, at the sociocultural stage of development, it is not correct to speak of the evolution of the species, but only of the evolution of societies. For purposes of the theory of social evolution, then, it is the evolutionary process of this sociocultural stage of development that we are interested in, and it is at this stage of the development of the species that the individuation and the socialization of the individual ego become interconnected.

Habermas identifies three sets of homologous structures of consciousness: (1) between moral consciousness and law and morality; (2) between ego development and worldviews; and (3) between ego and group identities (CES, 99). It should be noted that Habermas does not make any explicit claims as to the completeness of this list. This is indicative of a deeper ambiguity involving the status of the homological arguments in the theory in general. On the one hand, his presentation seems to leave the door open for additional, yet to be discovered homologies. If Habermas's proposed homologies are only examples, and not exhaustive, then his homological arguments (that there are parallel developmental patterns in ontogenesis and the development in history of the normative structures of society) must be seen as merely supporting evidence for the developmental logic thesis. On the other hand, the three homologies that he proposes seem to anticipate his later analysis of Weber's three rationality complexes. On this interpretation, one could understand the developmental homology between the (cognitive) ego and worldviews as paradigmatic of the cognitive-technical rationality complex he later analyzes following Weber. Similarly, the developmental homology between moral consciousness and formal legal and moral representations would be paradigmatic of what he later analyzes as the moral-practical rationality complex; and the developmental homology between ego and group identities would be paradigmatic of the aesthetic-practical rationality complex. Indeed, in *Communication and the Evolution of Society* he speaks of the "rationality structures that find expression in worldviews, moral representations, and identity formations . . ." (CES, 98), thus suggesting that he considers these three homologies to be the keys to accessing the deeper rationality structures. If this reading is correct, the homological arguments would be more than supporting evidence; they would be of singular importance in understanding the structure of rationality in each of the three dimensions. The fact that Habermas proposes exactly three homological arguments, then, seems not to be entirely accidental, and for this reason I propose that we interpret Habermas as maintaining that these three homologies are exhaustive.

Although the homologies Habermas identifies exhibit a prima facie plausibility, there are significant nonhomologous relations that would appear to weaken if not refute the homology hypotheses. Habermas is fully aware of this, and he carefully qualifies the homological arguments in order to avoid the many pitfalls that await an oversimplified analysis of the similarities between ego development and social evolution: "If we go on now to seek homologies between ego development and the evolution of world-views, *we must take care not to draw hasty parallels*" (CES, 102, emphasis added). Thus, Habermas enumerates various provisos that must be incorporated into a proper understanding of the homological arguments. These provisos serve an important clarificatory function, and, as I will show below, are often overlooked in critiques of Habermas's theory. The general provisos that apply to each of the homological arguments will be discussed in this section, and the specific provisos applicable to individual arguments will be in the appropriate sections.

Proviso (1): "The confusion of structure and content can easily lead to errors—individual consciousness and cultural tradition can agree in their content without expressing the same structures of consciousness" (CES, 102). With the first proviso Habermas emphasizes that one must carefully distinguish between the surface content, the observable behavior, and the deep structure—the generative rules of the observed behavior. To be sure, drawing this distinction in an unambiguous manner is a difficult challenge for any reconstructive theory. The difficulty rests, in part, on the fact that the same surface phenomena can reflect different deep structures, or, to put it differently, the same content can be expressed by differing deep structures. For instance, the moral obligation not to kill innocent persons (content) could be justified by reference to either the Ten Commandments as in the Judeo-Christian tradition, or the universalizability of the maxim as in the Kantian tradition (structure). Each tradition generates the same moral maxim, to not kill innocent persons, but for different kinds of reasons. Habermas is not simply pointing out the obvious fact that each of these traditions has different reasons for its justifications, but that the kinds of reasons acceptable to each are different.

While the problem of unambiguously distinguishing surface phenomena from deep structures is a conceptual one, there is an analogous methodological problem in developmental psychology involving the distinction between the measurement of performance and competence.[90] The problem can be stated as follows: How does the researcher distinguish behavior that reflects a deep competence from that which instantiates mere performance? This is not a conceptual problem but rather a methodological one; that is, there is no conceptual difficulty in distinguishing competence from performance. Indeed, the concept of performance in this sense presupposes the concept of competence, and there is no logical necessity associated with the concept of performance such that actions will always express underlying competencies. To be sure, the same conceptual analysis does not apply straightforwardly to the deep structure/surface phenomena distinction. The existence of surface phenomena does not in the case of the deep structure/surface phenomena distinction presuppose the existence of deep structures. Nevertheless, one can still make sense of the distinction, despite any attached methodological difficulties of identifying particular instances of it.

In any case, the problem lies not at the conceptual level, but in the methodology which the investigator uses to identify the distinction in scientific inquiry. While this is an important question in the field of developmental psychology, it becomes significantly more problematic in the domain of social theory. The problem arises because sociohistorical research is constrained to a finite number of given sociohistorical formations, and thus cannot construct controlled experiments to test its hypotheses. The problem, then, is not whether we can conceive of the distinction between deep structures and surface phenomena, or competence and performance, for surely we can, but whether we indeed can validly make the distinction in the course of social scientific research. That is, can social scientists devise research procedures that can reliably make this distinction in practice? Now, it seems that since researchers in the discipline of developmental psychology utilize repeatable experiments, and statistical analysis of those experiments, they have access to a methodology that can reliably make the distinction. For whenever the distinction is placed in doubt, researchers can go back and repeat a given experiment, perhaps expanding the sample or revising the experiment in order to test for the distinction. Furthermore, statistical analysis should be able to differentiate the competence/performance distinction in individual experiments from results that disconfirm the hypothesis being tested for. That is, when a given result is a significant deviation, statistical analysis should be able to determine whether that deviation is due to mere performance of the subject or to a hypothesis-refuting competence.

When applying the idea of developmental logic to sociohistorical research in the form of rational reconstruction of the development of normative structures, however, the competence/performance problem becomes reinvigorated. For sociohistorical research in this sense is reconstructive, and thus not purely empirical-analytic. Experiments are not performed, and thus are not repeatable; the data derives from the results of sociohistorical inquiry. The data one has to work with is finite, and statistical analysis becomes much less useful, if not useless. In this case, it becomes much more difficult to identify in practice the competencies of the members of a given historical society based solely on whatever records they may have left. Nevertheless, as was shown above, the distinction between deep structures and surface phenomena is sound, so it can, at least conceptually, serve as grounds for a developmental logic thesis. There is no good reason to think that this distinction is not valid. The so-called burden of proof rests, then, on the empirical side, in comparing the thesis with the data. Habermas has made at least a prima facie case for the explanatory strength of this thesis, and so it rests with the skeptics to provide concrete evidence of the falsity of the thesis. In any case, further empirical research needs to be done before Habermas's hypotheses can be considered implausible based on the objection that one cannot identify universal competencies in sociohistorical investigations. Any research intended to confirm or disconfirm his hypotheses requires, however, further conceptual clarification of the theory, which is the guiding intention of this study.

Proviso (2): "Not all individuals are equally representative of the developmental stage of their society" (CES, 102). The claim expressed here is that there is de facto no direct relationship between the stage of development of each member of a society and that society's institutionalized evolutionary level. In any given society, there can be found individuals whose level of development either exceeds or falls short of the general societal level of development. Habermas states that in modern societies, which institutionalize universalistic structures of law, there are individuals who are not capable of making principled moral judgments, that is, they have not attained the level of development necessary to do so (CES, 102). And in archaic societies, he suggests, there can be found individuals who have achieved the level of formal-operational cognitive development, whereas their society institutionalizes a lower level of cognitive development, for example, in a mythological worldview (CES, 102).

In this proviso Habermas is expressing two claims: a logical one and an empirical one. With this proviso he asserts that there is no logical reason why the level of development of each individual of a society necessarily corresponds to the societal level of development. The logical component of the proviso states that in any given society there exists at least the possibility that some individual member of that society will either attain a level of development that exceeds that of the society or fall short of it. The logical component of this proviso has the theoretical function of limiting the scope of the homology hypotheses, and in this way plays a critical role in determining the meaning of the hypotheses. For this proviso (in its logical form) makes it clear that Habermas is not suggesting that the structures of consciousness of the individuals and those institutionalized in societies are identical. There can be, and there are, discrepancies between individual and social structures of consciousness.

The empirical component of the proviso, on the other hand, heightens the probability of the proviso from mere possibility to likelihood. That is, the empirical component asserts that it is indeed likely that in any given society some individuals will diverge from the predominate structures of consciousness. There is little disagreement that in historical societies there are at least some individuals whose level of cognitive or moral development either exceeds or falls below that embodied in the society's institutions. The theoretical function of the empirical component is to raise the force of the claim from logical possibility to likelihood. Both components play an important role in the proviso: the logical component asserts that there is a logical possibility of nonrepresentative individuals in any given society, and the empirical component asserts that there is indeed a likelihood that such nonrepresentative individuals will be found in any given society.

Proviso (3): "The ontogenetic pattern of development cannot mirror the structure of species history for the obvious reason that collective structures of consciousness hold only for adult members—ontogenetically early stages of incomplete interaction have no correspondents, even in the oldest societies, for (with the family organization) social relations have had from the beginning the form of complementarily connected, generalized expectations of behavior (i.e. the form of complete interaction)" (CES, 102).

This is a difficult passage to interpret, in part, because of the confusing vocabulary Habermas utilizes. In particular, in the first clause he uses the term "species history" *(Gattungsgeschichte)*, but in the second half of the sentence he makes reference to "societies" *(Gesellschaften)* and "social relations" *(gesellschaftliche Beziehungen)*. The problem rests with the meaning intended by Habermas of the term *Gattungsgeschichte.* Does he mean to refer with this term to the history of human societies, from primitive clans to developed civilizations? Or, does he mean to refer to the history of the human species, including prehistorical hominids who lacked the developed interactive capacities afforded by language? In support of the second meaning, one could perhaps cite Habermas's reconstruction of Mead's arguments concerning the logical genesis of normatively regulated and linguistically mediated interaction, as well as of generalized role-taking capacities in language (TCA II, 3–43). There Habermas is interested in understanding the origins of the structures of intersubjectivity that are constituted by language use. Is this part of what he means by *Gattungsgeschichte*?

I do not think so. Another way to understand these two interpretations is that with this proviso Habermas is claiming that his homology hypothesis is comparing the pattern of development of the individual ego only with that of sociocultural evolution, and not with that of the natural history of Homo sapiens. The key distinction here is between the evolution of societies, which includes both processes of material development and sociocultural evolution, and the anthropogenesis of the species. Habermas is not concerned primarily with the developmental logic of the natural history of the species, despite his reconstruction of the Meadian theory of communication, but only with the developmental logic of the evolution of human societies. Thus, on this reading, there are no asserted homologies between ontogenesis and anthropogenesis, since the maturation of the individual ego is, inter alia, a process involving the development of interactive competence, and the evolution of societies occurs only when sociocultural evolutionary processes become differentiated from processes of natural evolution, that is, only when interactive competence has been achieved by the members of the society. The interactive competence Habermas refers to here is not a minimal competence, but one of "complete interaction," which means forms of interaction that are based on generalized expectations of behavior. This level of complete interaction is precisely that level at which the sociocultural level of species evolution becomes differentiated from natural evolution (CES, 131–138). Thus, I understand Habermas's use of *Gattungsgeschichte* to refer only to sociocultural evolution.

This interpretation would seem to be further supported by Habermas's terminology. He uses here the term *Gattungsgeschichte*, rather than *soziale Evolution,* when discussing the proposed homologies. This might suggest that he intends to include more than just sociocultural evolution in the homology hypothesis. But this evidence is spurious at best, since Habermas uses the term *Gattungsgeschichte* in other passages when he clearly intends its scope to cover only sociocultural evolution. For example, in the very next proviso, he emphasizes the differing modes of embodiment of the same structures of consciousness in *Individual- und Gattungsgeschichte* (RHM, 16). Thus, Habermas's usage of the term *Gattungsgeschichte* lends support to the interpretation that its scope covers only sociocultural evolution.

It might be objected that the interpretation of *Gattungseschichte* as sociocultural evolution (that is, that the homologous structures are between individual development and sociocultural evolution) is less plausible than the claim that such structures can be found between individual development and the history of the species (including both anthropogenesis and sociocultural evolution). The pattern of cognitive development can be seen to occur in two distinct periods: the first, the sensorimotor period, involves actions that do not involve language or conceptual representation, and the second involves actions which are then combined with linguistically-mediated conceptual representations.[91] If cognitive development is conceived in this way, as involving a prelinguistic and a linguistic stage of development, then we can see an homologous structure in the history of the species in the distinction between the stages of natural and sociocultural evolution. The initial stage of natural evolution proceeds on the basis of natural determinants, and the successive stage of sociocultural evolution is linguistically mediated.

So what does Habermas mean by this proviso? Perhaps he means simply that the pattern of development of the individual ego does not mirror, in a strict way, the pattern of social evolution. While there are homologies in the developmental logics of the structures of consciousness of each, we should not expect that they are mirror images of each other. In other words, we might understand Habermas to be claiming that while there are homologies between these phenomena, there are also disanalogies in content to be found. But I think Habermas means more than this. Careful attention to the proviso makes it clear that Habermas emphasizes the importance of intersubjective communication to his claims. This suggests that Habermas is concerned in this proviso to restrict the proposed homological arguments to structures of intersubjective communication. If this is the case, then we can understand the proviso to be claiming that the pattern of ego development does not necessarily reflect the pattern of sociocultural evolution, which presupposes fully developed structures of symbolically mediated intersubjective communication.

Proviso (4): "[T]he points of reference from which the same structures of consciousness are embodied are different in the history of the individual and in that of the species. The maintenance of the personality system poses quite different imperatives than the maintenance of the social system" (CES, 102). Ostensibly, here Habermas is simply pointing to the fact that the structures of consciousness, which are asserted to be homologous in the individual and in society, serve different functions in each. In both cases the structure of consciousness functions as a fundamental coordinating mechanism; that is, it maintains the integrity of the system—whether it is a system of the personality or of a society. As Habermas states, however, the imperatives of the maintenance of the personality are significantly different from those of the social system. While the maintenance of both the personality and the social system is guided by the imperative of identity maintenance, the social system faces the special task of defining its own identity in terms of its structures and boundaries. In other words, the personality system is embodied in a physical body, which is bound in time by birth and death. But the social system is embodied only in a set of institutions whose functional coherence defines the identity of the system. In the social system there is no unambiguous equivalent of bodily birth or death. Moreover, the conditions of the maintenance of the personality and the social system differ. Maintenance of a personality requires certain sociocultural institutions and practices, such as the family (for socialization) and an educational system (to develop the necessary functional competencies). So, with this proviso, Habermas seems to be reminding us that while personality and social systems may share homologous structures of consciousness, these structures do not necessarily function in the same way in each of these systems, and furthermore, that each requires different conditions for its maintenance.[92]

The significance of these general provisos is in their emphasis on the claim that the hypotheses Habermas is proposing involve homological structures and not an analogy between individual cognitive development and social evolution. Habermas wants to be clear that he is asserting that there are only structurally (or formally) similar patterns between ontogenetic development and social evolution. He is not asserting that analogies can be identified in their respective contents, and, of course, this is not ruled out. His thesis is restricted only to the claim that the relevant similarities between cognitive development and social evolution are structural, and are carried specifically in their structures of consciousness. In addition to these four general provisos, which are applicable to all proposed homologies, Habermas identifies provisos that are valid only for specific homological arguments. These specific provisos will be discussed below in the context of each relevant argument.

The first homology Habermas proposes is that between the development of the individual ego and the development of worldviews (CES, 99–106). Habermas uses the term "ego" to represent the capabilities or capacities that constitute the individual. These three capabilities are cognition, speech and action. Thus, Habermas uses "ego development" *(Ichentwicklung)* to refer to the development of the individual into a competently acting and speaking subject under these three aspects. Habermas understands the process of ego development as one in which the subjectivity of the individual ego is constituted in and through its construction of an objective world: "From Hegel through Freud to Piaget, the idea has developed that subject and object are reciprocally constituted, that the subject can grasp hold of itself only in relation to and by way of the construction of an objective world" (CES, 100). Habermas here assumes the distinction between the ego in general (the "me") and the individual ego (the "I"). The ego in general refers to the ego's capacity for cognition, speech and action, whereas the individual ego refers to those properties that distinguish a particular ego from all others.

The development of the ego can be understood generally as a process of demarcation of a subject from its environment. As the ego develops, it gradually distinguishes itself in a constructive process from its environment, thereby constituting its own subjectivity. The environment from which the ego distinguishes itself is not homogeneous, however. The external environment consists of both external nature and society. External nature is composed of perceptible objects, and society is composed of socially constituted meanings and other egos. Habermas proposes that, based on the empirical evidence, ego development occurs in four stages, and that we can recognize similar stages in the development of worldviews.[93] The four stages of ego development are the *symbiotic*, the *egocentric*, the *sociocentric-objectivistic*, and the *universalistic*. In the symbiotic stage of development the ego is not capable of distinguishing itself from its environment: "During the first year of life we can find no clear indicators for a subjective separation between subject and object. Apparently in this phase the child cannot perceive its own corporeal substance as a body, as a boundary-maintaining system. The symbiosis between child, reference person, and physical environment is so intimate that we cannot meaningfully speak of a demarcation of subjectivity in the strict sense" (CES, 100–101).

The initial subjective distinction between ego and environment occurs in the second, the egocentric, stage of development. While the ego distinguishes between itself and the permanent objects of its environment, it cannot yet differentiate between the natural and the social domains of the external environment; it only distinguishes between itself and the external environment in general. Nor can the ego at this stage reflect upon itself in an objective manner, thus seeing itself also as an object: "The child cannot perceive, understand, and judge situations independently of its own standpoint—it thinks and acts from a body-bound perspective" (CES, 101).

In the third stage of development, the sociocentric, the ego achieves the capacity to differentiate between the natural and the social domains of the external environment. This, according to Habermas, is a decisive step in the developmental process, for the ego "now differentiates between perceptible and manipulable things and events, on the one hand, and understandable action-subjects and their utterances, on the other; and it no longer confuses linguistic signs with the reference and meaning of symbols" (CES, 101). Furthermore, the ego becomes aware of its own subjectivity; that is, it recognizes that its own viewpoint is perspectival. Thus, the ego now distinguishes between itself as one subject among many from both the natural environment and the social environment. This stage is referred to as "sociocentric" because this stage allows for the development of complementary, generalized expectations of behavior; that is, only at this stage do social norms become recognized and gain currency with the individual.

In the final stage of development, the universalistic stage, the ego achieves the ability to reflect upon its beliefs and norms: "With the ability to think hypothetically and to conduct discourses, the system of ego-demarcations becomes reflective" (CES, 101).[94] Thus, the dogmatism of pregiven beliefs and norms is shattered, and validity claims concerning both objects in the natural environment and norms in the social environment become open to reflection.

Habermas claims that there are "certain homologies" between these stages of cognitive development and the evolution of worldviews. Homologies can be found in the developmental sequences of both basic concepts and logical structures. Concerning basic concepts Habermas mentions as examples the differentiation of temporal horizons, the articulation of the concept of causality, and the differentiation of the concept of substance (CES, 103). The homology hypothesis as applied to these basic concepts is simply that the development of each of these concepts, traced as an increase in differentiation or articulation, as the case may be, follows similar structural patterns—logics of development—in both ego development and the evolution of worldviews. Homologous structures of development can also be found, according to Habermas, in logical structures, for example in structures of explanation and justification: the ontogenetic stage of egocentrism is homologous to mythological narrative explanations; the stage of sociocentrism is homologous to the deductive explanations from first principles found in cosmologies, philosophies, and higher religions; and the stage of universalism is homologous to the reflective explanatory practices of modern science with its nomological explanations and practical justifications (CES, 104). Habermas states, however, that he is less interested in these homologies than in the homologies between the evolution of worldviews and the development of ego demarcations (CES, 104). By "ego demarcations" Habermas is referring to the structural differentiations between the individual ego, the natural environment and the social environment. Thus, Habermas's homology hypothesis regarding the system of ego demarcations is that just as the individual ego progressively distinguishes itself from its environments, the social structure progressively distinguishes itself from its environments (see CES, 104–105). Just as at the symbiotic stage the ego does not distinguish itself in any way from its environment, paleolithic societies did not possess worldviews that distinguished themselves from their environments. The magical-animistic worldviews of these paleolithic societies were not coherent, and were highly particularistic. With the development of mythological worldviews, archaic societies were capable of distinguishing themselves from their environment. They did not yet, however, distinguish between the natural and social environments. The formal properties of this stage of the evolution of worldviews is homologous to the stage of egocentric development of the individual ego. With the modern development of the nation-state as the central organizing feature of societies, developed civilizations became capable of distinguishing the normative from the natural spheres. This is homologous to the sociocentric stage of ego development, in which the individual ego is first capable of distinguishing the social and natural environments. Finally, the appearance of secular world interpretations on the basis of modern empirical science, institutionalized capitalist economic systems, and democratically legitimated political systems is homologous to the universalistic stage of ego development. At this stage of development of the ego and the evolution of worldviews, the ego or the society understands its own relationship to its environments in a universalistic and reflective manner. In this way the totalizing character of worldviews is dissolved and theoretical and practical reason become differentiated.

In addition to the four general provisos discussed above, Habermas adds a proviso specifically applicable to ego development and the evolution of worldviews: "The unifying power of worldviews is directed not only against cognitive dissonance but also against social disintegration. The concordant structuration of the stock of knowledge stored and harmonized in interpretive systems is related, therefore, not only to the unity of the epistemic ego, but also to that of the practical ego." (CES, 102–103). The consequence of this observation is that the various structures underlying worldviews perform different functions, and thus we need to exercise care in attempting to locate homologous structures between ego development and the evolution of worldviews. In particular, we need to identify specific reference points for our comparisons, and, hence, we cannot make a "global comparison between ego development and the development of worldviews" (CES, 103).

As this specific proviso makes clear, Habermas does not view the structures of worldviews, legal representations, and group identities on the same theoretical plane. Rather, worldviews are the general, overarching "interpretive systems" that structure the interaction of human and environment (both natural and social). And within worldviews we can distinguish between, on the one hand, structures that serve primarily epistemic purposes, that is, functioning to prevent cognitive dissonance, and, on the other hand, structures that serve primarily practical purposes, that is, functioning to prevent social disintegration. Furthermore, Habermas notes, within the practical structures we can distinguish those oriented towards harmonizing intersubjective relations—legal and moral representations—and those oriented towards unifying and stabilizing the individual identity—ego and group identities (CES, 103).

The distinctions Habermas draws here provide the groundwork, albeit in unclarified form, for his later distinctions between cognitive-technical, moral-practical, and aesthetic-practical forms of rationality (see esp. TCA I, 216–242). The point he is making with these distinctions is critical to a proper understanding of his homology hypothesis. The homology hypothesis asserts only that certain homologies can be found between ego development and social evolution, and that these homologies are valid only with respect to particular reference points. So, while we cannot validly claim that the pattern of development of interpretive structures is generally homologous to the structure of ego development, we can identify a homology between worldview development and cognitive development with respect to an increasing decentration: "In both dimensions [of ego development and the evolution of worldviews], development apparently leads to a growing decentration of interpretive systems and to an ever-clearer categorical demarcation of the subjectivity of internal nature from the objectivity of external nature, as well as from the normativity of social reality and the intersubjectivity of linguistic reality" (CES, 106). The idea of decentration is derived from cognitive developmental psychology. There it refers to a certain property of ontogenesis in which the individual ego develops through successive stages an increasingly impartial and reflexive perspective. In the process of gradually distinguishing, at first, between itself (the subject) and the external world, and later, between itself, the objective (that is, natural) world, and the social world, the child's epistemic perspective moves from one that is highly subjective, being centered in the ego, to one that is decentered in adopting the third-person epistemic perspective. This move from an egoistic perspective to an (ideally) impartial perspective is what is referred to as "decentering." From an epistemic point of view, both worldviews and cognitive structures develop in such a way that the perspective from which valid knowledge is judged becomes increasingly decentered. This, then, is the central claim of the homology hypothesis regarding ego development and the development of worldviews.

But why does Habermas focus on decentration as the key homology between cognitive development and the development of worldviews? Recall that he presents these hypotheses in the context of a reconstruction of historical materialism understood as a theory of social evolution. And while it is not always apparent in the essays in *Zur Rekonstruktion des Historischen Materialismus*, Habermas is developing this theory of social evolution within the context of the idea of communicative action. By the time of the writing of those essays, Habermas had laid the key cornerstones of his theory of communicative action. Indeed, he turns to social evolutionary considerations in order to secure the normative grounds of the universalistic claims of his formal pragmatics. This explains, then, Habermas's emphasis on decentration as a key homologous developmental structure of both individual egos and societies.

One of the central themes of Habermas's work is the integration of social action, and the consensual reintegration of social action in cases of action conflicts—all of which rests on an explanation of the social order. Thus, his argument concerning the homologous structures in individual moral consciousness and legal systems is central to the justification of the developmental logic thesis. And although his comments with respect to this homological relation are more fully developed than those regarding both the ego development/evolution of worldview and the ego/group identity homologies, his remarks are also more scattered. My reconstruction of this homological argument will rely primarily upon three essays: "Moral Development and Ego Identity" (CES, 69–94); "Toward a Reconstruction of Historical Materialism" (CES, 130–177); and "Moral Consciousness and Communicative Action" (MCCA, 116–194).[95]

Habermas refers to the work of Lawrence Kohlberg in describing the stages of development of moral consciousness.[96] According to Kohlberg, there are three primary levels of the development of moral consciousness, which are further subdivided into six (total) stages of moral judgment. The three levels of moral consciousness are the *preconventional, conventional,* and *postconventional* levels.

At the preconventional level, moral agents do not yet distinguish between actions, agents, and motives; action conflicts are resolved at this level with reference to only the consequences of actions (CES, 156).[97] The cultural categories of good and bad and right and wrong are interpreted in hedonistic terms such as punishment, reward, and so forth, or in terms of the physical superiority of adults (CES, 79). Within the preconventional level of moral consciousness there are two identifiable stages of moral judgment. In the first stage, which Kohlberg refers to as the stage of punishment and obedience, right actions consist only in obeying the rules and authorities that minimize punishment and maximize reward: "The physical consequences of action determine its goodness or badness regardless of the human meaning or value of these consequences. Avoidance of punishment and unquestioning deference to power are valued in their own right, not in terms of respect for an underlying moral order supported by punishment and authority (the latter being stage 4)" (CES, 79).

In the second stage, the stage of "individual instrumental purpose and exchange" (MCCA, 123), right action is determined by one's own immediate interests, and the following of rules which satisfy those interests; right is also doing what is fair, as determined by the principle of equal exchange: "Right action consists of that which instrumentally satisfies one's own needs and occasionally the needs of others. Human relations are viewed in terms like those of the market place. Elements of fairness, reciprocity, and of equal sharing are present, but they are always interpreted in a physical pragmatic way. Reciprocity is a matter of 'you scratch my back and I'll scratch yours,' not of loyalty, gratitude, or justice" (CES, 79, quoting from Kohlberg 1971).

At the conventional level of the development of moral consciousness, motives are distinguished from action consequences, and right action is determined by conformity to social roles or norms (CES, 156). Again there are two substages that constitute this level. The first (Stage 3) is the stage of "mutual interpersonal expectations, relationships and conformity" (MCCA, 123). At this stage right action consists in following the socially given rules and norms in order to maintain good interpersonal relations for their own sake: "Good behavior is that which pleases or helps others and is approved by them. There is much conformity to stereotypical images of what is majority or 'natural' behavior. Behavior is frequently judged by intention—'he means well' becomes important for the first time. One earns approval by being 'nice'" (CES, 79-80).

In the second substage (Stage 4) of this level, the stage of "social system and conscience maintenance" (MCCA, 124), right action is determined primarily by the maintenance of the social order, which is achieved by the following of socially given rules and norms.

The third and highest level of the development of moral consciousness is the postconventional level. Systems of norms and social roles lose their quasi-natural validity, resulting in the independent (that is, from a universal and impartial perspective) justification of moral actions (CES, 156). The key feature of this level of moral consciousness is the development of a universalistic orientation. Moral norms now require justification that can meet the logical demands of universal validity. The substages of this level are differentiated as follows. Right action in the first substage (Stage 5), the stage of "prior rights and social contract or utility" (MCCA, 124), consists in the maintenance of basic individual rights and the social contracts:

> Right action tends to be defined in terms of general individual rights, and standards which have been critically examined and agreed upon by the whole society. There is a clear awareness of the relativism of personal values and opinions and a corresponding emphasis upon procedural rules for reaching consensus. Aside from what is constitutionally and democratically agreed upon, the right is a matter of personal "values" and "opinion." The result is an emphasis upon the "legal point of view," but with an emphasis upon the possibility of changing law in terms of rational considerations of social utility (rather than freezing it in terms of stage 4 "law and order"). Outside the legal realm, free agreement and contract is the binding element of obligation. (CES, 80)

And the final stage (Stage 6) is the stage of "universal ethical principles" (MCCA, 124). At this stage, what is morally right behavior is determined by certain principles that are reflectively justified and universally valid: "Right is defined by the decision of conscience in accord with self-chosen *ethical principles* appealing to logical comprehensiveness, universality, and consistency. These principles are abstract and ethical (the Golden Rule, the categorical imperative); they are not concrete moral rules like the Ten Commandments. At heart, these are universal principles of *justice,* of the *reciprocity* and *equality* of human *rights,* and of respect for the dignity of human beings as *individual persons*" (CES, 80)

Given Kohlberg's schema of the developmental stages of moral consciousness, Habermas claims that the developmental pattern of legal institutions is homologous to that of moral consciousness, that is, the developmental structures of these two domains have interesting similarities. This claim plays a role in the homological argument for the developmental logic thesis (that there is an autonomous developmental logic of normative structures); this argument is as follows. Given the apparent developmental logic of structures of moral consciousness in the individual, and given the homologous relation between these structures and the structures of the evolution of legal institutions, we can conclude that there is a developmental logic of normative structures (legal systems being an instantiation of such normative structures).

This argument rests, of course, on the claim that there are homologous structures between the development of moral consciousness and the evolution of legal institutions. What, then, are the homologous structures of the evolution of legal systems? Habermas's sketch runs as follows (see CES, 157–158, and TCA I, 254–271). In neolithic societies the legal regulation of action conflicts proceeds from the preconventional point of view, where the reestablishment of the status quo is a key factor and legal obligations are not recognized in their own right (TCAI, 258). Actions and norms are not yet differentiated, and actions are assessed strictly according to their consequences, and consequences are assessed with respect to custom or self-interest. The structurally significant properties, then, of neolithic or primitive societies can be said to be homologous to the structural properties of the preconventional level of moral consciousness.

In early civilizations (or, alternatively, "archaic societies") organized around mythological worldviews which in turn legitimate the authority of the rulers, action conflicts are institutionally regulated at the conventional level with respect to the authority of the rulers (CES, 157). Just as at the conventional level of moral consciousness, right action is determined by the given set of social roles and norms, which are in turn grounded in the authority of the ruler. The legal norms that are determined by the given social norms remain particularistic at this level, because they are not based on universalistic principles, but on the mythologically founded authority of the ruler. There appear to be homologous structures between the legal institutions of early civilizations and the conventional level of moral consciousness.

Developed civilizations arise in conjunction with the development from mythological worldviews to metaphysical-religious worldviews. This transition can be characterized as a decentering one, since in the transition the legal institutions become detached from the authority of the ruler, and are grounded only in a general tradition, for example, in natural law (CES, 157). This natural law tradition presupposes a greater degree of rationality and universality in the justification of legal norms; nevertheless, this justification is not yet reflexive. That is, the justificatory procedures are not themselves explicitly justified at this level. The achievement of natural law is their basis in universalistic legal principles, "which supposes that such principles can be rationally derived. With this, however, law is given not only a principled basis, but at the same time a metajurisitc basis. Existing law must now be legitimized through such principles; and it can and must be changed when it contradicts them. With this, the idea of enacting law was given a decisive impulse. To be sure, law still held fast to the idea of the giveness of legal principles. Only when this idea was shattered, when the principles themselves became reflective, could law become positive in the strict sense. This was achieved in the modern legal process" (TCA I, 259, quoting Schluchter 1979, 146).

Despite the structural differences between developed and early civilizations (especially the rationalization of law), Habermas concludes that the legal structures of developed civilizations are homologous to the conventional level of structure of moral consciousness. The differences can be understood as reflecting the distinction at the conventional level of moral consciousness between Stages 3 and 4.

Finally, with the appearance of modern, secularized world interpretations, the law becomes reflexive, and thus postconventional. The social roles and norms that previously had served to ground natural law lose their quasi-natural validity, and consequently, legal norms must now be justified on a truly universalistic basis. Modern legal systems are positive, "expressing the will of the sovereign law-giver," legalistic, meaning that law and morality are strictly separated, and formal, in that they define the "domains in which individuals may legitimately exercise free choice" (TCA I, 259). Just as the postconventional level of moral consciousness defines right actions in terms of individual rights and social contracts, positive law is also based on these fundamental ideas. And, most importantly, the principles of the justification of legal norms become reflexive: "[In modern legal systems] [a]lmost all law can be considered as enacted and thus as open to revision. And its 'anchoring' is therefore shifted from metajuristic to juristic principles. These now have a merely hypothetical status, which is an expression of the fact that law has become autonomous while at the same time retaining its relation to extralegal contexts" (TCA I, 259, quoting Schluchter 1979, 146). Here again there appear to be homologous structures between modern legal institutions and postconventional moral consciousness.

Thus, Habermas asserts that there are good reasons to believe that "[t]he rationalization of law reflects the same series of stages of preconventional, conventional, and postconventional basic concepts that developmental psychology has shown to obtain in ontogenesis" (TCA I, 258). Although Habermas does not mention specific provisos for this claim, the same general provisos discussed above continue to apply here.

A third homology Habermas identifies is that between the development of ego and group identities. This homology presupposes the distinction between the epistemic ego (the "me") and the practical ego (the "I") to which Habermas draws attention:

> The epistemic ego (as the ego in general) is characterized by those general structures of cognitive, linguistic, and active ability that every individual ego has in common with all other egos; the practical ego, however, forms and maintains itself as individual in performing its actions. It secures the identity of the person within the epistemic structures of the ego in general. It maintains the continuity of life history and the symbolic boundaries of the personality system through repeatedly actualized self-identifications; and it does so in such a way that it can locate itself clearly—that is, unmistakably and recognizedly—in the intersubjective relations of its social life world. Indeed the identity of the person is in a certain way the result of identifying achievements of the person himself. (CES, 106)

Habermas emphasizes that the identifying achievements of the individual ego (the "I") are accomplished through practical actions, in particular, communicative actions. And since the participants in communicative actions must presuppose partners in communication, a reciprocal structure of recognition is constituted; that is, the performance of a communicative action presupposes that there is a partner (alter) with whom one (ego) is communicating, and that alter also recognizes ego as a communicative partner. Thus, the practical act of self-identification is not one that is monological, but one that involves the recognition of others (see CES, 107).

Habermas notes, however, that there is an interesting asymmetry between the self-identifications of individual egos and those of groups. Whereas self-identification of an individual is necessarily accomplished through intersubjective recognition, the self-identification of a group does not require the recognition of other groups. This is because, Habermas argues, the personal pronoun "we" can be addressed either to individuals outside of the group or to other members of the same group. He illustrates this with the following sentences:

(1) "We took part in the demonstration (while you sat at home)."

(2) "We are all in the same boat" (CES, 108).

Sentence (1) is addressed to someone outside of the group of individuals that participated in the demonstration. Sentence (2) is addressed to other members of the group, and not to individuals outside of the group; sentence (2) has both self-referential meaning and self-identificational meaning (CES, 108). Habermas concludes from this observation of the asymmetry between the addressees of "I" and "we" that group identity is not dependent upon recognition: "The expression *I* can also be used for purposes of self-identification; but the self-identification of an *I* requires intersubjective recognition by other *I's*, who must in turn assume the role of *thou*. By contrast, the self-identification of a group is not dependent on intersubjective recognition by *another* group; an *I* that identifies itself as *we* can be confirmed through another *I* that identifies with the same *we*. The reciprocal recognition of group members requires I-thou-we relations" (CES, 108).

Habermas's argument rests fundamentally upon the distinction between self-referentiality and self-identification. But when the notion of self-referentiality is understood in terms of formal identity, in contrast to the substantive identity of self-identification, we can see that the distinction is only analytical. While this analytical distinction is valid, it is not at all clear that the distinction can be made in practice. Is it indeed possible to refer to oneself as a member of a group (formal identity) without also at the same time making reference to the unique characteristics of that group (substantive identity)? The objection might be made that if formal identity cannot be separated from substantive identity in practice, then Habermas's conclusion that group identity is not founded in reciprocal recognition does not follow. In other words, if in practice a necessary part of group identity is its substantive identity, then group identity is also necessarily constituted in part by relationships of reciprocal recognition between groups.[98] Another way to put this is to say that while a group can identify itself as a group, as an aggregate of individuals, without reference to other groups, it cannot specify its substantive identity without reference to at least one other group. For to specify the identity of a group (its "I") requires that this identity be contrasted with at least one other identity that the first group is not. The first group possesses its substantive identity by virtue of the fact that it is not each and every other group (in terms of identification).

If this objection is sound, then the consequences that Habermas asserts to follow from his argument are also undermined. Habermas defines "collective identity" as referring to "reference groups that are essential to the identity of their members, which are in a certain way 'ascribed' to individuals, cannot be freely chosen by them, and which have a continuity that extends beyond the life-historical perspectives of their members" (CES, 108). Habermas apparently has in mind such reference groups as "women," "Jews," "African-Americans," "Germans," "homosexuals," and so forth. Now, Habermas claims that for such collective identities, self-identification can be accomplished without the recognition of other groups. This opens up the possibility, though, that a group can identify itself as a totality, thereby relegating nonmembers to the class of objects with which communication is impossible: "[A] group can understand and define itself so exclusively as a totality that they live in the idea of embracing all possible participants in interaction, whereas everything that doesn't belong thereto becomes a neuter, about which one can make statements in the third person, but with which one cannot take up interpersonal relations in the strict sense—as was the case, for instance, with the barbarians on the borders of ancient civilizations" (CES, 108).

This does not seem to be an unreasonable conclusion. There are, of course, innumerable examples from history, for example colonialism, where one group viewed another group as unequal in status, perhaps even subhuman, and they thus entered into noncommunicative relations with this "outsider" group. Since the oppressors viewed the oppressed as unequals, they could not conceive of communication (in the sense of equal partners in dialogue) between the two groups.[99] Nevertheless, the truth of the conclusion says nothing about the validity of the argument. Perhaps these noncommunicative relationships between groups that Habermas refers to could be explained as instances of distorted communication, rather than noncommunication: "We tried to communicate with them, but they were unable to comprehend us." In any case, it is not entirely clear that group identity does not necessarily depend upon recognition in some form.

For Habermas, the essential property of ego identity is "the ability to sustain one's own identity," and this, as we will see, is the key to understanding collective identities as well (CES, 109). Accordingly, Habermas traces the development of ego identity through the various stages of ontogenesis from the perspective of the maintenance of identity. At the first stage of ontogenesis, what Habermas refers to as "natural identity," the maintenance of identity is conceived on the model of the boundary-maintaining organism. Here, the child's identity is maintained by its body, which physically separates it from its environment. At the second stage of ontogenesis the maintenance of identity develops into a process of self-identification through intersubjective recognition, and here Habermas relies on the work of G. H. Mead. At this stage the unity of the person is based on the identification with, and internalization of, social roles, that is, roles defined intersubjectively within the symbolic social order of the group. In this way individuals identify themselves with the group while at the same time distinguishing themselves from the group. "The unity of the person is formed through internalization of roles that are originally attached to concrete reference persons and later detached from them—primarily the generation and sex roles that determine the structure of the family" (CES, 109). The ability to maintain one's own identity is directly dependent upon the validity and stability of the behavioral expectations of the group; it thus can be characterized as conventional. The third stage of ontogenesis, which Habermas calls "ego identity," is marked from the point at which the individual breaks out of this conventional moral consciousness by beginning to abstract from particular role identities and to consider these identities in a hypothetical attitude.[100] By hypothetically reflecting upon its own identity, the individual ego is faced with the task of justifying its own identity, and this involves the ego constructively in identity maintenance:

> An ego expected to judge any given norm in the light of internalized principles, that is, to consider them hypothetically and to provide justifications, can no longer tie its identity to particular pregiven roles and sets of norms. Now continuity can be established only through the ego's own integrating accomplishment. . . . To the extent that the ego generalizes this ability to overcome an old identity and to construct a new one and learns to resolve identity crises by re-establishing at a higher level the disturbed balance between itself and a changed social reality, role identity is replaced by ego identity. The ego can then maintain his identity in relation to others, expressing in all relevant role games the paradoxical relationship of being like and yet being absolutely different from the other, and represent himself as the one who organizes his interactions in an unmistakable complex of life history. (CES, 110)[101]

Habermas argues that there are structures of collective identity that are homologous to this three-tiered conception of the ontogenesis of identity (natural, role, and ego identity). Although here he does so implicitly, Habermas approaches collective identity, as he does regarding ego identity, from the perspective of the maintenance of identity. Again, one should keep in mind that there are certain provisos, both general and specific, that condition these claims. These provisos will be discussed immediately following the explication of the proposed homologies.

Habermas discusses homologous structures in four general types of societies: neolithic, "states," great empires, and modern nation-states. The collective identity of neolithic societies was secured through the structure of kinship relationships (CES, 111–112). The kinship structure itself was anchored in the descent from ancestors that, by means of a mythological worldview, were not distinguishable from the origins of the cosmos. In other words, there was no distinction made between natural and social environments: the collective identity was secured in, and maintained by means of, the kinship structure's role in the mythological worldview. Personal identity was secured and maintained in the same way, through its place in the kinship structure, and thereby its place in the cosmos. Habermas notes that contact with alien civilizations that could not be assimilated into the mythological kinship structure presented challenges (although not the only ones) to the identity of these neolithic societies (CES, 112).

The challenge to the collective identities of these archaic tribal societies presented by increasing contacts with other unassimilable societies (as the result of population growth and territorial expansion) led to the development of more abstract collective identities. There is no necessity implied here with respect to the transition from archaic tribal identities to identities secured by the political structure of a state (or for that matter the transition from any one social form to another); the challenge faced by a given society should be conceived only as an external pressure that threatens the stable maintenance of that society's collective identity. This external challenge thus encourages attempts to reconceive the collective identity in order to resecure its stability. The form of collective identity that followed archaic societies, what I will call "political identity" to avoid confusion with the identity of the nation-state, secured the identity of the society by means of control over a given territory (CES, 112). The formal properties of this political identity are homologous to those of the role-identity stage in ontogenetic ego development; that is, the structure of this stage of collective identity (the political) is homologous to the structure of the stage of individual identity formation in which the individual's identity is shaped essentially by role identifications. Whereas the identity of the individual at this stage of ontogenesis is constituted by identifications with certain socially constituted roles, the collective identity in these political states is determined with reference to, and identification with, a ruler who has claimed a special association to the originary mythological powers.

Despite the greater abstraction of this form of collective identity, it remained unstable due to continuous external challenges presented by interactions with alien societies. Habermas asserts that alien societies were assimilated by the expansion of the world of the gods, "a solution that would prove to be rather unstable" (CES, 112). Since the limitations of the mythological worldviews were the determining factor, further developments in the form of collective identity necessitated a break with them. Habermas points to the "universalistic world interpretations of the great founders of religions and of the great philosophers [which] grounded a commonality of conviction mediated through a teaching tradition and permitting only abstract objects of identification" (CES, 112). This form of the collective identity of the great empires represents a further development of what I have called political identity, because in both membership is determined by identification with a ruler, who has a special relation to the transcendental order. In contrast to the earlier form of political identity, which was based in mythological worldviews, the collective identity of the great empires is grounded in the universalistic worldviews of the great religions and metaphysical philosophies, and mediated by the rulers.

The universality of these metaphysical-religious worldviews contributed significantly to the stabilization of the collective identities of the great empires. The initial cohesiveness of the Roman Empire's identity, for example, rested fundamentally upon the Christian worldview. The external challenge of other empires, based on different yet universal worldviews, was not, however, eliminated. The Roman Empire faced external challenges from not only barbarians, but also the Parthian Empire of southwest Asia, the Kushan Empire of northern India, and the Han Empire of eastern Asia.[102] But despite trade relations, the empires shielded themselves from these challenges. Habermas cites in support of this the fact that they maintained no formal diplomatic relations with each other. Habermas wants to emphasize here that "their political existence was not dependent on a system of reciprocal recognition" (CES, 113). That is, they did not recognize formally each other's right to exist as independent political units. This is in contrast, Habermas claims, to the collective identities of modern nation-states, which are based on such a system of reciprocal recognition. The maintenance of the collective identities of the great empires faced internal challenges as well. In contrast to societies based on mythological worldviews which could accommodate discrepancies of collective identity (by, for instance, expanding the number of gods, and thus explanatory hypotheses), the great empires faced the challenge of synchronizing the identities of various social domains: "[T]he integrating power of the identity of the empire had to confirm itself precisely in unifying the evolutionarily nonsynchronous structures of consciousness of the country, the aristocracy, city tradesmen, priests and officials, and in binding them to the same political order" (CES, 113). Thus the tension between the universalism of the form of collective identity and the particularism of the political form of domination gave rise to crises and certain evolutionary pressures.

With the transition to the modern nation-states and capitalist economies, the form of collective identity becomes even more general and abstract in the form of citizenship. This modern form of citizenship was constituted by the three aspects of a free and equal subject of civil law, a morally free subject, and a politically free citizen (CES, 114). But under this identity construction there was a tension between the universalism of the legal and moral subject, and the particularism of the citizen of a sovereign state. On the one hand, the collective identity was determined by the universal principles of equality before the law and moral autonomy, and on the other hand, this collective identity was determined by the citizen as a politically free subject. As Habermas notes, "[T]hese abstract determinations are best suited to the identity of world citizens, not to that of citizens of a particular state that has to maintain itself against other states" (CES, 114). The solution to this tension was the development of the nation-state in which the tension between the universalistic perspective of modern law and morality and the particularism of the citizen of a state can be suppressed. Habermas suggests, however, that the nation is a solution that is "no longer stable" (CES, 115).[103] He points in particular to the widespread emergence of "[c]onflicts that are ignited below the threshold of national identity . . . in connection with questions of race, creed, language, regional differences, and other subcultures" (CES, 115). Among the initial solutions that have been attempted, Habermas mentions the European working-class movement, and suggests that the solution to the instability of collective identities based on the nation will involve a reflective turn: "[Socialism] was the first example of an identity that had become reflective, of a collective identity no longer tied retrospectively to specific doctrines and forms of life but prospectively to programs and rules for bringing about something" (CES,

115).[104] The reflexive nature of socialism lies in its orientation to the future. As a project, it seeks to change current social conditions based on a conception of a better future. It is far from clear, Habermas admits, whether a reflective sort of collective identity of this type can be developed within modern societies. This is because of the high complexity of modern societies, and because of the greater significance of value pluralism in modern societies.

In addition to the general provisos discussed above, there are also three special provisos that apply to homologies between ego and group identity.

(1) "The collective identity of a group or a society secures continuity and recognizability. For this reason it varies with the temporal concepts *[Zeitbegriffen]* in terms of which the society can specify the requirements for remaining the same" (CES, 110–111). Whereas individual ego identities are objectively bounded by birth and death, societies are not. Societies have the capacity to define their own births and deaths in linguistically-mediated interaction; that is, they must subjectively determined their own identities in order to constitute a society.

(2) "[C]ollective identity determines how a society demarcates itself from its natural and social environments" (CES, 111). Here Habermas is pointing out how the boundaries between the subject and the environment, whether in the case of the ego or the group, are different in each case. Whereas the boundary of the ego's identity is determined by its exchanges with its environment, the boundary of the group's identity is determined primarily by the internal relations of its members: "[T]he symbolic boundaries of a society are formed primarily as the horizon of the actions that members reciprocally attribute to themselves internally" (CES, 111). This is not to say that in the case of group identities external influences have no effect on the group's identity, but only that the external influences are greatly outweighed by the internal determinations. Since this proviso follows from Habermas's earlier claim that the identity of a group does not depend upon the recognition of another group, its soundness rests upon the soundness of this earlier premise (see CES, 108).

(3) "[C]ollective identity regulates the membership of individuals in the society (and exclusion therefrom)" (CES, 111). In contrast, ego identity serves no such regulatory function. There is, however, a complementary relationship between the regulation by the collective identity of membership in the group and the formation of individual identities through interaction with other members of the group (CES, 111). Individual and group identities are complementary in the sense that on the one hand, the individual's identity is determined, in part, by interaction with other members of the group, and on the other hand, the group's identity is determined, in part, by who is included and who is excluded.

Keeping in mind both the general and particular provisos, the essence of Habermas's proposed homology between the development of ego and group identities lies in the process of generalization and abstraction shared by both. By using psychological theories of the development of ego identities as the key, we can describe the process of the change of collective identities as becoming more general and abstract, until the identity of the group becomes reflective. An identity is reflective to the extent that individuals (or groups) consciously choose their own identities (to the extent that they can). Identities (in both the individual and group) develop in the sense that they become more general, and at the same time more abstract. They become more general, meaning that the categories of identity formation progressively expand. The child thus goes from a natural identity of "me, here, now" to a role identity of "son of X and Y, brother to A, classmate of B," and so on, and finally to an ego identity of "morally autonomous person, legally equal property owner, citizen of country X." As the categories of identity formation become more general, they also become more abstract. They are more abstract because the identity is formed from increasingly decentered perspectives. Thus the development of identities is not a simple extension of a given empirical identity over a larger domain; rather, the identities become at the same time more abstract, and their extension to new members is justified and not in conflict with the previous form of identity. The end result of this developmental process is the identity becoming reflective; that is, the process of identity formation itself becomes conscious: "In both dimensions [of the ego and the group] identity projections apparently become more and more general and abstract, until finally the projection mechanism as such becomes conscious, and identity formation takes on a reflective form, in the knowledge that to a certain extent individuals and societies themselves establish their identities" (CES, 116). In the course of maturation an individual becomes conscious of the formation of her identity, steps out of the conventionally (and naturally) determined categories of identity, and is able to reflectively consider who she wants to be. The same holds true for group identity. The homologous structures proposed by Habermas, then, are the structures of development or change. The development of identity in both the ego and the group shares the same structure: they become more general and reflective (as a complementary pair).

At this point, one might reasonably ask, Just how plausible are Habermas's proposed homologies? Do they indeed provide the intended support for the developmental logic thesis? Of course, it is not within the scope of this study to attempt an evaluation of his interpretation of the historical record, but, given his carefully posed provisos, the homology arguments have a prima facie plausibility.

In his paper entitled "The Ontogenetic Fallacy: The Immanent Critique of Habermas's Developmental Logical Theory of Social Evolution," Piet Strydom traces the contours of what he sees as a "significant immanent critique" that has emerged in the work of many of the younger critical theorists such as Johann Arnason, Axel Honneth, Hans Joas, and Klaus Eder.[105] Strydom finds the first clear outline of this critique in Honneth and Joas, and it is further elaborated by Eder.[106] The critique Strydom identifies in the literature focuses on the validity of transferring the structures of ontogenetic development to social evolution, that is, that the "theory of socio-cultural evolution is a developmental logical one which, as such, rests on the employment of the ontogenetic model of development in a manner which must be regarded as involving the commitment of the ontogenetic fallacy."[107] Although Strydom never explicitly defines the ontogenetic fallacy, presumably what he has in mind is that it involves the improper projection of "the structure of ontogenetic learning processes on to the process of evolutionary learning."[108] This involves assuming that Habermas is making the following argument:

(1) The maturational process of the individual (ontogenesis) can be explained by a developmental logic;

(2) Society is analogous to the individual;

(3) Therefore, the evolution of society can be explained by a developmental logic.

The ontogenetic fallacy, then, is committed since premise (2) is false.[109]

Does Habermas commit the ontogenetic fallacy, as Strydom and others argue? In various places above I have attempted to make the case for the reasonableness of the developmental logic thesis, and my arguments have been based primarily on two considerations. First, the developmental logic thesis proposes to borrow only the formal features of the concept of developmental logic from its psychological roots. That is, Habermas is not suggesting that the empirical investigation of ontogenesis can contribute substantive content to the theory of social evolution, but only that the formal properties of the concept of developmental logic can legitimately be claimed to be relevant to the theorization of social evolution. Habermas's enumeration of the provisos pertaining to the homological arguments is an integral part of this claim, and the substance of the provisos is intended to avoid this misunderstanding. It is crucial here to understand the difference between an homology and an analogy. Habermas asserts only that there are similarities between the schemes of development of individuals and societies. He does not assert that there are substantive similarities—in terms of determinate content—between the development of individuals and societies. Unfortunately, Strydom falls into this misunderstanding by conflating the argument from homology, which Habermas does make, with the argument from analogy, which he does not. Second, assuming that the processes of ontogenesis and social evolution both are constituted in structures of linguistically mediated interaction, then it is not entirely unreasonable to infer that the same developmental constraints will apply to both ontogenesis and social evolution. If both ontogenesis and social evolution are in fact constituted in communicative structures, and these communicative structures can be formally analyzed, then the results of an homological analysis will be valid for both ontogenesis and social evolution. Furthermore, since Habermas conceives of the constitution of ego identity and the socialization of the ego as reciprocal processes, a further link between the structures of ego development and those of social development can be established. These two observations, that there are homologies between ego and societal development and that ego and society are reciprocally constituted, provide at least a prima facie case for the plausibility of borrowing of the concept of developmental logic for the theory of social evolution.

Thus, a careful reconstruction of Habermas's theory of social evolution provides an initial response to the basic claim of the ontogenetic fallacy, for Habermas does give a plausible argument for the validity of the developmental logic thesis. Given this initial response, the burden of argument shifts back to the critics. It is now their obligation to show in detail just how the developmental logic thesis succumbs to the ontogenetic fallacy; that is, they must show—given the premises of Habermas's theory—precisely why one cannot legitimately infer social evolutionary explanations from the model of ontogenetic development, in the way that Habermas's theory does.

One possible response by the critics at this point would be to argue that the numerous dis-analogies between ontogenesis and the evolution of societies make any inferences about shared developmental structures highly implausible. For instance, there seem to be no societies in the historical record that are as immaturely developed as is an infant or small child. Whereas an infant lacks any notion of the social and thus of social norms, any society, by definition, is ordered according to some set of social norms. Therefore, the argument goes, any inferences about social evolution based upon the analogy with ontogenesis would be highly problematic at best. The weakness in this argument, however, lies in its failure to carefully distinguish between analogy and homology. Habermas's theory of social evolution claims only that there is an homology between ontogenesis and social evolution, that is, that the structures of development are similar. An analogy refers primarily to a comparison of the substantive properties of two items, and an homology refers primarily to a comparison of the structural (or formal) properties of two items. Habermas's critics often conflate these two forms of comparison, thus interpreting his homological arguments as asserting analogical rather than homological claims. But Habermas's claim is not that we should view less developed societies (according to his theory) as analogous to children, but that we should understand these societies as constituted by intersubjective structures that are homologous to those that constitute ontogenesis. For example, an earlier society might possess a worldview that in its structural properties is homologous to the egocentric outlook of the child. Again, this is not to say that this means that the society is immature in a substantive sense, only that the intersubjective structures of that society have developed only to a given level.

Another objection would be that since ontogenesis presupposes a subject that learns, asserting a homological relation to the evolution of societies would entail that there is some macrosubject that learns in the process of social evolution. This is tantamount to classifying Habermas's theory of social evolution with Hegel's philosophy of history, or Marx's (on some interpretations) theory of history. But Habermas has explicitly denied that the theory of social evolution needs to assume such a macrosubject of history. Moreover, a careful reconstruction of his theory shows that in fact it does not presuppose any such macrosubject of history. In Habermas's theory of social evolution the learning that characterizes social evolution is a collective learning that inheres in the intersubjective structures that constitute society as such. To be sure, structures do not learn, individuals do, but through such means as social movements individual learning achievements are transferred to the social structure in the form of norms and institutions. Thus, Habermas's theory, properly understood, is not susceptible to the objection that it presupposes a macrosubject of history.

Despite my efforts above to distinguish the social-theoretic conception of developmental logic from its psychological-theoretic counterpart, the question remains concerning the implications of ongoing research in developmental psychology for the theory of social evolution. Specifically, given the shared structures of intersubjectivity of both ontogenesis and social evolution, would not empirical research that had implications for the psychological-theoretic conception of developmental logic also have implications for the social-theoretic conception? For example, if further empirical research suggested that ontogenesis, while being stagelike, does not follow an invariant sequence, would we need to reconsider the social-theoretic conception of developmental logic? This is not merely a hypothetical question; there is considerable on-going debate among developmental psychologists about the proper conception of a developmental logic. Now, on the one hand, one might argue that since Habermas's developmental logic thesis intends to borrow only the formal concept of developmental logic from psychological theory, the relation between the psychological-theoretic and the social-theoretic conceptions is only a weak one. The relationship, on this view, is little more than one of inspiration: social theory needs a conception of development, and psychological theory has one, so why not borrow this conception for social-theoretic use? On the other hand, however, one might argue that since Habermas has explicitly called attention to the shared intersubjective structures of ontogenesis and social evolution, he cannot now disentangle the two conceptions of developmental logic when it becomes inconvenient for social theory.

The solution of this problem rests squarely on the characterization adopted of the relationship between ontogenesis and social evolution, and Habermas's explicit statements regarding this relationship do not clarify the ambiguity involved here. A proponent of Habermas's theory of social evolution would want to characterize this relationship in such a way that it avoids both too close a connection, so that the ontogenetic fallacy arguments do not apply, and too distant a connection, in which the shared intersubjective structures are no longer a factor. Another way to put this is that an adequate characterization of the relationship between ontogenesis and social evolution is bounded on the one side by the ontogenetic fallacy, and on the other by the shared structures of linguistically-mediated intersubjectivity. The question is, Can an adequate characterization be conceived that avoids these two limitations? This, it seems to me, is the absolute crux of Habermas's theory of social evolution. An adequate evaluation of this theory requires a clear-cut position on this point. Until the relation between ontogenesis and social evolution is unambiguously characterized, the theory cannot be either defended or criticized.

I think the best approach to this problem would be from a pragmatic perspective, which here means from the perspective of social theory. I have argued above that an adequate critical social theory requires a conception of progressive social change. Since in Habermas's theory of social evolution this conception is provided by the notion of developmental logic, it is worthwhile to ask just what function the concept of developmental logic is intended to fulfill. Habermas introduced the concept in order to provide the theory of social evolution with a way of conceiving social change from the inside, that is, from the perspective of the participants; the concept of developmental logic is intended to capture the inner history of social change as viewed by the participants themselves.[110] Moreover, this history is interpreted as a learning process. The basic structures of social change are characterized as a process in which higher levels of development dialectically sublate earlier levels. This aspect is fundamental to Habermas's conception of social evolution, and it is this feature of the concept of developmental logic that is most important in Habermas's theory of social evolution. Ontogenesis can be characterized relatively uncontroversially as a learning process, I think, and this is how Habermas wants to characterize social evolution. It is the dialectical aspect of developmental logic that he wants to utilize in social theory. I think that given the current state of psychological research we can say that whatever else is involved in ontogenesis (regressions, stagnations, environmental factors, and so forth), part of the process is indeed developmental in this dialectical sense. As long as this is the case, then the borrowing of the concept of developmental logic for social theory is justified. Of course, the soundness of the developmental logic thesis cannot be determined a priori. If further empirical research were to show that ontogenesis was not structured according to any sort of a developmental logic, then this would significantly weaken the plausibility of Habermas's developmental logic thesis. This, it seems to me, is not likely. Moreover, the appearance of one or two studies that reach this conclusion would not affect Habermas's thesis. For empirical research to have a significant affect on this thesis, a broad consensus among researchers would first need to obtain.

The Formal-Pragmatic Argument

As we have seen, an all too common objection to the developmental model is that its justification on the basis of an homology between the development of the individual and of society is far too weak to support the claim that the evolution of societies follows a universal developmental logic. This objection is significant because it argues that Habermas's developmental model of social evolution is conceptually problematic from the start. Although I think that while this objection is important and carries some force against Habermas's initial arguments for the developmental model, it is not relevant to the arguments Habermas later formulated in *The Theory of Communicative Action* and which appeal to different grounds. Nevertheless, there is a different though related problem with this later justification. As before, the problem lies with the difficulty in justifying the universal claims of the developmental model. If the developmental logic of social evolution cannot be shown to be universally valid, then it is open to the charge of being ethnocentric. I will argue that Habermas cannot sustain the claim that the developmental logic of lifeworld structures is universally valid on the basis of only the conceptual and theoretical resources of the theory of communicative action.[111]

The elaboration of the formal pragmatic analysis of language that culminated in *The Theory of Communicative Action* provided Habermas with the conceptual and theoretical resources to justify the developmental logic thesis on grounds other than homological arguments. The formulation of the argument for the developmental logic thesis found in *The Theory of Communicative Action* is grounded explicitly in formal pragmatics. In the course of an explication of the communications-theoretic conception of the lifeworld, Habermas makes the following argument:

> [T]he fact that sociocultural developments are subject to the structural constraints of communicative action can have a systematic effect. We can speak of a developmental logic—in the sense of the tradition stemming from Piaget, a sense that calls for further clarification—if the structures of historical lifeworlds vary within the scope defined by the structural constraints of communicative action not accidentally but directionally, that is, in dependence on learning processes. For instance, there would be a *directional variation of lifeworld structures* if we could bring evolutionary changes under the description of a structural differentiation between culture, society, and personality. One would have to postulate learning processes for such a structural differentiation of the lifeworld if one could show that this meant an increase in rationality. (TCA II, 144–5).

This argument can be reconstructed as follows: if sociocultural developments are in fact structurally constrained by the formal-pragmatic properties of communicative action, and if the variation of lifeworld structures are dependent upon learning processes, then we can claim that the variation of sociocultural lifeworld structures follows a developmental logic, in terms of which rationalization can be analyzed. The first step in analyzing this argument will be to clarify the sense in which communicative action constrains the development of the sociocultural lifeworld, and the second will be to explain in what sense the variation of lifeworld structures is dependent upon learning processes.[112]

How, then, are sociocultural developments subject to the constraints of communicative action? Habermas analyzes communicative action in terms of speech acts. In communicative action a speaker generates an utterance that unavoidably raises validity claims. The hearer to whom the speech act is directed is then compelled to respond to the validity claims implicit in the utterance with either a yes or a no. In other words, in communicative action a speaker raises certain validity claims in her utterances and the hearer is obligated either to accept or reject those validity claims. Speech acts, however, do not occur in a decontextualized space; they occur within and against a background lifeworld. The lifeworld is a background in two senses. First, it serves as a reservoir of shared semantic resources or meanings which constitute individual utterances. And second, it serves as a storehouse of common knowledge, which provides a stabilizing force against the risk of dissension in determinate communicative exchanges. But the relation between communicative action and the lifeworld is not one-sided. The lifeworld is renewed and maintained in and through communicative actions, and it is altered by means of discourse. Communicative action is the process through which the sociocultural lifeworld is reproduced, and conversely, the sociocultural lifeworld generates the context and provides the resources for determinate communicative interchanges.

In addition to serving as a complementary concept to communicative action, the lifeworld's internal differentiation reflects the formal-pragmatic structure of communicative action. This structural reflection is a consequence of the sociocultural functions of communicative action—these functions are the reproduction of cultural knowledge, the establishment and maintenance of intersubjective relationships, and the socialization of individuals. By means of these functions, communicative actions renew the lifeworld in the dimensions of culture, society, and personality. This formal-pragmatic structure is reflected in the sociocultural lifeworld, because, in a sense, both communicative action and the lifeworld occupy the same intersubjective space. The formal pragmatic structure of communicative interaction exists in between individual interlocutors, and it functions to reproduce the sociocultural conditions of communicative action itself, that is, the coordination of social actions, the reaching of intersubjective understanding, and the socialization of individuals.

Thus, if we assume for the sake of argument that Habermas's formal-pragmatic analysis of communicative action is correct, and if we assume the complementarity of communicative action and the lifeworld, then we can establish the claim that the communicative infrastructure of the sociocultural lifeworld is internally related to, and hence logically constrained by, the formal-pragmatic properties of communicative action. Although the argument appears to be valid, the soundness of the argument is primarily grounded in the cogency of Habermas's formal-pragmatic analysis of communicative action, where the confirmation or disconfirmation of this formal-pragmatic analysis is achieved by the intuitive plausibility it has for competent acting and speaking subjects. The question of the cogency of the theory of communicative action lies well beyond our immediate interests, and so its cogency will simply be assumed in the remainder of this paper.

The second premise of the argument for the developmental logic thesis is that the variation of lifeworld structures is dependent upon learning processes. We have seen how the complementarity of communicative action and the lifeworld function to reproduce lifeworld structures, but how are these structures altered and transformed by communicative action? In mundane communicative actions the lifeworld is maintained and reproduced as it is, without (significant) change, because on the basis of the shared lifeworld communication generally proceeds uninterrupted by disagreement. But when disagreement erupts, and a speech act offer is challenged by the hearer, a validity claim becomes problematized. By challenging a validity claim the hearer invites the speaker to provide reasons in support of the problematized claim. This involves, however, a transition from uninterrupted communicative action to the level of argumentation, or discourse in Habermas's sense. On Habermas's understanding of discourse, participants bracket practical imperatives and attempt to reach a rational agreement concerning the problematic validity claim. In doing so, they unavoidably presuppose that ideally an agreement could be reached based only on the "unforced force" of good reasons. By raising validity claims in communicative actions we unavoidably rely on certain idealizing presuppositions, presuppositions concerning the possibility of their uncoerced redemption in discourse. Thus, the unavoidable raising of criticizable validity claims in communicative actions possesses a rational potential—the potential of communicative rationality. This means that "[a]rgumentation makes possible behavior that counts as rational in a specific sense, namely learning from explicit mistakes" (TCA I, 22). And since "learning processes . . . themselves *rely* on argumentation," the tapping of this rational potential in argumentation constitutes a learning process that results in an intersubjective understanding or agreement (TCA I, 22).

In discourse, interlocutors learn in the process of rational argumentation on the basis of the mutual consideration and evaluation of reasons. If by means of discourse the parties reach a rational agreement, they have, based only on the power of good reasons, corrected their mistakes and adopted new understandings, which then become part of their shared lifeworld. Through innumerable iterations by ever more members of the society, the structures and content of the sociocultural lifeworld gradually become transformed. But this is not simply a process of random variation, for the lifeworld has not been changed arbitrarily. Rather, to the extent that the variation of the lifeworld is a product of rational argumentation—and only to that extent—the rationality of discourse is transferred by means of new understandings into the lifeworld, resulting in a rationalization of the lifeworld itself.

If this analysis of the complementarity of communicative action and the lifeworld is correct, it is reasonable to ask whether these considerations can ground the claim that the developmental logic of structures of the lifeworld is universally valid. This claim to universal validity is especially problematic in light of the radical underdetermination of the theory by the sociohistorical evidence. The theory is underdetermined in part because we are dealing with historical data that requires interpretation, and in part because the theory explains development only in terms of the infrastructure of the lifeworld. To be sure, Habermas recognizes this challenge, for he notes that once one replaces the phenomenological concept of the lifeworld with the communications-theoretical one, "the idea of approaching *any society whatsoever* by means of [the communications-theoretical concept] is not at all trivial" (TCA II, 143, emphasis added). But he goes on to claim that in adopting the communications-theoretical concept, the "burden of truth for the universal validity of the lifeworld concept—a validity reaching across cultures and epochs—shifts then to the complementary concept of communicative action" (TCA II, 143–4). Presumably, the argument for this can be reconstructed as follows. The formal pragmatic analysis of communicative action has elucidated the invariant structures of the use of language in communication, and this analysis will be universally valid for all users of propositionally differentiated languages. Communicative action and the lifeworld are complementary; as such they mutually presuppose one another. Given this complementarity, and since the formal pragmatic structures of communicative action are universal, we can conclude that the formal pragmatic structures of the sociocultural lifeworld are also universal.

It is far from evident, however, that this conclusion is warranted. First of all, suppose that the developmental structures of the lifeworld are not universal and invariant. If communicative action and lifeworld are in fact complementary, as Habermas maintains, then we might just as reasonably infer that it is the results of our formal pragmatic analysis of communicative action that are not universal and invariant. If the two concepts of communicative action and lifeworld are indeed symmetrically complementary in the way that Habermas claims, then it is not entirely clear on what grounds he asserts the asymmetrical relationship between them. In order to make good on this claim, Habermas owes us an argument for asserting this asymmetrical relation between communicative action and lifeworld in which communicative action is in some sense more basic and fundamental in relation to the lifeworld, since given the explication of these two concepts in *The Theory of Communicative Action* we would expect a symmetrical rather than an asymmetrical relation between them.

Second, Habermas maintains that the structural differentiation of the three formal world concepts—the objective, the social, and the subjective worlds—is itself the interpretive achievement of acting and speaking subjects: "In their interpretive accomplishments the members of a communication community demarcate the one objective world and their intersubjectively shared social world from the subjective worlds of individuals and (other) collectives" (TCA I, 70). This suggests that the formal pragmatic analysis of communicative action, which rests heavily upon the relations actors can take to each of these three formal worlds, may be uncovering structures that are not necessarily invariant and universal, but are the result of interpretive practices that occur in the medium of language and against a lifeworld background.[113] In other words, if the elements of the formal pragmatic analysis are themselves the results of interpretive accomplishments, then the claim that the formal pragmatic analysis of communicative action uncovers invariant structures becomes problematic.

Suppose, however, that my arguments here are mistaken and that the formal-pragmatic structures of communicative action are in fact universal, and that these structures are functionally reflected in the infrastructure of the sociocultural lifeworld. In this case, it is still necessary to clarify the way that the communicative rationality inherent in discourse shapes the developmental logic of the sociocultural lifeworld. Habermas argues that for both communicative action and the sociocultural lifeworld an increase in rationality is constituted by a decentering of the egocentric perspective. This strategy presents itself naturally to a theory of society that begins from the intersubjective character of communicative action. For it is clear that the process of reaching an understanding with someone requires that I overcome my egocentric perspective and be capable of adopting the perspective of the Other, and in doing so my reflexivity increases. This increase in reflexivity indicates an increased capacity for learning; hence Habermas speaks of progressing to new "learning levels." Once again, developmental psychology is useful in clarifying this idea. For just as the child moves from egocentric, to sociocentric, and finally to universalistic action orientations, worldviews develop from the mythological, to the metaphysical-religious, to the postmetaphysical (universal). This rationalization process of decentration results in an increase in the learning potential of both the child (in ontogenesis) and the lifeworld (in phylogenesis). Sociocultural decentration occurs such that the infrastructure of the lifeworld is transformed in such a way that the *formal* characteristics of the new learning level more adequately realize the *functional* properties of communicative action. As the lifeworld becomes increasingly rationalized, the rational potential inherent in communicative action is released; that is, the reproduction processes of the lifeworld rely less on uninterrogated traditions that are dogmatically reproduced and they become increasingly subject to the imperatives of reaching an understanding by means of communicative action. Most importantly, Habermas argues that this rationalization process is universal; insofar as a society develops, it must do so within the developmental logical structure of an increasing decentration.

If such a concept of developmental logic could then be utilized to explain sociohistorical change, then we would have good conceptual grounds for describing those tendencies as processes of rationalization. Indeed, in the second volume of *The Theory of Communicative Action* Habermas draws upon the empirical research of George Herbert Mead and Emile Durkheim to indicate how we can understand various sociocultural changes as rationalization processes. He cites the increasing differentiation between the lifeworld components of culture, society, and personality; the increasing distinction between form and content; and the increasing formalization of the distinct reproductive functions of the lifeworld, resulting in an increase in the reflexivity of lifeworld reproduction (see TCA II, 145–6).

But the claim that this account is universally valid does not yet seem to be warranted. Supposing that the formal-pragmatic structures of communicative action are universal, and that these structures are functionally reflected in the lifeworld, it does not follow that the logic of the development of these structures in the lifeworld is universal. To be sure, Habermas is not making any such a priori arguments; his is a reconstructive project that seeks to uncover the development of the infrastructure of the lifeworld in a retrospective manner. Nonetheless, the method of rational reconstruction will also fail to warrant the claim to universality. This argument fails because the claim to universality is radically underdetermined by the available empirical sociohistorical evidence, and it is underdetermined in principle. For a developmental-logical reconstruction of the historical structures of the lifeworld must be highly abstract in order to be at all plausible. But the level of abstraction necessary to satisfy the condition of plausibility will preclude the possibility of a single best interpretation of the evidence. That is, we could not accumulate sufficient historical evidence that would be needed to make a case that the reconstructive interpretation offered is the single best interpretation of the evidence: the theory will be chronically underdetermined by the evidence. The consequence is that any proposed rational reconstruction cannot be shown to be the best interpretation of the available evidence without at the same time relying on unexamined normative assumptions.

Thus, it appears that the resources of the theory of communicative action are insufficient in themselves to warrant the claim that the developmental logic of the lifeworld is universally valid. A consequence of this conclusion is that it can be argued that since Habermas has asserted the universal validity of this developmental logic without sufficient warrant, he has in effect permitted a Eurocentric bias to seep into his theory of social evolution. To be sure, the social theorist can never completely avoid ethnocentrism, and Habermas does acknowledge the force of this concern, but he believes that the problem of ethnocentrism can be mitigated, if not avoided, by emphasizing both the theory's reconstructive methodology and its fallibility. On this account, the Eurocentric bias of his theory of social evolution, to the extent that it in fact has one, will be continually reduced and corrected for in the course of an ongoing social-scientific research program. But merely pointing out that the theory is capable of being falsified is inadequate since, as we have seen, the theory is radically underdetermined by the evidence. There is no guarantee that the Eurocentric bias will be gradually eliminated through the processes of empirical corroboration and theoretical reformulation because there simply is not sufficient evidence to determine theory choice.

I have argued that while Habermas's new argument in *The Theory of Communicative Action* for the developmental logic thesis avoids the problems that the earlier argument from analogy faced, it nevertheless has its own problems. On Habermas's own account of communicative action and the complementary concept of the sociocultural lifeworld it is not clear what justifies the asymmetry that is necessary to warrant the claim that the structures of the lifeworld are universally valid on the basis of a universal formal pragmatics of communicative action. Since the formal pragmatic analysis of communicative action is always already situated within the lifeworld it is difficult to see how the fundamental interpretive nature of these analyses can be sidestepped. But unless this interpretive nature is somehow transcended, the claim to universality will be very difficult to vindicate. This is not to suggest that Habermas's developmental model of social evolution is invalidated by this difficulty. Rather, only its claim to have reconstructed a universally valid developmental logic of the structures of the sociocultural lifeworld is put into question. In my view, Habermas's developmental model of social evolution remains particularly promising if it foregoes the claim to universality. Instead of attempting to reconstruct a universal developmental logic it would be more plausible simply to reduce the scope of validity of the developmental logic to the sociocultural formation or form of life under investigation. In that case, it would be necessary to reconstruct the developmental logics for different sociocultural complexes and forms of life, but these would no longer claim universal validity. This approach would have the result of generating a plurality of developmental logics that would be commensurable only on the methodological level. It would be a mistake, however, to think that this revision would result in an invidious cultural relativism that would be inconsistent with the interests of a critical social theory. Habermas's developmental model of social evolution is an element of a critical social theory that can still be understood as applying the method of immanent critique. And since the suggested revision retains the developmental model, thus allowing identification of unrealized rationality potentials within any given sociocultural configuration, the methods of immanent critique remain applicable. Moreover, it would also seem to be empirically evident—though an unfortunate fact in many ways—that what were in previous ages separate and distinct sociocultural complexes are interacting to increasingly greater degrees under the pressures of globalization processes. Globalization of the economy, greater mobility, and global communications networks all put pressure on individual societies to assimilate to one another. Under this pressure, it will become increasingly difficult for societies to resist such a convergence nonrepressively. This will have the effect of creating a contingent convergence of these diverse developmental logics. The result is that given the conditions of modernity, such a convergence appears inevitable, and so the proposal of thinking in terms of a plurality of developmental logics should not, in the long run, be especially problematic for proponents of universalism such as Habermas. For insofar as cultures learn from each other, the infrastructure of their lifeworlds will increasingly overlap.

Further Questions

Habermas appeals to the concept of a developmental logic of normative structures in order to overcome two weaknesses that he sees in functionalist theories of social evolution.[114] In a debate in the mid-1970s with Niklas Luhmann, a leading exponent of systems-theoretical approach to social theorizing, Habermas argued that functionalist theories of social change face two primary weaknesses (HE). First, functionalist explanations of evolutionary changes do not adequately explain the uniqueness of the given changes. Functionalist theories explain functionally equivalent mutations of a social system, but they fail to specify why any one particular change has occurred, and not another: "An observable change of systemic conditions or structure cannot be explained by allusion to the function it fulfills from an externally adduced point of reference. For depending on the choice of the reference point, the same process can assume very different functions, while given a fixed reference point, other processes can fulfill the same function. Social-scientific functionalism serves to detect classes of functionally equivalent changes of conditions or structural formations, but not to explain the genesis of newly emerging states and structures" (HE, 26–27).

The second primary weakness of functionalist theories of social change is that they cannot determine unambiguously the identity of social systems as they change over time. The identity of any given society, Habermas claims, must be determined, at least in part, from the internal perspective of the members of that society. Thus, since functionalist theories adopt by definition only an external perspective with respect to a given society, they fail to adequately capture the society's identity. One consequence of this is that they lack the explanatory capacity to determine the death of a social system; that is, they cannot determine which changes are considered so radical that they entail the death of a given society. Functionalism simply fails "to identify the important constituent structures of a society that determine the range of variation that must not be exceeded if this society is to preserve its identity. . . ." (HE, 27).

Habermas contends, then, that functionalist explanations lack certain necessary determinants of social change. For example, functionalist theories of social change lack the theoretical resources to adequately describe the continued existence of societies undergoing radical change. When, in response to a crisis, a society changes both its internal structure and its boundaries with its environment, it is not clear on the functionalist model (which can only adopt the observer's perspective) whether the society has survived the change or is now a different society. Only by adopting the first-person perspective of members of the society can an adequate self-identification of a society be determined. The lack of the ability to analyze social change from the inside also prevents functionalist theories from adequately distinguishing between functionally equivalent solutions to crises. In other words, functionalist theories of social change cannot unambiguously determine crisis solutions that are progressive in terms of the maintenance of the collective identity. The role of the developmental logic thesis, then, is to provide this capacity; specifically, it provides the theory of social evolution with the conceptual means for unambiguously distinguishing progressive from regressive crisis resolutions. My intent here is not to enter into the debate between Habermas and the functionalists, but rather to consider further the soundness of Habermas's claim that an adequate theory of social evolution requires some notion of developmental logic.

A functionalist critic of Habermas, Michael Schmid, has written an essay directly challenging the theoretic value of the concept of developmental logic for theories of social evolution.[115] While recognizing much of value in Habermas's theory of social evolution, Schmid nevertheless sides with the functionalists, arguing that Habermas's theory simply does not need the concept of developmental logic because it does no substantive theoretical work. He thinks that if Habermas abandoned the concept of developmental logic, his theory would be much more plausible: "I think it possible to prove not only that the postulation of a developmental logic leads to questionable assumptions about the relation between ontogenesis and the development of worldviews, but also that such a logic has no explanatory powers whatsoever and in fact only burdens an evolutionary theory with irrelevant logical problems. I should like therefore to prescribe a radical cure for Habermas's theory by suggesting that *it be freed of all developmental-logical elements*."[116]

Schmid marshals two arguments against Habermas's use of the concept of developmental logic. In the first argument he worries that if the developmental logic of sociocultural stages is meant to have an empirical referent, then it is not clear just what would count as corroborating empirical evidence. He begins by asserting that Habermas provides no unambiguous account of how we are to understand the homologies between ontogenetic and sociohistorical structures. He asserts that Habermas's "description of the relation between the two processes as an 'homology' or a 'copy' points to a factual connection but provides no clear interpretation of it."[117] Although Schmid reads Habermas as asserting that the homology "points to a factual connection," he does not provide us with the reasons why he adopts this reading. Schmid claims further that he "can find no detailed argument for what the connection between ontogenesis and the developmental logic of worldviews should look like."[118] Based on these assertions, which Schmid backs with little or no textual evidence, he goes on to argue that if we take Habermas literally and understand the homology in a factual manner, then Habermas's theory encounters the objection that its explanatory hypothesis for the (relatively) undeveloped action competencies of individuals of earlier epochs is underdetermined. That is, given Habermas's theory of social evolution, and assuming that it postulates a factual connection between the development of the structures of cognition and the evolution of a society's normative structures, how can we explain the limited development of members of earlier societies? "[I]f, taking Habermas's terms as literally as possible, we do assert that there is an empirical connection between the conditions of evolutionary learning and an ontogenetic developmental logic, then we come upon what seems to me to be an obscure empirical problem: can we connect the fact that different problem-solving capacities are institutionalized in structures of collective consciousness according to the organization principle and the learning level (which is what the ascription of a developmental logic to learning levels amounts to) with the fact that the people of earlier social formations did not pass through all the stages of their possible ontogenetic development?"[119]

Schmid does not think so, and indeed he thinks that if in fact there is a correlation between individual action competencies and worldviews, for example, then we do not need to postulate an empirically problematic developmental logic to explain the correlation. He suggests that the correlation can only be explained by reference to "the factual structures which determine the institutionalized expansions of the stock of knowledge and also of the relevant intra- and extra-social environments of the societies under examination."[120] The limited development of the cognitive and moral competencies of these individuals could thus be explained by the relation of the given level of development of structures of consciousness to certain environmental conditions: "The moral conservativism of traditional societies would then be the factual consequence of this complex of conditions, and we would not fall back on the highly dubious assumption that the people of earlier societies were *incapable* of reflecting upon their norms. The stability of their environment would have removed the *need* for them to do this."[121] We can account for the apparent correlation between the development of individual structures of consciousness and the evolution of worldviews with a functional explanation, according to Schmid, thus avoiding the need for the excessive theoretical baggage of the concept of developmental logic.

In his second argument, Schmid objects to the heuristic understanding of the concept of developmental logic on the grounds that it is too speculative. On this interpretation of the concept, developmental logic is understood only as an interpretative procedure or method. In this sense the historical record is interpreted as if it satisfied the criteria of a developmental logic. Positing a developmental logic of normative structures would be no more than an interpretive framework for social theorists and historians. This heuristic understanding of the developmental logic thesis stands in contrast to the formal-pragmatic interpretation in which the reconstruction of a developmental logic is said to uncover the historical pattern of the development of quasi-transcendental structures of consciousness which have been operative throughout history. Schmid argues that if the heuristic interpretation is indeed Habermas's understanding of developmental logic, then he needs to specify the limits of this sort of reconstructive historical explanation; otherwise it is not clear just how much of the explanatory burden is being carried by the "as if" hypothesis of developmental logic: "Any 'as if' philosophy is obliged to define the limits of its proposed powers of explanation in the face of the all too 'freely creative moment' of such fictions. Otherwise, in the context of an empirically understood theory of social evolution, the question remains as to exactly how much of the burden of explanation is in fact carried by the reconstruction of the developmental logic."[122] Moreover, if Habermas is proposing a way to interpret the process of social evolution that is based on a developmental logic, and that developmental logic cannot be empirically tested (since there is no empirical referent), then the empirical status of the theory of social evolution is placed into question. A theory of social evolution based on a developmental logic in the heuristic sense risks being indistinguishable in this respect from speculative philosophies of history, which purport to explain the meaning of history without any way to empirically evaluate their claims.

Schmid feels compelled to present both of these arguments against Habermas's use of the concept of developmental logic because he believes that Habermas is not entirely clear as to which understanding of developmental logic, the formal-pragmatic or the heuristic interpretation, is entailed by the theory of social evolution. Schmid does admit, however, that on his reading Habermas is proposing the heuristic understanding of developmental logic, despite certain textual evidence to the contrary. He gives two reasons for this reading: first, since Habermas does not consider social evolution to be a macroprocess of a species subject, there is nothing for the developmental logic to inhere in; and second, Habermas explicitly states that the epistemological status of the theory of social evolution is one of rational reconstruction, and the retrospective nature of this type of explanation entails "as if" types of interpretations. I presume his argument here is that since reconstructive sciences do not generate explanations capable of empirical predictions, they are effectively narratives constructed to make our historical self-understanding coherent.

The first question to consider, then, is the sense of developmental logic entailed by Habermas's theory of social evolution. Only when this question is answered will it be productive to consider Schmid's specific criticisms. The ambiguity presented by the two alternative senses of developmental logic does not originate with Habermas's theory. It can be traced back to an original ambiguity in Piaget's own conception of structures of developmental logic.[123] Rotenstreich notes that while Piaget is not entirely unambiguous with respect to the sense of (developmental logical) structure, structures can be said generally to be understood in the heuristic (or methodical) sense: "[Structures] serve as tools for establishing the order of data by imposing on them a certain pattern."[124]

A careful reading, however, leads one unavoidably to the conclusion that Habermas understands the developmental logic of normative structures to be inherent in history. Indeed, he explicitly states, "The systematically reconstructable patterns of development of normative structures. . . depict a *developmental logic* inherent in cultural traditions and institutional change" (CES, 98). Moreover, it is clear from Habermas's characterization of reconstructive sciences as empirical that a reconstruction of a developmental logic of normative structures must be grounded in the historical data. Finally, the structures of consciousness which are conditions of both ontogenesis and sociocultural evolution are said to be constituted in linguistically mediated interaction, in the formal-pragmatic structures of intersubjectivity (CES, 98–99). The developmental logic of normative structures forms the pattern of change of these linguistically mediated structures of interaction. For these reasons we can conclude that Habermas understands the developmental logic of normative structures not merely as a heuristic, as Schmid claims, but as actually operative in determining the horizons of consciousness.

In disentangling these various interpretations of the reality of developmental logical structures, however, it is important to consider the various points of view from which they can be considered. When one considers structures from the point of view of the participants who (unintentionally) constructed them, they definitely have a heuristic character. From this perspective, structures, whether they be cognitive or social, are constructs that function to order and make comprehensible the flux of experience. To be sure, the range of possible structures that can be constructed is determined, at least in part, by the given, the objective world. Since structures function to mediate the interaction of the system and the environment, they are constructed through learning processes by the system (or its members) with the intention of ordering the given chaos presented by the environment. On this view, the heuristic character of structure stands out; structures are constructed only for the function of ordering in a meaningful way the flux of the given. Note that this is how structures of consciousness appear from the first-person perspective of the participant (although not consciously).

Another perspective from which structures can be viewed is that of the third-person observer, from which the developmental logic of normative structures is reconstructed by abstracting from concrete historical descriptions. Here, developmental structures are reconstructed from an analysis of the historical record, and so their empirical character comes to the fore. Of course the soundness of this reconstruction depends upon the quality of this historical knowledge, and also upon how we interpret these historical facts. Recall, however, that reconstructive sciences are fallible and grounded in empirical evidence; therefore Schmid's charge of speculation is unfounded. This is the perspective adopted by a social theorist interested in reconstructing the developmental logical structures of history.

Schmid's critique operates within the perspective of the social theorist, and so his argument against the realistic understanding of developmental logic is particularly relevant. He is concerned at first about how the theory would explain the limited developmental progression of earlier societies: "[W]as the process by which the action competencies of people of earlier epochs came to maturity restricted (perhaps by disruptions of their learning capacities) to preconventional or conventional stages of development? If this is the case, what kind of empirical grounds could we produce for this, independently of the fact that the relevant worldview had *no* universal or postconventional features?"[125] This question suggests that Schmid has failed to grasp the distinction Habermas makes between the developmental logic of structures and the empirical and contingent mechanisms of development. The answer to Schmid's first question is no, the developmental processes were not restricted in some way to a lower level of development. They did not achieve higher levels of development for strictly contingent empirical reasons. What this means is that the society, for whatever reasons, did not face challenges of the sort that would impel development to a higher level (or face social disintegration or stagnation). This can be viewed from two perspectives: either the challenges faced by the society, that is, the system problems it encountered, were of the sort that could be solved within the given learning level, or the society did not face the extreme challenges that would require development for its continued survival. So there was no limitation of learning levels in earlier societies; they simply had not faced the sorts of challenges that would compel development. Just as in the cognitive development of the child, social evolution occurs over time. Schmid's question is comparable to asking why the infant doesn't develop formal operational skills, or why the five year old doesn't develop a postconventional moral consciousness. Just as in the child, societal development occurs over a period of time and through a continuous process of facing challenges and constructing solutions.

Schmid then generalizes this concern into the skeptical question: What is the empirical referent of the developmental sequences? In other words, what factual evidence could be produced to substantiate the claim of a developmental logic of normative structures, and how could one empirically test this hypothesis? The factual understanding of developmental logical structures implies that an adequate theory of social change would need to uncover them. To be sure, they are not uncovered in the sense of traditional empirical inquiry, but in the sense of a reconstructive science, which abstracts from the empirical data. Whereas empirical-analytic sciences describe observable objects and events, reconstructive sciences explicate symbolically prestructured reality. But reconstructive sciences do not explicate surface meanings, which is the task of hermeneutics; they explicate the deep meanings of symbolic interaction. Reconstructive sciences seek to explicate the intuitive know-how of competent speaking and acting subjects. This does not mean that reconstructive sciences do not involve any interpretation. For them, the data must be interpreted just as in any other form of theory construction. Habermas's theory of social evolution with its concept of a developmental logic of normative structures seeks to explicate those symbolic structures of the social world that constitute the intuitive know-how of the mature members of the society. The structures of consciousness that are to be reconstructed, however, are not directly observable; they can only be inferred by abstracting formal structures from everyday pragmatic activities.

In his essay on the ontogenetic fallacy, Strydom also points out three consequences that result from Habermas's commitment to a developmental approach to sociocultural evolution. First, a theory of social evolution based on the ontogenetic model of development, that is, on structures of possible evolutionary changes, "necessarily abstracts from historically specific events and unique collective experiences within the framework of which social groups engage in historical action, and thus detaches itself from the real historical process."[126] Evidence of this abstraction is found in Habermas's rigorous separation of theories of social evolution from the practice of historiography (see HE). The second consequence is that Habermas's theory of social evolution "operates with an ambiguous concept of 'social learning.'"[127] On the one hand, his theory of social evolution explicitly relies on a systems-theoretic conception of evolutionary learning, and on the other hand, the theory asserts that moral-practical learning occurs in and through communicative action, and such learning processes are exemplified by social movements. Systems theory conceives of collective learning as a functional response to a disturbance that threatens the stability of the system (that is, crisis). This, however, is in tension with conceptions of collective learning based on social movements. Social movements arise in response to consciously experienced oppression and social injustice, and not to anonymous system disturbances. The third and final consequence of the ontogenetic fallacy is that it results in a theory of social evolution that is too abstract to satisfy the emancipatory interest of critical social theory: "[Habermas's] theory's high degree of abstraction from everyday plexuses of meaning . . . renders it incapable of vindicating the critical theoretical claim of being concerned with the development of enlightening hermeneutic interpretations which have a bearing on social agents' self-understanding and help them in orienting their action."[128]

The undesirable consequences of (1) excessive abstraction of the theory of social evolution, (2) ambiguity of the concept of collective learning, and (3) the lack of any direct sociocritical and practical impact strike at the foundation of the developmental theory of social evolution. The first implication, that Habermas's theory of social evolution necessarily abstracts from concrete historical events, and thus from the historical process, does not carefully state in what sense this is problematic for the theory. Presumably, this abstraction is undesirable because a theory of history (or in this case a theory of social evolution) should take account of the historical evidence. It is not clear why, in general, a theory of history that is distinguished from narrative historiography cannot in principle be abstract and take into account historical evidence as well. A theory of history, just like any other scientific theory, attempts to explain the facts with general and abstract laws. Of course, Habermas's theory of social evolution is a reconstructive theory, and so does not posit laws of history; rather, it reconstructs through a process of abstraction the pattern or structure of the development of history, or, more precisely, it reconstructs the developmental structures of societal evolution. Since Habermas's theory proceeds by a method of abstracting from historical evidence, it is not clear that this objection applies to his theory.

The second undesirable implication, according to Strydom, of the developmental logic thesis is that it is said to entail an ambiguous conception of collective learning. On the one hand, the theory explains social evolution in systems-theoretic terms, that is, as a functional process of adaptation, and on the other hand, it asserts that moral-practical learning occurs in and through communicative action, an emphatically nonfunctional form of learning. This objection is based upon a misunderstanding of Habermas's theory of social evolution. Although Habermas's theory explains the total process of social evolution in both functional and developmental terms, the conception of collective learning it entails refers only to developmental changes between levels of learning. Evolutionarily significant changes are understood as developments from one learning level to a higher one. But changes within a given learning level are indeed explained as functional adaptations. Both types of change are necessary to the theory. For without the intralevel functional adaptations a level of crisis would not develop that would be sufficient to impel the leap to a higher learning level. Therefore, once properly understood Habermas's theory of social evolution does not entail an ambiguous conception of collective learning.

The third undesirable consequence in Strydom's view is that Habermas's theory is too abstract both to provide practical orientation and to ground concrete social critique. This is a common reaction upon first encountering Habermas's theory because of its scope, complexity, and lack of systematic development. I have attempted in this study to clarify and systematize the theory, nevertheless, one might still object that it is too abstract to be of any value to a critical social theory. This objection, I think, is unjustified. As I have shown, the theory of social evolution is valuable in two respects to critical social theory (at least as it is conceived by Habermas). First, the theory of social evolution provides the framework in which a nontranscendental yet universalistic grounding of norms of communication can be located. Without such a framework, Habermas's formal pragmatics—which lies at the core of the theory of communicative action—would be open to the charge of historicism. Providing an historical-theoretic framework for the theory of communicative action contributes to the clarification of the normative claims of a critical theory based in such a theory of communicative action. Second, the theory of social evolution entails a theory of modernity, which in turn provides a concrete normative framework for a critical theory of society. Habermas's theory of modernity grounds the arguments for the claim that the processes of rationalization in the West have been distorted with the transition to modernity. This distortion has resulted in the systemic imperatives of the economic and bureaucratic subsystems colonizing or invading processes of lifeworld reproduction. Specifically, processes of social integration, cultural reproduction, and socialization have become increasingly oriented towards the goals of accumulation of money and power. But, as Habermas argues, the lifeworld (that is, society, culture, and personality) must be reproduced by means of communicative action, which by definition excludes the coercive systemic imperatives of the accumulation of money and power. The solution implied by this diagnosis is the reassertion of forms of communicative interaction within these lifeworld spheres. Pragmatically, this means that we, as members of a society, need to assert our interests in the communicative reproduction of the lifeworld by democratic means against the subsystems of the economy and the bureaucracy. Moreover, Habermas's theory of modernity entails that we should not retreat behind modern science and technology to a romantic conception of a society based only on communion with nature. Of course, neither should we champion science and technology as the answers to all of our problems; indeed, this path has led to many of the problems with which we Westerners are faced today. The point I am making here is that although Habermas's theory of social evolution at first appears too abstract to be of practical service to critical theory, it indeed makes significant contributions to the task of emancipation.

Chapter 5

Progress and Social Evolution

In the opening chapters of this study I argued that the concept of progress plays an important and necessary function both in the very idea of critical social theory and in Habermas's particular conception of it. In order to practice a rational social criticism it is unavoidable to presuppose a conception of social change that gives an account of progressive change. That is, if we want to critique existing social conditions, say the oppression of women or of people of color, then my critique can be well grounded only if I can specify what counts as progressive social change and how such change is possible given existing sociocultural conditions; the practice of social critique necessarily presupposes some conception of progress.[1]

As we have seen, Habermas's critical social theory refers essentially to a developmental theory of social evolution to ground its normative claims, such that the concept of developmental logic formalizes the conditions of social change so that progressive social change is understood as a collective learning process. But is this conception of progress an adequate one? Does it give an adequate account of the necessary conditions of progressive social change required by critical theory? For present purposes I am only interested in whether the conception of progress entailed by the theory of social evolution is adequate for the purposes of a critical theory of society.

I will begin by explicating the conception of progress entailed by Habermas's theory of social evolution. We will see that this conception of progress is dialectical in the manner that it explains the paradox of development. I will attempt to show that Habermas's development of the theory of social evolution has been unbalanced; I will argue that he has not given an adequate account of progress with respect to happiness and fulfillment, with which—alongside freedom from oppression—critical theory has been traditionally concerned. Next, I will attempt to show that the dialectical conception of progress entails a differentiated notion of progress that accounts for progress in the dimensions of material well-being, liberty and autonomy, and happiness and fulfillment. While Habermas has expounded on progress in the dimensions of well-being and justice, he has had little to say about progress with respect to happiness and fulfillment. I suggest that a promising direction to go in at this point would be to examine the expressive/creative moment of action and interaction; in this way we can complete Habermas's theory of social evolution in the dimension of happiness and fulfillment. I will conclude by briefly reviewing the central themes of this study, and will consider some of its implications.

Habermas's Conception of Progress

Despite the analysis of the concept of developmental logic above, the concept of progress it entails remains unclear. How does the concept of a developmental logic translate into a concept of progress? The short answer is that Habermas understands societal evolution, following Weber, as a rationalization process. Unlike Weber, however, Habermas postulates that rationalization occurs in two dimensions: the cognitive-technical and the moral-practical: "The development of productive forces depends on the application of technically useful knowledge; and the basic institutions of a society embody moral-practical knowledge. Progress in these two dimensions is measured against the two universal validity claims we also use to measure the progress of empirical knowledge and of moral-practical insight, namely, the truth of propositions and the rightness of norms. I would like, therefore, to defend the thesis that the criteria of social progress singled out by historical materialism as the development of productive forces and the maturity of forms of social intercourse can be systematically justified" (CES, 142).

On this view, rationalization processes in each of the dimensions of cognitive-technical knowledge and moral-practical insight are progressive in the sense that they increase our capacity for true knowledge and right action. Progressive changes in productive forces (cognitive-technical knowledge) are determined according to the criterion of truth, and progressive changes in social formations are determined according to the criterion of rightness. If we understand rationalization with respect to outer nature as constituting progress in the dimension of material well-being, and rationalization with respect to social interaction as constituting progress in the dimension of freedom, what is missing is an account of progress with respect to individual happiness and fulfillment, which, along with freedom from unnecessary domination, is a traditional concern of critical theory. Of course, this assumes that material well-being and freedom from oppression are not sufficient conditions for happiness and fulfillment. We will return to this issue below.

In what sense, however, is this conceived as a rationalization process? The key to Habermas's conception of progress is his understanding of development as a process of rationalization. As was shown in the analysis of the concept of developmental logic above, a logic of development is defined by the properties of structure, qualitativeness, hierarchization, and integration. The two properties of structure and qualitativeness capture the notion that a developmental logic is a logical space that exhibits (contingent) transformations of form, in which successive structures differ qualitatively from each other. Structural transformations are necessarily (but not sufficiently) conditioned by system problems; that is, they occur only to the extent that the contingent, empirical conditions present the need for change, and they are evolutionary in the sense that they constitute advances in the learning capacity of a society. Thus evolutionary advances occur when a society advances from one learning level to another, where a learning level is defined as the structures of consciousness collectively attained by the society at the given level of development.[2] The key here is that the structures of consciousness determine the logical space in which learning can occur. In social-theoretic terms this logical space is the collective structure of consciousness that determines the conditions or the range of possible forms a society can empirically realize. Occasionally, certain empirical conditions impel the structure to transform, thus reorganizing the content into a qualitatively new structural form. For example, the structural conditions of the scholastic tradition of law constrained justifications of legal norms to reference to God's will as expressed in the Judeo-Christian Bible, or indirectly through the Pope, priests, and the like. The historical transition known as the Enlightenment transformed this structure such that the justification of legal norms could no longer legitimately refer to God's will. The new structure constrained legal justification to reference to natural law. This change in the collective structure of consciousness is accompanied by a change in the backing, or general types of reasons, which were considered legitimate in justificatory argumentation. With the transformation, some reasons became illegitimate (appeal to God's will), and others were introduced as valid (appeal to human nature). Of course, since the Enlightenment natural law theory has come to be replaced by positive law, in which appeal to human nature is no longer considered a valid reason in the justification of legal norms.[3] The properties of structure and qualitativeness capture the characteristically developmental properties of rationalization processes. The rationalization processes of Habermas's theory of social evolution are conceived as progressive changes in structures of consciousness which determine the range of possible variations a society can embody. Thus, the institutions of two empirical societies may appear significantly different, while they are both conditioned by the same deep structure of consciousness.

The properties of hierarchization and integration are also central to Habermas's notion of progress, and these two properties capture the characteristic rationality of rationalization processes. Replacing one structure with a qualitatively different one would be meaningless from the perspective of rationalization if one could not specify in what sense (if any) the new structure is better than the old one and how they are internally related. This addresses one of the problems with functionalist theories of social evolution. While they give functionalist explanations for social change, and justify that change on functionalist grounds, what they cannot explain is why that change is good for a determinate community. In other words, functionalist theories of social evolution do not give an adequate account of social change from the perspective of the participants; by their very nature functionalist accounts are constrained to the external perspective of the observer. The properties of hierarchization and integration specify the sense in which successive developmental structures are rationally ordered. Successively ordered developmental stages can be said to be hierarchically arranged because each stage integrates those prior to it. As we saw above, integration involves both generalization and differentiation. The combination of the two results in a decentering of justificatory perspectives in which egoistic backings become gradually replaced by backings that are intersubjectively valid. Thus, actions and beliefs become increasingly justified with respect the third person perspective, for example, the moral point of view.

It is helpful to think of Habermas as in a sense empirically reformulating Hegel's concept of *Aufhebung*.[4] The concepts of developmental logic and *Aufhebung* are not strictly analogous, but they share a general structure. *Aufhebung* is Hegel's term for the pattern generated by the dialectical synthesis of a concept and its contradiction into a higher unity which preserves and transforms the two lower moments. Likewise, the concept of developmental logic refers to the pattern that results from the transformation of an inadequate structure of consciousness into a higher, more adequate structure that preserves and reorganizes the contents of consciousness. This interpretation of the concept of developmental logic is made plausible by Habermas's intentions and his relationship to his predecessors. The aim of the theory of social evolution is to explain the historical development of structures of consciousness, just as Hegel attempted to explain the development of *Geist*. Moreover, since Habermas stands in the tradition of critical theory which runs from Marx through the Hegelian-Marxism of the Frankfurt School, Hegel has undeniably been a significant influence on his thought.

Progress, however, is not entailed solely by an advance to a higher learning level. Advancement to an evolutionarily higher level is also characterized by a cumulative and continuous production of cognitive-technical knowledge and moral-practical insight (see for example TCA I, 239). For Habermas, then, there are two necessary conditions of social change that is characterized as progressive: first, a developmentally significant structural change (advancement to a higher learning level) must occur, and second, the accumulation of content (the accumulation of empirical knowledge or of moral-practical insight) must be continuous between the levels of development. This sense of progress, however, should not be understood in a pre-Kuhnian sense of a continuous and linear accumulation of knowledge. Habermas conceives of development processes in both the cognitive-technical and moral-practical dimensions as continuous only insofar as these processes can be understood as learning processes. If Habermas's thesis is correct, and there are reconstructable developmental logics in these two dimensions, then progress (understood in terms of development) possesses this moment of continuity. Yet the moment of continuity should not be overemphasized. Evolutionary changes between levels of learning can also be characterized as radically discontinuous in the sense that they involve radical transformations of structures of consciousness. The Enlightenment ushered in just such a radical transformation in our very conceptions of science, morality, and the law (among others). Habermas's theory of social evolution understands this transition to modern forms of consciousness as a learning process that occurred in both the cognitive-technical and moral-practical dimensions.

Moreover, the accumulation of content should not be understood only in the sense of the addition of new content to old. The addition of new content is indeed part of what accumulation means here, since the advancement to a higher learning level does increase structural capacity for accumulating new content in this sense. But accumulation also means that at a higher learning level the old content is reinterpreted according to the new structure such that the content is better understood. The transition from the scholastic understanding of the natural world to modern empirical science resulted not only in a revision of how we understand facts about the world, but it also greatly expanded our capacity to gather more facts that have greater predictive value. The transition from scholasticism to empiricism did not result in a loss of content or understanding about the world; rather, it resulted in a structural reorganization of how we understand the natural world, and this structural reorganization is characterized by its differentiation and generalization of the scholastic worldview.

Now a critic might object that Habermas's characterization of rationalization as progressive exhibits the Eurocentric bias of the whole project. The celebration of reason is a notable feature of Western, especially European, thought since the Enlightenment (or even since the first philosophical systems of ancient Greece). The Eurocentric objection has been further sharpened and hardened by poststructuralist thinkers such as Derrida, who now refer to the logocentrism of such thinking. The valorization of reason, they argue, is misguided at best and disastrous at worst, since reason epitomizes and perpetuates domination and oppression. The dichotomies and hierarchies entailed by rational thought embody precisely the unnecessary forms of domination that reason claims to be eradicating.

These poststructuralist arguments are powerful, and certainly have had a sobering effect upon all of philosophy. Nevertheless, as Habermas has argued at length (see PDM), their complete rejection of reason and rationality is unwarranted and self-contradictory. According to Habermas's notion of communicative rationality, in which in every speech act validity claims are raised that require a yes or no response, the poststructuralists cannot both completely reject all conceptions of reason and give arguments defending this rejection without becoming enmeshed in a "performative contradiction." It is not my intention to enter into this debate here, but only to show that the charge of Eurocentrism or logocentrism needs to be deepened in order to provide any bite.

Nor can one simply object that Habermas's theory of social evolution is Eurocentric because it has a superficial appearance of Eurocentrism without further justifying the charge. Habermas has performed the (initial, at least) formal-pragmatic analysis of practices of communication and has identified certain structural presuppositions of these practices. Given our practices of language use, he claims, we cannot avoid raising exactly the three validity claims of truth, rightness, and sincerity in each and every speech act. The raising of validity claims in speech acts requires a response, which can take the simple form of either a yes or a no. Accordingly, Habermas develops a procedural conception of communicative rationality that rests fundamentally on a process of argumentation in which the reasons given in support of a validity claim are intersubjectively evaluated. This notion of rationality is derived from an analysis of our everyday practices of communicative action. This analysis identifies the unavoidable conditions of these practices; the unavoidable presuppositions we must make in order to engage in communication processes. Any grammatically differentiated language is determined by such presuppositions. Indeed, (communicative) rationality is an integral part of the very possibility of social existence constituted in language. The point is that Habermas's conception of communicative rationality, which is presupposed by his theory of social evolution, is grounded in an analysis of the very communicative practices that constitute society. In order to substantiate the objection of Eurocentrism, the critic would need to show specifically where Habermas's analysis goes wrong, or where there lies a specific Eurocentric bias in his analysis. The burden of proof rests not on Habermas to demonstrate empirically that every known linguistic form of communication is susceptible to such an analysis; rather, it rests on the critic, who must cite specific counterexamples in which the unavoidable presuppositions identified by Habermas are indeed not made. Until such an argument is made in detail, the charge of Eurocentrism (in the sense of logocentrism) cannot be taken seriously.

There is another meaning of the charge of Eurocentrism that does not involve a critique of reason as such, but rather involves the claim that the particular understanding of reason (in this case, Habermas's) has oppressive consequences. For example, the argument is made that the Enlightenment conception of reason justified in the minds of Europeans their colonial exploitation of non-European societies and cultures. The question is, does this sense of the charge of Eurocentrism apply to Habermas? This is certainly a more significant critique than the sense of Eurocentrism considered above, and it deserves a more careful consideration than can be given here. There is little doubt that what we take to be rational in a given sociohistorical context often involves oppressive consequences. This is implied by the historical character of reason. For if our conception of reason is historically variable, then it follows that there is no true conception (even ideally) to which we might appeal. The best we can do, being historical beings in this sense, is to continually reflect upon the possible oppressive consequence of our current conception in order to replace that conception with a better one. If Habermas is correct, and the history of reason follows a developmental logic, then we have a basis for claiming that our current conceptions are better than preceding ones. This does not entail that the current conception is the best one possible, only that it is better than the others. The model of progress that is implied by Habermas's conception of reason does not specify that history as such is progressive, only that there is a dialectic of progress—meaning that there are both progressive and regressive moments. Thus, he interprets existent sociohistorical structures to be incomplete and deformed forms of underlying possibilities. To be sure, Habermas does draw upon certain Enlightenment ideals in constructing his conception of reason, but this does not in itself undermine his arguments. For not all moments of modern reason are oppressive. The modern conception of reason grounds the universality that is a key element of a critical perspective. The question that needs to be considered further is, does Habermas leave out of his conception of reason all of the oppressive moments of modern reason, or are some smuggled in surreptitiously?

The Dialectic of Progress

A related objection, which derives from the Eurocentric one, is that Habermas's theory of social evolution, and the conception of progress it entails, are nothing more than a Hegelian, "triumphalist" reading of history in which the course of history is interpreted as a continuous progressive development culminating in Western structures of consciousness. In proposing that we analyze social evolution in terms of a developmental logic, Habermas must be careful to anticipate such misinterpretations that understand him as proposing a triumphalist theory of social evolution in which the West is seen as the pinnacle of historical development. Vulgar theories of social evolution typically imply such linear conceptions of progress in which the development of humankind is interpreted to be a smooth, continuous realization of reason, such that the present social conditions represent the highest degree of development.

A superficial reading of Habermas's theory of social evolution might encourage one to conclude that his theory implies such a linear conception of progress. Given such a reading, the theory would be understood to imply the claim that the evolution of humanity is constituted by the expansion of power over nature, and by the growth of insight into moral social relations. As we evolve, we expand our learning capacities, and this allows us to accumulate in a continuous manner cognitive-technical knowledge and moral-practical insight, and this ever increasing accumulation of knowledge and insight reflects a rationalization process that increases our freedom. A careful reading of Habermas's theory of social evolution, however, does not allow such an interpretation, for Habermas explicitly recognizes the dialectical nature of progress: "When we assume learning processes not only in the dimension of technically useful knowledge but also in that of moral-practical consciousness, we are maintaining [the existence of] developmental stages both for productive forces and for the forms of social integration. But the extent of exploitation and repression by no means stands in inverse proportion to these levels of development" (CES, 163). The paradox of development that Habermas is concerned with here is manifested in both objective and subjective forms. Objectively, while undeniable advances in cognitive-technical knowledge and moral-practical insight have indeed been made, these rationalization processes have often produced horrifying consequences. Subjectively, especially with respect to the transition from traditional forms of life to modern ones, members of modern societies have had ambivalent reactions to this progress. On the one hand, technological progress has expanded the capacity to satisfy material needs, but on the other, this same technological progress has resulted in a significant increase in the domination of one over another, as well as a sense of dislocation, isolation, fragmentation, and alienation.

After pointing out the apparent paradox of evolution, Habermas asks, "How is this *dialectic* of progress to be explained?" (CES, 163). The emphasis on "dialectic" here provides the clue: progressive developments can be understood as constituted by a dialectic of structures of consciousness and the problems specific to those structures. Although development to a new learning level generates an expanded capacity to solve certain problems, new problems appear at this higher level of development. A given level of development generates its own problems that lead to crises, which are contingently overcome when a new learning level is achieved. At the new learning level, however, new problems that are unique to that level are generated, and the dialectical process continues. The ambivalent nature of development is explained, according to Habermas, by the fact that the problems that appear at the new level of development can increase in intensity: "A higher stage of development of productive forces and of social integration does bring relief from problems of the superseded social formation. But the problems that arise at the new stage of development can—insofar as they are at all comparable with the old ones—increase in intensity. This seems to be the case, at least intuitively, with the burdens that arise in the transition to societies organized through a state" (CES, 163–164).

But, what does Habermas mean by the claim that the new problems "increase in intensity"? This is not simple to determine. A plausible reading would be to understand the increase in intensity as an increase in psychological pressure felt by the individual members of the society, in the sense of an increase in the subjectively felt impact of problems, and this only makes sense from a first-person point of view. It would be tautological, however, to maintain that we subjectively experience the current set of given problems more intensely than the problems associated with the previous learning level (which has since been overcome). Surely the set of problems currently being experienced will feel more intense than previously overcome problems, if only for the reason that the present ones are more immediate and thus more pressing. So it seems that Habermas has a different understanding of the claim that the new problems increase in intensity. He asserts that "the exploitation and oppression *necessarily* practiced in political class societies has to be considered retrogressive in comparison with the less significant social inequalities *permitted* by the kinship system" (CES, 163). Perhaps he means, then, that at least with respect to the criteria of exploitation and oppression, an increase in intensity is associated with the pervasiveness of the problems faced by a given social formation. Whereas societies based on both the kinship system and political class systems fail to adequately legitimize political rule, this is a deeper problem for political class societies because their very principles generate the demand for political legitimization: "[C]lass societies are structurally unable to satisfy the need for legitimation that they themselves generate" (CES, 163). Another possible interpretation would be that at each higher learning level the problems faced by the society in question become more difficult to solve. Given the plausibility of these various interpretations, what Habermas means by an increase in intensity remains somewhat ambiguous and is in need of further clarification.

Nonetheless, the specific criteria according to which we gauge increases in intensity are determined by the given learning level. According to Habermas, the concepts of exploitation and oppression, by which we currently measure progress, are not necessarily adequate criteria of progress at other learning levels. We cannot simply apply the standards of exploitation and oppression to societies that have attained different levels of learning, since those societies, by virtue of their structurally different learning levels, would face different sets of probems:

> [T]he perspective from which we make this comparison [between a given stage of development and the previous one] is distorted so long as we do not also take into account the specific burdens of prestate societies; societies organized along kinship lines have to come off better if we examine them in the light of the kinds of problems first typical of class societies. The socialist battle-concepts of exploitation and oppression do not adequately discriminate among evolutionarily different problem situations. In [certain] heretical traditions one can indeed find suggestions for differentiating not only the concept of progress but that of exploitation. It is possible to differentiate according to bodily harm (hunger, exhaustion, illness), personal injury (degradation, servitude, fear), and finally spiritual desperation (loneliness, emptiness)—to which in turn there correspond various hopes—for well-being and security, freedom and dignity, happiness and fulfillment (CES, 164).

Habermas maintains here that the different problem situations that arise from the given levels of learning, that is, different historical contexts, necessitate different criteria according to which the increase in intensity is measured. So while the elimination of exploitation and oppression is an appropriate criterion of progress in advanced capitalist societies according to Habermas, this criterion would be inadequate for an analysis of the social pathologies of, say, feudal societies. The cognitive-technical level of development of feudal societies was lower than in modern, industrialized societies; thus they faced, unlike in modern, industrial societies, pressing technical problems of satisfying basic material needs. To be sure, this does not mean that hunger and disease have been eradicated from the modern world; while moderns have the technical means to eradicate hunger and improve health, these problems have been shifted to the dimension of social relations as socio-political problems of justice. Given the three dimensions of progress—material well-being and security, freedom and dignity, and happiness and fulfillment—the socio-structural properties of any concrete historical context will determine which of these dimensions of progress is the historically adequate criterion.

The problem with Habermas's claim is that it implies that since only one criterion of progress is most relevant to a given situation, in any given historical context two of the three dimensions of progress will be either adequately satisfied or not yet germane, and thus that social critique should utilize only one of the three criteria. For example, Habermas seems to suggest that in advanced capitalist societies the technical capabilities to satisfy material needs and security exist, so sociocritical analyses of these societies need not be concerned with the lack of progress in this dimension; and in advanced capitalist societies progress in the dimension of happiness and fulfillment is not yet germane since exploitation and oppression, which block the achievement of freedom and dignity, remain the overriding burden of these societies. While the structural properties of different historical contexts bring to the fore one or another dimension of progress, the other dimensions do not then become of no interest to the progressive social critic. Indeed, conditions of exploitation and oppression are often intermingled with identity crises and loss of meaning. The social critic needs to remain vigilant for the need for emancipation in each of these dimensions. To be sure, Habermas would likely reply that in any given historical situation all dimensions of progress should be given consideration, but that the specific problem situation demands that one dimension override the others. In contrast, I want to suggest that a sociocritical analysis of any historical context should not suppress any of the dimensions of progress, and that each of the three dimensions of material well-being and security, freedom and dignity, and happiness and fulfillment need to be accorded critical attention. Which of these sociocritical criteria is most relevant for a given sociohistorical context remains an open question. Moreover, the specific meaning of each of these criteria is sociohistorically variable. Nevertheless, in any given context, all three criteria are relevant to some extent. Thus, distinguishing between progressive changes in each of these dimensions would allow a more subtle analysis of the progressive character of social change in general. While progress might be made in one dimension, regressions might occur in another dimension, thus making an apparently progressive trend, at the least, appear highly ambivalent. There is little doubt that there is an ambivalence of development in general, but this ambivalence is problematic only so long as an undifferentiated conception of progress is being used. This ambivalence can be better explained by a differentiated conception of progress that accounts for the different types of progressive change that constitute social evolution. For example, in the era of industrial capitalism, capabilities in the dimension of material well-being and security were greatly increased; however, change in the dimension of freedom and dignity was ostensibly regressive, as witnessed by the increase in exploitation and oppression. At that time, rampant exploitation and oppression were the most pressing problems. With the arrival of advanced, post-industrial capitalism, exploitation and oppression remain problematic—although they have been suppressed by consumerism, and now they are coupled to problems of identity, which are increasing in importance as various mechanisms serve to repress the negative effects of the market. A differentiated conception of progress, then, would seem to account more adequately for the dialectical nature of social change.

A Differentiated Conception of Progress

In an earlier essay, in which he comes to terms with the mysticism of Walter Benjamin, Habermas explores the idea of a differentiated conception of progress and the implications that such a concept has for critical social theory (WB, 129–163).[5] While he rejects Benjamin's conception of progress, Habermas does recognize the insights it provides. In the final section of that essay Habermas asserts, "Benjamin was one of the first to emphasize a further moment in the concepts of exploitation and progress: besides hunger and repression, failure; besides prosperity and liberty, happiness" (WB, 156). But while Benjamin recognized the need to distinguish the moments of prosperity, liberty, and happiness in the conception of progress, he considered only happiness to be an adequate criterion of real progress. Accordingly, Benjamin can plausibly argue (according to Habermas) "that prosperity without liberty is not prosperity and that liberty without happiness is not liberty" (WB, 157). Given this hierarchy of the moments of prosperity, liberty and happiness, in which real liberty presupposes prosperity, and real happiness presupposes liberty (and prosperity), Benjamin argues that we can speak of real progress only when there is progress in the dimension of happiness: "Before Benjamin's Manichean gaze, progress can be perceived only at the solar prominences of happiness. . . ." (WB, 157).

Habermas worries, however, that by demanding that real progress be measured only according to the criterion of happiness, Benjamin's proposal will undermine political action: "In the melancholy of remembering what has been missed and in conjuring up moments of happiness that are in the process of being extinguished, the historical sense for secular progress is in danger of atrophy. No doubt these advances generate their regressions, but this is where political action starts" (WB, 157). In the progressive demand for an increase of meaningful fulfillment Benjamin bypasses other criteria of progress, that, while they are not meaning-generating changes, nevertheless increase prosperity and self-determination. The criteria of prosperity and liberty possess their own value for determining progress; increased prosperity and liberty "create no new memories, but they dissolve old and dangerous ones" (WB, 157). In other words, while the improvement of the material conditions of life and of the conditions of self-determination are certainly valuable objectives to pursue, material well-being and autonomy cannot themselves inject life with meaningfulness. But the development of new structures of consciousness in the dimensions of cognitive-technical knowledge and moral-practical insight can allow us to overcome inadequate worldviews that had appeared to bring meaning to life. Nevertheless, Habermas maintains that we should not forego pursuing material well-being and autonomy by measuring social change only by the criteria of happiness and fulfillment, as Benjamin suggests. For if we do, we will shunt aside much needed political action in the service of emancipation from domination. By focusing our political efforts on only change that brings happiness and fulfillment we effectively ignore the exploitation and oppression that obtain in the meantime. Thus, Habermas argues that we ought not determine progress only by the criterion of happiness to the exclusion of the criteria of prosperity and liberty.

Despite these doubts regarding Benjamin's particular conception of progress, Habermas applauds Benjamin's insight that emancipation without fulfillment might be empty. The significant doubt raised by Benjamin is this:

> Can we preclude the possibility of a meaningless emancipation? In complex societies, emancipation means the participatory transformation of administrative decision structures. Is it possible that one day an emancipated human race could encounter itself within an expanded space of discursive formation of will and yet be robbed of the light in which it is capable of interpreting its life as something good? The revenge of a culture exploited over millennia for the legitimation of domination would then take this form: Right at the moment of overcoming age-old repressions, it would harbor no violence but it would have no content either. Without the influx of those semantic energies with which Benjamin's rescuing criticism was concerned, the structures of practical discourse—finally well established—would necessarily become desolate. (WB, 158)

Thus Habermas acknowledges the insight contained in Benjamin's critique of those overconfident notions of progress that are concerned primarily with emancipation. According to Habermas, an adequate conception of progress needs to account for meaninglessness as well as repression and poverty, but without overemphasizing the concern for happiness at the cost of concrete, emancipatory political action with respect to exploitation and oppression. To be sure, improving the conditions of self-determination brings with it a greater degree of happiness and fulfillment, but it does not, in itself, bring about sufficient conditions of happiness and fulfillment. Habermas acknowledges here that while we should focus our political efforts on the elimination of all unnecessary domination, we should also not eschew striving to bring about the conditions necessary to lead happy and fulfilled lives.

Habermas concludes that despite the possibility of achieving a meaningless freedom, understanding progress only as the achievement of happiness and fulfillment would be an undesirable form of utopianism since it would drain energies from political action seeking emancipation from exploitation and oppression. Only a conception of progress that is differentiated along the dimensions of material prosperity (well-being), freedom (self-determination), and happiness (self-realization), such that progress can be determined independently in each dimension according to the given sociohistorical conditions, will be adequate. A conception of progress that is adequate will retain a sufficiently well-grounded utopian moment to provide hope, it will be subtle enough to determine real progress (and not an empty, desolate progress in which we are autonomous and self-determining, but not happy), and it will at the least not obstruct concrete political action. Moreover, Habermas asserts that a differentiated and balanced conception of progress will not impede political action, but enhance it: "I, of course, think that a differentiated concept of progress opens a perspective that does not simply obstruct courage but can make political action more sure of hitting its mark, for under historical circumstances that prohibit the thought of revolution and give one reason to expect revolutionary processes of long duration, the idea of the revolution as the process of forming a new subjectivity must also be transformed" (WB, 158–159). Thus, in modern, complex societies we need a more differentiated conception of progress in order to refine the effectiveness of our political action in the name of emancipation from domination in all its forms.

While Habermas's endorsement in the Benjamin essay of a differentiated, dialectical conception of progress is a promising suggestion, his later work on the theory of communicative action does not always fulfill the intentions here expressed. The suspicion Habermas acknowledges in the Benjamin essay, that "an emancipation without happiness and lacking in fulfillment might not be just as possible as relative prosperity without the elimination of repression," becomes marginalized in his later work in an effort to theorize the possibility of the rational grounding of modern moral and legal norms (WB, 156). The claim that Habermas has marginalized the moments of happiness and fulfillment in emancipation is further supported by his theoretical treatment of the different cultural "value-spheres" of modern forms of understanding. Associated with each of the cultural value spheres of science, law, and art are specialized forms of discourse. The theory of communicative action understands each of these specialized forms of discourse as thematizing one of the three validity claims contained in speech acts. Thus, scientific discourse thematizes the validity claim to the truth of our statements about the objective world. Moral and legal discourses thematize the validity claim to the normative rightness of our statements about the social world. And aesthetic discourses, exemplified by art criticism, thematize the validity claim to the truthfulness of our statements about subjectively accessible phenomena. Furthermore, each type of specialized discourse indexed to a specific validity claim forms a complex of rationalization. A cumulative production of knowledge, that is, rationalization, is associated with the rationalization complexes of cognitive-technical rationality, moral-practical rationality, and aesthetic-practical rationality.

We have discussed above Habermas's extensive analyses of both cognitive-technical and moral-practical complexes of rationality, but Habermas's analysis is curiously thin with respect to the third, aesthetic-practical rationality complex. At this point one might notice a certain symmetry between Habermas's earlier acknowledgment of the virtues of a dialectical theory of progress in which progress can be determined in each of the three dimensions of material well-being, autonomy, and happiness and fulfillment, and the three complexes of cognitive-technical, moral-practical, and aesthetic-practical rationality. The question arises: Is the complex of aesthetic-practical rationality the key to understanding a conception of progress in the dimension of happiness and fulfillment? Exploring this question requires a careful treatment that I cannot provide here. However, I would suggest that there is a link between the notion of aesthetic reason or aesthetic truth and happiness and fulfillment, and that an analysis of the creative/expressive dimension of action and speech would help to clarify this relation.

Summary and Conclusions

The two primary aims of this work have been to argue for the claims that (1) some conception of progress is presupposed by the very practice of social critique; and (2) Habermas's theory of social evolution entails an adequate (for the purposes of critical social theory) conception of progress. Let me briefly summarize the main lines of argument.

I began this study by arguing that the concept of critical social theory originally formulated by Horkheimer entails a conception of progressive social change. I further argued that the practice of social critique presupposes that the critic operate with some conception of progress. Thus, if social critics in general and critical theorists in particular want to perform social critique, they cannot avoid reference (either implicit or explicit) to some conception of progress. That is, in order to critique existing sociohistorical conditions, we need to be capable of specifying what would count as a progressive change, and a nondogmatic critic will attempt to be explicit about the notion of progress she relies upon. And we saw that Habermas's unique conception of critical social theory, centrally incorporating a theory of social evolution, does explicitly give an account of progressive social change.

Habermas's theory of social evolution explains progress in terms of a bidimensional rationalization process. On the one hand, societies develop in terms of cognitive-technical knowledge, and on the other hand, they develop in terms of moral-practical knowledge. The introduction of a concept of communicative rationality (based, in turn, on a concept of communicative action) allows Habermas to conceive of rationalization in terms of both knowledge about the objective world, and insight into social relations. Significantly, developments in each dimension are logically independent of the other; in Marxist terms, the superstructure possesses its own history, that is not a functional response to changes in the base. These rationalization processes are interpreted as learning processes, in which we achieve increasingly decentered and open perspectives. This conception of learning is grounded on a concept of developmental logic, which is distinguished from the contingent content of determinate historical processes, where a developmental logic denotes an invariant, hierarchically ordered sequence of stages, and refers only to the formal or structural properties of development, and not to the content.

Based on these analyses of Habermas's theory of social evolution and the concept of developmental logic I then examined the question of whether Habermas's conception of progress—differentiated as it is between the dimensions of cognitive-technical and moral-practical—is a conceptually adequate one. I argue that in general it is adequate for the purposes of a critical social theory, because it is well grounded in the theory of communicative action, and it is sufficiently rigorous for the purposes of social critique. Of course, the theory of communicative action itself is far from uncontroversial, and Habermas's theory of social evolution rests squarely on this theory. So if that theory is ultimately refuted, then the theory of social evolution would be radically undermined as well. With respect to social critique, it adequately identifies and explains the structural preconditions that are necessary for progress. It cannot and does not determine the contingent empirical conditions necessary for progressive social change, for these conditions can only be specified by reference to the given sociohistorical phenomena of determinate societies. In other words, Habermas's theory of social evolution explains only the progressive development of the structures of consciousness that determine the potentials for rationalization in concrete sociohistorical contexts; it does not pretend to narrate a story about the progress of some "universal history." For example, Habermas's theory postulates a developmental logic of cognitive-technical knowledge which entails that we moderns have a greater understanding of natural processes than did premoderns. His theory does not claim, however, that this knowledge has been successfully or appropriately utilized. While we know how to control nature better than our predecessors, this does not imply that we have applied that knowledge in a wise manner—indeed, as various ecological critiques demonstrate, we have not. This does not invalidate the claim, which Habermas's theory does make, that our knowledge in the cognitive-technical domain has expanded. Such is also the case concerning matters of autonomy and freedom. The horizon of our moral-practical consciousness has shifted with the emergence of modernity such that we now understand autonomy and freedom in universal terms; this does not mean that the potential of this shifted consciousness has been utilized. The distortions of this potential are readily apparent in the many injustices of the colonialist expansion of Europe that has accompanied its entrance onto the modern stage. Nonetheless, distorted historical developments do not undermine the concept of progress; on the contrary, they call for its application in a critique of such distortions.

Habermas's conception of progress is especially well suited to ground such a critique of social pathologies. For by distinguishing between the universal structure of development and the contingent and unfathomably complex historical process, Habermas's theory of social evolution provides a standard by which distortions of development, manifested as social pathologies, can be identified and critiqued. Without such a standard, it is difficult to ground sufficiently and in a generally convincing manner critiques of injustice, domination, or alienation.

While Habermas's conception of progress is adequate in general respects, it was found lacking in certain particulars. Specifically, his "differentiated" conception of progress is insufficiently differentiated. Habermas's conception is differentiated into progress in the dimensions of material well-being and self-determination (autonomy), but it lacks an account of progress in terms of happiness and fulfillment.

My critique and proposals are presented with a collaborative intent. Habermas's explicit understanding of both his critical theory and the theory of social evolution is that both are research programs; that is, they are open-ended attempts to clarify concepts and theses. Since they are research programs, it is expected that they would be revised and refined in the course of social scientific inquiry. The theory's validity rests on its fruitfulness for such a program, and its validity cannot be fully evaluated until such a research program has been engaged in. I hope this study has contributed to the furtherance of such a program.

Notes

Notes to Introduction

1. Karl Marx, "Theses on Feuerbach," in Karl Marx and Frederick Engels, *The German Ideology: Part I, With Selections from Parts II and III, and Supplementary Texts*, ed. and intro. C. J. Arthur (New York: International Publishers, 1970), 123.

2. G. W. F. Hegel, *Elements of the Philosophy of Right*, ed. Allen W. Wood, trans. H. B. Nisbet (Cambridge: Cambridge University Press, 1991), §§105–107, 121–123.

3. It is argued that Habermas has become increasingly enchanted with liberal universalism and thus moved away from his critical theoretical roots. There is some justification for this argument, but for my purposes here, we can focus on his work insofar as it represents an attempt to formulate a critical theory of society. In particular, I will focus largely upon his work culminating in *The Theory of Communicative Action*.

Notes to Chapter 1

1. Max Horkheimer, "Traditional and Critical Theory," in *Critical Theory: Selected Essays*, trans. Matthew J. O'Connell et al. (New York: Continuum, 1972).

2. See Martin Jay, *The Dialectical Imagination: A History of the Frankfurt School and the Institute of Social Research 1923–1950* (Boston: Little, Brown and Company, 1973), and Rolf Wiggershaus, *The Frankfurt School: Its History, Theories, and Political Significance*, trans. Michael Robertson (Cambridge, Mass.: MIT Press, 1994).

3. The arrangement between the *Institut* and the university was unusual in that the *Institut* was financially and scientifically independent of the university, but the *Institut's* faculty taught seminars for the university, and graduate students did research for and obtained fellowships and scholarships from the *Institut*. Furthermore, the building that housed the *Institut* was financed by Weil, but was located on university grounds.

4. Wiggershaus, 2–3; Jay, *Dialectical Imagination*, xv.

5. John Rawls, *A Theory of Justice* (Cambridge, Mass.: Harvard University Press, 1971), 5–6.

6. Jay, *Dialectical Imagination*, 41.

7. Ibid., 42.

8. Max Horkheimer, "The Present Situation of Social Philosophy and the Tasks of an Institute for Social Research," in *Between Philosophy and Social Science: Selected Early Writings*, trans. John Torpey (Cambridge, Mass.: MIT Press, 1993), 1–14.

9. Wiggershaus, 2.

10. Horkheimer, "Present Situation," 7–8.

11. Ibid., 8–9.
12. Ibid., 9–10.
13. Horkheimer, "Traditional and Critical Theory," 188–243.
14. Ibid., 188.
15. Ibid., 191.
16. Ibid., 191.
17. Ibid., 191.
18. Ibid., 195.
19. Ibid., 196.
20. Ibid., 197.
21. Ibid., 198–199.
22. Ibid., 200.
23. See also David Couzens Hoy and Thomas McCarthy, *Critical Theory* (Oxford: Blackwell, 1994), 16.
24. Jürgen Habermas, *Knowledge and Human Interests* (Boston: Beacon Press, 1971).
25. Max Horkheimer, "A New Concept of Ideology?" in *Between Philosophy and Social Science: Selected Early Writings*, trans. John Torpey (Cambridge, Mass.: MIT Press, 1993), 129.
26. Hoy and McCarthy, 17.
27. Marcuse is an obvious counter-example. He represented, especially after World War II, the utopian end of the Frankfurt School. Nevertheless, the idea of critical theory does not require the specification of a utopia in detail.
28. Horkheimer, "Traditional and Critical Theory," 210–211.
29. David Ingram, *Critical Theory and Philosophy* (New York: Paragon, 1990), ixx–xxvi.
30. Particular conceptions of critical social theory do not always acknowledge that their normative orientation requires justification. For example, the post–World War II critical theories of both Horkheimer and Adorno relied on the notion of immanent critique because they believed that substantive norms of action did not admit of rational justification. It can be argued, however, that even immanent critique, in the sense of comparing the ideals to their concrete embodiments without attempting to justify the ideals themselves, presupposes some normative orientation, and that orientation itself requires justification.
31. Albrecht Wellmer, "Practical Philosophy and the Theory of Society: On the Normative Foundations of a Critical Social Science," in *The Communicative Ethics Controversy*, ed. Seyla Benhabib and Fred Dallmayr (Cambridge, Mass.: MIT Press, 1990), 293.
32. Stephen Toulmin, Richard Rieke, and Allan Janik, *An Introduction to Reasoning* (New York: Macmillan, 1979). There is the *claim* that is asserted and in need of justification, for example, "Jim treats Betty unfairly and inconsiderately." The claim is based on certain facts of the situation, the *grounds*, for example, "Jim habitually leaves Betty at home baby-sitting while he goes drinking with his buddies, and he never even bothers to ask her if that is OK." The inference from the grounds to the conclusion (the claim) is based on a *warrant*, for example, "These days, a husband has no business leaving his wife to spend all her evenings tied to the house, while he goes out without her." And finally, the warrant itself is inferred from the *backing*, for example, "Given the present-day understanding of what the demands of equity in human relations require." (This analysis of the basic elements of argumentation simplifies somewhat the analysis of Toulmin, Rieke, and Janik, 88).
33. Toulmin, Rieke, and Janik, *Reasoning*, 88.

34. Don Herzog, *Without Foundations: Justification in Political Theory* (Ithaca: Cornell University Press, 1985), 15–28, 218–243.

35. Ibid., 20.

36. Assuming, of course, the validity of Toulmin, Ricke, and Janik's analysis of rational argumentation.

37. Stephen K. White, "The Normative Basis of Critical Theory," *Polity* (fall 1983): 151.

38. Kenneth Baynes, *The Normative Grounds of Social Criticism: Kant, Rawls, and Habermas* (Albany: State University of New York Press, 1992).

39. Part of what this means is that the historical process has become disenchanted. That is, in modernity, the belief that there is a creator who determines human history has become untenable. Beliefs of this sort are untenable because with the advent of the Enlightenment, humans came to rely upon the giving and the redeeming of reasons for their justifications. This process of rational argumentation presupposes that the grounds appealed to are intersubjectively acceptable. The result is that revelation is no longer considered to be rationally justifiable in this way. And since there is a lack of empirical evidence for the existence of some creator who determines human history, religious worldviews have difficulty meeting modern criteria of rational justification. Therefore, we have come to look elsewhere for the source (or sources) of the dynamic force underlying history.

40. To be sure, this claim does not entail a radical historicism. It would be compatible with a convergence of our representations and insights towards the truth. But the issue of convergence is not germane to my argument here.

41. I mean "impartial" in the sense of intersubjectively valid.

42. Cf. Hoy and McCarthy, 138.

43. It is significant that in seeking emancipation, critical social theory has a utopian moment but it is not itself utopian. Critical social theory is constrained by the real conditions of existence, and the possibilities for emancipation are likewise constrained. Typically, normative social and political philosophy is utopian in the sense that it tries to determine the ideally just social order. An abyss is then opened up between what is and what ought to be. That is, normative social and political philosophy lacks the capacity for concrete practical guidance.

44. See Hoy and McCarthy, 138.

45. David Couzens Hoy, "Taking History Seriously: Foucault, Gadamer, Habermas," *Union Seminary Quarterly Review* 34, no. 2 (1979): 85–95.

46. Ibid., 95.

47. Hoy and McCarthy, esp. chap. 6.

48. Ibid., 103.

49. Ibid., 202.

50. For example, in Horkheimer's "Traditional and Critical Theory."

51. Hoy and McCarthy, 207.

52. Hoy, "Taking History Seriously, 95.

53. Hoy and McCarthy, 207.

54. Ibid.

55. Ibid.

56. Ibid.

57. Ibid., 202.

Notes to Chapter 2

1. Max Horkheimer and Theodor W. Adorno, *Dialectic of Enlightenment*, trans. John Cumming (New York: Continuum, 1944), xi.

2. Ibid., xiii.

3. Strictly speaking, Habermas discusses the relation of the theory of rationality to sociology considered as a theory of society. His discussion of the special importance of the science of sociology to his project is not relevant to my purposes here, so I have left it out. See TCA I, 1–7.

4. See also MCCA, 134.

5. On this account, a notion such as Aristotle's *theōria* is nothing more than a chimera. Habermas makes the critical-theoretic assumption that all forms of knowledge are imbued with interests, so there is no such thing as passionless, disinterested contemplation of objects or truths.

6. Habermas elaborates further on the tasks and social-theoretical relevance of formal-pragmatics in TCA I, 328–337.

7. Thomas McCarthy, *The Critical Theory of Jürgen Habermas* (Cambridge, Mass.: MIT Press, 1978), 274; Noam Chomsky, *Aspects of the Theory of Syntax* (Cambridge, Mass.: MIT Press, 1965).

8. McCarthy, *Critical Theory of Jürgen Habermas*, 274.

9. This advantage of the speech act analysis will be particularly useful for the grounding of the normative moment of a critical social theory.

10. J. L. Austin, *How to Do Things With Words*, ed. J. O. Urmson and Marina Sbisà, 2nd ed. (Cambridge, Mass.: Harvard University Press, 1962), esp. lectures 8, 9, and 11.

11. Ibid., 94–120.

12. Ibid., 99–100.

13. David Ingram makes the interesting point that while Habermas interprets the illocutionary/perlocutionary distinction as a distinction of action types, Austin understood the distinction as one of action effects (David Ingram, "Nussbaum's 'Habermas on Austin's Perlocutionary Effects,'" paper read at the Central Division Meeting of the American Philosophical Association, 1995, 3).

14. See Jürgen Habermas, "A Reply," in *Communicative Action: Essays on Jürgen Habermas's "The Theory of Communicative Action,"* ed. Axel Honneth and Hans Joas, trans. Jeremy Gaines and Doris L. Jones (Cambridge, Mass.: MIT Press, 1991); and Ingram, "Nussbaum's 'Habermas.'"

15. Habermas, "A Reply," 239–240.

16. The case of the robber's command of "Hands up!" is a manifestly strategic demand, in which the obligation is not supplied by any illocutionary force, but by the threat of sanctions (see Habermas, "A Reply," 239).

17. Habermas considers three prima facie objections to this thesis at TCA I, 310–319.

18. While my intent in this chapter is not to critically examine Habermas's conception of critical social theory but to simply explicate it, I would like to make a brief critical comment. Since the lifeworld is fundamental to Habermas's conception of society, this adoption of the everyday concept of the lifeworld in place of the communication-theoretic conception for its capacity to give an account of narration seems somewhat troubling. It would seem to open the door to less theoretically inclined conceptions of social critique, and especially critiques that place special emphasis on the narrative structure of social relations, as in for example philosophical hermeneutics.

19. For my purposes here I have simplified Habermas's schema. In his schema, each of the three reproduction processes contributes to the maintenance of each of the three structural elements of the lifeworld. So there are nine different ways that the reproduction processes interact with the components of the lifeworld. See TCA II, 140–143.

20. Jürgen Habermas, "Towards a Theory of Communicative Competence," *Inquiry* 13, no. 3 (1970): 370–376; "Wahrheitstheorien," in *Wirklichkeit und Reflexion*, ed. Helmut Fahrenbach (Neske: Pfullingen, 1973).

21. Habermas carefully qualifies his use of Alexy's analysis. First, he thinks that Alexy's characterization of these conditions as "rules" can lead to misunderstandings (MCCA, 91). Second, this use of Alexy's analysis is meant to provide only examples of the type of presuppositions of argumentation we are concerned with, and not as a comprehensive catalog of conditions.

22. There is no contradiction between this rule of argumentative discourse and the assertion that persons can "try out" ideas that they are not committed to. It is important to keep in mind that these are formal-pragmatic rules of discourse, and as such they are operative only in the course of redeeming contested validity claims, and not at the level of everyday speech. In everyday speech, speakers may try out ideas they are not committed to. The implication, however, is that one is sincere in what one says, so in trying out ideas, the utterance is open to being contested on grounds of insincerity. But at the level of discourse, where contested validity claims are assessed argumentatively, certain idealizing presuppositions hold, and one of these is that the reasons given and arguments made are done so sincerely, that is, with the intention of reaching an understanding.

23. Note that the rules 3.1–3.3 do not demand that all competent subjects participate. They only state that any interested party may participate, and that those who so desire must be allowed to participate freely and without coercion. These are idealizing suppositions of everyday speech (as operative at the level of discourse), and as such regulatively include all interested parties in the discourse. These rules do not imply that everyday conversations (not at the level of discourse) are somehow distorted if they are not open to all.

24. For a successful and illuminating study of Habermas's discursive theory of truth, see James Swindal, *Reflection Revisited: Jürgen Habermas's Discursive Theory of Truth* (New York: Fordham University Press, 1999).

25. Jürgen Habermas, *Autonomy and Solidarity: Interviews with Jürgen Habermas*, ed. Peter Dews, rev. and enlarged ed. (London: Verso, 1992), 160–161.

26. Ibid., 171.

27. For the purposes of this study, I will refrain from assessing the adequacy of Habermas's interpretation of either Marx's writings or of orthodox historical materialism. Tom Rockmore has convincingly argued that Habermas does not always adequately distinguish the writings of Marx from the work of his interpreters. See Tom Rockmore, *Habermas on Historical Materialism* (Bloomington: Indiana University Press, 1989). Since in this chapter I am primarily concerned to introduce the theory of social evolution, I will attempt only to distinguish it from a generic reading of Marx's theory. For this, I draw on the discussions in David Ingram, *Habermas and the Dialectic of Reason* (New Haven: Yale University Press, 1987), esp. chap. 8; and McCarthy, *Critical Theory of Jürgen Habermas*, esp. chap. 3.

28. One might ask why we should think that there is one unique distinguishing feature of the human species. One reason is that social and political theorists unavoidably must specify certain norms and ideals, and to avoid privileging the interests of a select individual or group over those of others, these norms and ideals are typically related to a determinate

conception of the person, that is, what it means to be human. While there is no a priori reason to think that there is one feature, or even a set of features, that uniquely distinguishes the human species, searching for some feature (or set of features) is desirable from the perspective of social and political theory.

29. Jürgen Habermas, "Technology and Science as 'Ideology,'" in *Toward a Rational Society: Student Protest, Science, and Politics*, trans. Jeremy J. Shapiro (Boston: Beacon Press, 1970), 91–92; see also McCarthy, *Critical Theory of Jürgen Habermas*, 391, note 33.

30. G. A. Cohen, *Karl Marx's Theory of History: A Defence*, (Princeton: Princeton University Press, 1978), 32; but cf. Charles W. Mills, "Is it Immaterial that there's a 'Material' in 'Historical Materialism,'" *Inquiry* 32 (1989): 323–342.

31. Ingram, *Dialectic of Reason*, 118.

32. CES, 143; Ingram, *Dialectic of Reason*, 119.

33. Social roles are here understood in the sociological sense. While a primate can assume the biological roles of mate and father or mother, he or she cannot adopt the socially defined roles of husband or wife and father or mother, in the sociological sense. The sociological sense of social roles implies a set of normative expectations attached to those roles. These normative expectations should be distinguished from instinctual interests.

34. McCarthy, *Critical Theory of Jürgen Habermas*, 246.

35. Ibid.

36. In his later essay "A Reply," in which he defends the arguments of *The Theory of Communicative Action*, Habermas clarifies the motives for incorporating a systems concept of society into his critical social theory. First, the two theoretical approaches that have dominated the tradition of social theory (action theory and systems theory) result from the dissolution of the philosophy of history and its attempt to conceive of society and history as a totality. Second, Habermas asserts that systems theory uniquely provides a perspective "for outlining certain pathological phenomena of modern society, namely what Marx termed 'real abstractions'" (251). In other words, action theory cannot adequately explain systemic distortions of social relations. Third, while action theory is inadequate to the tasks of critical social theory, systems theory also cannot in itself give an adequate explanation of social phenomena. Specifically, there are certain methodological problems endemic to systems theory, especially with respect to the definitions of boundaries and goal states of social systems. Fourth, Habermas confesses that certain problems in his own attempts to develop an adequate conception of critical social theory persuaded him of the theoretical and methodological value of the systems-theoretic perspective.

37. Habermas, "A Reply," 252.

Notes to Chapter 3

1. Throughout this study I will use "social evolution" in the conventional sense to refer to the evolution of society as a whole. It perhaps would be less ambiguous to label this idea "societal evolution," since it refers to the evolution of human society and not to the evolution of just the social sphere as a subset of society in general. When I am referring to the social sphere (as a subset of society) I make this reference explicit.

2. Habermas served as codirector from 1971 until 1982, after which he returned to the University of Frankfurt.

3. The most relevant of his writings directly concerning this theory are collected in *Zur Rekonstruktion des Historischen Materialismus* (Frankfurt am Main: Suhrkamp Verlag, 1976), much of which has been translated by Thomas McCarthy and collected in *Commu-*

nication and the Evolution of Society (Boston: Beacon Press, 1979). And as I have already indicated, Habermas's more recent work specifically concerning critical social theory, *The Theory of Communicative Action* (1984, 1987), largely presupposes the theory of social evolution. It thus adds little to the theoretical structure, although Habermas develops it into a more concrete and substantive theory of modernity by making connections to Weber's concept of rationalization.

4. See, for example, John B. Thompson and David Held, eds., *Habermas: Critical Debates* (Cambridge, Mass.: MIT Press, 1982); Axel Honneth and Hans Joas, eds., *Communicative Action,* trans. Jeremy Gaines and Doris L. Jones (Cambridge, Mass.: MIT Press, 1991); Peter Dews, ed., *Autonomy and Solidarity: Interviews with Jürgen Habermas*, rev. ed. (London: Verso, 1992).

5. Thompson and Held, 220.

6. Charles A. Beard and Sydney Hook, "Problems of Terminology in Historical Writing," in *Social Science Research Council, Theory and Practice in Historical Study: A Report of the Committee on Historiography* (New York: Social Science Research Council, 1946), 103–130.

7. Ibid., 117. Compare the concepts of change and historical change with Ritter's preference for "process" and "historical process" (Harry Ritter, *Dictionary of Concepts in History* [New York: Greenwood Press, 1986], 330–331). Ritter adopts the *Oxford English Dictionary's* definition of process as "a continuous and regular action or succession of actions, taking place or carried on in a definite manner, and leading to the accomplishment of some result" (Ritter, 331). Accordingly, historical process "does not refer to mere change, but to 'an alteration in human affairs which seems to display direction, pattern, or purpose' " (Ibid., 331, quoted in R. Stephen Humphreys, "The Historian, His Documents, and the Elementary Modes of Historical Thought," *History and Theory* 19 (1980): 3.

8. Beard and Hook, 117.

9. Tom Bottomore, *Sociology: A Guide To Problems and Literature*, 3rd ed. (London: Allen & Unwin, 1987), 265–266.

10. Robert A. Nisbet, *Social Change and History: Aspects of the Western Theory of Development* (London: Oxford University Press, 1969), 161. Marshall Sahlins and Elman Service affirm this view: "Without meaning to minimize the profound biological contributions of [Charles Darwin], we should remember that the evolutionary study of society and culture long antedates him" (Marshall D. Sahlins and Elman R. Service, eds., *Evolution and Culture* [Ann Arbor: University of Michigan Press, 1960], 3–4).

11. As J. B. Bury notes in his classic work on progress, Spencer, although significantly boosted by the publication of *Origin of the Species*, had been "an evolutionist long before Darwin's decisive intervention" (*The Idea of Progress: An Inquiry into its Origin and Growth* [New York: Dover, 1932], 336).

12. Nisbet, 161–162.

13. See for example J. B. Bury: "Evolution itself, it must be remembered, does not necessarily mean, applied to society, the movement of man to a desirable goal. It is a neutral, scientific conception, compatible either with optimism or with pessimism. According to different estimates it may appear to be a cruel sentence or a guarantee of steady amelioration. And it has been actually interpreted in both ways" (335–336).

14. Piet Strydom, however, emphasizes the importance of the concept of development for theories of social evolution: "In the light of debates in both theoretical biology and social theory during the last twenty to thirty years, it has become clear that development,

far from resulting from and hence being secondary to evolution, has a primary and determinative influence on evolution. Development determines what kinds of change are possible and thus fixes what is evolutionarily accessible and what not. Consequently, an adequate understanding of evolution requires that a good deal of attention be paid to development" ("The Ontogenetic Fallacy: The Immanent Critique of Habermas's Developmental Logical Theory of Evolution," *Theory, Culture & Society* 9 [1992]: 65–66).

15. Beard and Hook, 117.

16. Bottomore, 267, quoting from the *Oxford English Dictionary*. Robert Nisbet also understands development on the model of the growth of an organism (Nisbet, 7–11).

17. Moreover, as Bottomore notes, there is another more recent sense in which development refers to economic growth, which is characterized by the expansion and improvement of the forces and relations of production. Development in this sense is also associated by some theorists with the economic aspect of the concept of modernization, where modernization refers to "the process through which a traditional or pretechnological society passes as it is transformed into a society characterized by machine technology, rational and secular attitudes, and highly differentiated social structures" (James O'Connell, "The Concept of Modernization," in *South Atlantic Quarterly* 64 (1965): 549, cited in Ritter, 275). In this sense, nation-states are often characterized as underdeveloped, developing, or developed based upon the relative stage of development of their economies (see also Richard T. Gill, *Economic Development: Past and Present*, 2nd ed. (Englewood Cliffs: Prentice-Hall, 1964). The differences between these senses reflect the conceptual confusion surrounding the notion of development. This sense, which I will refer to as "economic development," we can set aside as a specialized term that is only indirectly related to the general concept of development.

18. Beard and Hook, 117.

19. Nisbet, 163–164.

20. Note that McCarthy characterizes Habermas's theory of social evolution as teleological (*Critical Theory of Jürgen Habermas*, 239). As I have indicated, an account of directional social change need not be teleological if the directionality can be specified according to a criterion immanent to the process of social change but which does not specify a normative goal. On my reading of Habermas, this is what he attempts to achieve with the concept of developmental logic, which specifies a normative criterion of progress, that is, greater reflexivity in learning, without specifying a telos of the developmental process (See chapter 4 for more regarding this issue).

21. Brian J. Whitton, "Universal Pragmatics and the Formation of Western Civilization: A Critique of Habermas's Theory of Human Moral Evolution," *History and Theory* 31 (1992): 299–313.

22. Habermas fully recognizes that this understanding of formal analysis diverges from the standard understanding in the sense of logical analysis (see CES, 8).

23. I also rely on McCarthy's clear discussion of these issues (see *Critical Theory of Jürgen Habermas*, esp. 276–279).

24. McCarthy, *Critical Theory of Jürgen Habermas*, 278.

25. According to Habermas in a more recent essay, there are three characteristics of rational reconstructions that have misled some to understand them as ultimate justifications. These characteristics are the critical substance, the constructive role, and the transcendental justification of theoretical knowledge:

> Insofar as rational reconstructions explicate the conditions for the validity of utterances, they also explain deviant cases, and through this indirect legislative authority they acquire a *critical* function as well. Insofar as they extend the differentiation between individual claims to validity beyond traditional boundaries, they can even establish new analytic standards and thus assume a *constructive* role. And insofar as we succeed in analyzing very general conditions of validity, rational reconstructions can claim to be describing universals and thus to represent a *theoretical* knowledge capable of competing with other such knowledge. At this level, weak *transcendental* arguments make their appearance, arguments aimed at demonstrating that the presuppositions of relevant practices are inescapable, that is, they cannot be cast aside. (MCCA, 31–32)

It is unfortunate that Habermas here describes the type of justification as "weakly transcendental." This is misleading because it implies that the philosopher is able to escape her historical conditions and ascend to a perspective "outside" of the world from which she has a perspective on these universal structures of thought and action. This is not what Habermas has in mind, though. The philosopher engaged in rational reconstructions does not claim to escape her historical conditions in performing formal analysis, in the sense used by Habermas. This is why rational reconstructions are hypothetical claims just like any other sort of knowledge claim. However, through the methods of formal analysis the philosopher identifies those pragmatic structures of thought and action that we cannot escape in our everyday pragmatic attitudes. This does not mean that these structures are immutable; they do change in the course of history. But these structures are constitutive of our intuitive know-how, here and now, so we cannot pragmatically, by mere force of will, step outside of them.

26. Stephen K. White, *The Recent Work of Jürgen Habermas: Reason, Justice and Modernity* (Cambridge: Cambridge University Press, 1988), 5. Thus, Rorty's criticisms of Habermasian epistemology as found in *Knowledge and Human Interests* do not apply here, since they are directed at Habermas's earlier views (see Richard Rorty, *Philosophy and the Mirror of Nature*. [Princeton: Princeton University Press, 1979], 379–389).

27. McCarthy, *Critical Theory of Jürgen Habermas*, 36.

28. Habermas does not first make the labor/interaction distinction in *The Theory of Communicative Action*. Earlier formulations include a discussion of the distinction as found in Hegel's Jena lectures (TP, 142–169); a clarification and use of the distinction to rebut what Habermas takes to be Marcuse's identification of instrumental reason with the domination of both nature and persons (R); and a further development of the distinction, especially with relation to Marx's 1844 Manuscripts (KHI). Since the distinction remains substantially unchanged throughout these essays, and it receives its clearest analytic formulation in *The Theory of Communicative Action*, I will rely primarily upon the distinction as it is found in the latter work.

29. Rockmore, 92.

30. This, of course, is a contentious issue, and entering into this debate here would diverge too far from my primary purpose, so I will not provide here further arguments in support the concept of communicative action. For my purpose of systematically explicating the theory of social evolution I will assume the validity of this fundamental distinction of action types.

31. Although I refer to "structures of consciousness," this should not be understood in an idealistic sense. Structures of consciousness delimit the horizon of possible actions, while our actions determine the structures of consciousness.

32. See, for example, Cohen.

33. Cohen refers to this as the "Development Thesis": "The productive forces tend to develop throughout history" (Ibid., 134).

34. O'Connell, 549.

35. My presentation here does not follow the order of Habermas's presentation in the first volume of *The Theory of Communicative Action.* There, after an introductory chapter, Habermas begins with a systematic reconstruction and critique of Weber's theory of modernity. Essentially he argues that although Weber's understanding of rationalization was largely correct, he (Weber) relied on a too narrowly conceived conception of rationality. Weber did not recognize that a differentiated conception of rationality that included both purposive and communicative rationality would better serve to analyze the process of modernization. Only after the chapter on Weber does Habermas systematically distinguish between purposive and communicative rationality (although the distinction was introduced in the first chapter).

36. Ingram, *Dialectic of Reason,* 51.

37. Ibid., 51–52.

38. See Habermas, "A Reply," 238–250; TCA I, 233–242; "Questions and Counterquestions," in *Habermas and Modernity*, ed. and with an introduction by Richard J. Bernstein, trans. James Bohman (Cambridge, Mass.: MIT Press, 1985), 206–211.

39. There are nine possible formal-pragmatic relations that derive from combining the three attitudes with the three world-concepts. Habermas asserts that of these nine possible relations only six are rationalizable. McCarthy ("Reflections on Rationalization in *The Theory of Communicative Action*," in *Habermas and Modernity*, ed. Bernstein) challenges Habermas's assertion that only these six (natural science, social science, morality, law, eroticism, and art) of the nine possible relations are rationalizable. Habermas responds that he begins with the assumption that when facts, norms, and values are originally experienced as differentiated from each other, they are experienced as elements of their respective worlds, and are accessible only through their respective attitudes (Habermas, "Questions and Counterquestions," 208–209). So, for example, when facts are first experienced as distinct from norms and values, they are experienced as elements of the objective world, and in the objectivating attitude. The implication is that there is an internal relationship between the three attitudes with their respective world concepts. This is not to say that only these six relations are possible, only that they are the only ones to generate legitimate knowledge.

This, however, is a highly controversial claim. See, for example, McCarthy, "Reflections on Rationalization;" Ingram, *Dialectic of Reason*.

40. It should be noted that this essay was written in response to an essay by Niklas Luhmann bearing the same title (for both essays see *Geschichte und Gesellschaft* 2 no. 3 [1976]). While the arguments Habermas makes here have a wider import they are directed specifically against Luhmann's position. Ignoring this context can lead to misinterpretations.

41. My discussion here of social systems and crises generally follows LC, 1–31.

42. In the first part of *Legitimation Crisis*, Habermas relates the socioscientific conception of crisis back to the medical conception of crisis, where it is conceived to represent a deviation from the functional goal of the organism: health (LC, 1–8).

43. Thomas McCarthy, "Complexity and Democracy: or the Seducements of Systems Theory," in *Communicative Action*, ed. Axel Honneth and Hans Joas (Cambridge, Mass.: MIT Press, 1991), 138.

44. McCarthy, *Critical Theory of Jürgen Habermas*, 246.

45. Note that traditional, capitalist, and postcapitalist social formations are all class societies. Also, Habermas classifies state-socialist societies as postcapitalist (see LC, 17).

46. While my interest here is in prima facie problems with the distinction, there is some evidence that the distinction is empirically problematic. Piet Strydom refers to a study written by Günter Frankenberg and Ulrich Rödel in which they attempted to test this theory of social evolution against historical material, in particular, "selected doctrines of British common law and in particular legislation, judgments and political journalism bearing on the development of the freedom of political communication in the USA since the colonial period." Their conclusion was that the model "proved to be an empirical failure . . . in that the material simply did not admit of being ordered according to the chosen viewpoint" (Strydom, "Ontogenetic Fallacy," 77). See Günther Frankenberg and Ulrich Rödel, *Von der Volkssouveränität zum Minderheitenschutz* (Frankfurt: Europäische Verlagsanstalt, 1981).

Notes to Chapter 4

1. See, for example, Michael Schmid, "Habermas's Theory of Social Evolution," in Thompson and Held.
2. See, for example, Baynes.
3. White, "Normative Basis of Critical Theory." Strydom, "Ontogenetic Fallacy."
4. See Ingram, *Dialectic of Reason,* McCarthy, "Reflections on Rationalization"; McCarthy, "Practical Discourse: On the Relation of Morality to Politics," in *Ideals and Illusions* (Cambridge, Mass.: MIT Press, 1991); Axel Honneth and Hans Joas, eds., *Social Action and Human Nature* (Cambridge: Cambridge University Press, 1988).
5. Indeed, he explicitly refers to the earlier theory of social evolution at TCA II, 312–318.
6. In personal conversations with me in late 1995, Professor Habermas confirmed that he remains convinced of the general validity of the theory.
7. It should be noted that the exegesis presented here both of Piaget's developmental psychology in general and the concept of developmental logic in particular are not only glosses of the relevant psychological research, but also selective interpretations of the material with respect to the concept of developmental logic; there is by no means a consensus regarding the proper understanding of the concept of developmental logic.
8. For the following sketch I have relied primarily upon Jean Piaget's *Principles of Genetic Epistemology*, trans. Wolfe Mays (London: Routledge & Kegan Paul, 1972) in which he focuses on the epistemology of his system, and on the invaluable resource of John H. Flavell's *Developmental Psychology of Jean Piaget* (Princeton: Van Nostrand, 1963).
9. Piaget, 14.
10. Ibid., 17.
11. Flavell, *Developmental Psychology of Jean Piaget*, 15.
12. Ibid., 17–19.
13. Ibid., 17.
14. Ibid., 44–52.
15. Ibid., 17.
16. Ibid., 19.
17. Ibid., 20.
18. Ibid.
19. Piaget, 20.
20. Ibid., 21.

21. Ibid.

22. Ibid., 27.

23. Ibid., 30–31.

24. Ibid., 36. When a child possesses the concept of the conservation in his cognitive inventory, he understands that when a liquid is poured from a tall, narrow beaker into a short, wide beaker the same amount of liquid is in the short beaker as was in the tall one. Such a child also understands the conservation of mass.

25. Ibid., 46.

26. Ibid., 26.

27. This literature discusses both horizontal and vertical (or latitudinal and longitudinal) formal aspects of development simply as properties of the stage model. See, for example, Adrien Pinard and Monique Laurendeau, "'Stage' in Piaget's Cognitive-Developmental Theory: Exegesis of a Concept," in *Studies in Cognitive Development*, ed. David Elkind and John H. Flavell (New York: Oxford University Press, 1969).

28. John H. Flavell and Joachim F. Wohlwill, "Formal and Functional Aspects of Cognitive Development," in *Studies in Cognitive Development*, ed. David Elkind and John H. Flavell (New York: Oxford University Press, 1969), 91.

29. Flavell and Wohlwill, 91.

30. Elsewhere, Flavell claims that there are *four* properties that are true of the elements of stages. First, the elements must be describable as forming structures. Second, the elements of a given stage must be recognizable as qualitatively different from the elements of previous stages. Third, each element, once achieved, functions at adult level proficiency. And fourth, all elements of a given stage must be achieved, or appear, simultaneously. (John H. Flavell, "Stage-Related Properties of Cognitive Development,"*Cognitive Psychology* 2 [1971]: 421–453.)

My analysis is not concerned with the last two properties for the following reasons. Flavell himself admits that the last two may be "overdrawn," and I tend to agree. The genetic history of the achievement of any given element of a stage is of less interest for our purposes. It is conceded that any element possesses some time line of development from its first appearance to achievement of adult-level proficiency, but it does not appear that this variable is immediately salient to our formal analysis of developmental logic. Moreover, this would appear to be more of an empirical problem, perhaps of measurement, than a conceptual problem. The fourth property described by Flavell seems particularly overdrawn to me. What this property means is that the elements of a given stage must appear within a relatively short time span in order that the appearance of the achievement of a new, qualitatively different stage might be described. This, however, seems to be covered by the structuration and qualitativeness properties of stages. That is, if stages are seen as elements in a sequentially ordered set of qualitatively different structures, there is no need (at least for our purposes) to further specify the simultaneous appearance of the individual elements. Sufficient synchronicity can be implied by the characterization of the stages as structured and qualitative.

31. Pinard and Laurendeau, 136.

32. Ibid.

33. Ibid., 137.

34. Ibid., 129–136.

35. Note that Piaget has also observed the phenomenon of *vertical décalage,* in which a given concept is progressively restructured at successive levels of development (see Flavell,

Developmental Psychology of Jean Piaget, 21–24; Pinard and Laurendeau, 127–129). This concept will be discussed further below in connection with sequences.

36. Pinard and Laurendeau, 132–133.

37. See Nathan Rotenstreich, "An Analysis of Piaget's Concept of Structure," *Philosophy and Phenomenological Research* 37, no. 3 (1997): 368–380.

38. Ibid., 368.

39. Ibid.

40. Ibid.

41. Flavell and Wohlwill, 77.

42. Ibid.

43. See Flavell, "Stage-Related Properties," 423–424.

44. Flavell and Wohlwill, 76–78.

45. Flavell, "Stage-related Properties," 424.

46. While I have separated stage and sequence in an attempt to gain analytic clarity over the concept of developmental logic, one must remember that the concept of developmental logic characterizes nothing more than a genetic structuralism. In other words, when thinking developmental logic one must think, simultaneously so to speak, both structure and the transformation of that structure. Thus, it is extremely important to understand that Piaget's concept of structuralism is not a concept of a static but of a dynamic (or, more usually, genetic) structuralism. Piaget, of course, is interested in structuralism as a theoretical tool in explaining cognitive development, and so it necessarily must give an account of the change or transformation of structures.

47. Pinard and Laurendeau, 125.

48. Ibid., 127.

49. Ibid.

50. Ibid.

51. Ibid., 127–128.

52. Ibid., 128.

53. Ibid.

54. It is useful to examine Flavell's work on this topic since it explicitly analyzes and develops Piaget's concept of developmental logic.

55. John H. Flavell, "An Analysis of Cognitive-Developmental Sequences," *Genetic Psychology Monographs* 86 (1972): 279–350.

56. Flavell defines a "cognitive item" as "a structure, skill, concept, rule, operation, belief, attitude, bit of knowledge, or any other type of cognitive activity, large or small, that [the developmental psychologist] might define as X_1 or X_2 in analyzing a developmental sequence X_1–X_2" ("Analysis," 281).

57. Flavell, "Analysis," 252.

58. Ibid., 282.

59. Ibid., 282–283.

60. Ibid., 285.

61. Ibid., 286.

62. Ibid.

63. Ibid., 287.

64. Ibid.

65. Flavell notes, however, that pure cases of substitution, where the item replaced is never utilized again, are rare, but there do exist such relatively unequivocal cases ("Analysis,"

291–295). Flavell points to the cognitive differences exhibited between the preoperational and concrete-operational levels of development as good examples of substitution (295–297). For instance, the child's beliefs about dreams in the preoperational period—that they are real, physical manifestations with an external origin, and thus intersubjectively accessible—are replaced in a process of substitution by the belief that dreams are only subjective manifestations, with an internal origin, and thus not intersubjectively accessible. Flavell notes, however, that there is some evidence presented by Kohlberg that this is not such a clear instance of substitution as it at first might appear. There is significant evidence that many adults continue to believe that dreams possess an objective reality (295).

66. Flavell, "Analysis," 297–298.

67. Ibid., 298.

68. Ibid., 299.

69. Ibid., 299–300.

70. Ibid., 300.

71. Ibid., 302.

72. Ibid., 303.

73. Ibid.

74. Ibid., 306.

75. Ibid., 305. Flavell does not go on to clarify the meanings of the concepts of invariance, universality and necessity. Necessity, of course, is a much stronger condition than universality, and it is not clear that sequences of inclusion can or should be characterized as necessary.

76. Flavell, "Analysis," 309.

77. Ibid., 311.

78. Ibid., 312.

79. Ibid., 313.

80. Ibid., 304.

81. Ibid., 315.

82. Ibid.

83. Ibid., 316–317.

84. Flavell and Wohlwill, 91.

85. This ambiguity can be neutralized by interpreting Kohlberg's schema of moral development in the following way. The transitions between levels of moral consciousness, that is, between the preconventional, conventional, and postconventional, are developmental in the sense that they follow a developmental logic. The transitions between stages within levels of moral consciousness are functional and not developmental in the above sense. (Of course, the transition from Stage 2 to Stage 3, which also represents a change of learning level, is a developmental change.) These transitions between stages within learning levels do not involve fundamental transformations of the deep structures of moral consciousness; rather, they can be understood as functional alternatives within the given levels of learning.

86. Pinard and Laurendeau, 128.

87. Flavell, "Analysis," 298.

88. See, for example, Axel Honneth, *The Critique of Power: Reflective Stages in a Critical Social Theory*, trans. Kenneth Baynes (Cambridge, Mass.: MIT Press, 1991), chapters 7, 8, and 9.

89. See CES, 131–138; and Habermas's discussion of G. H. Mead in TCA II, 3–42.

90. McCarthy discusses this same problem in *Ideals and Illusions,* 136–145, esp. 140–142.

91. See Piaget, 20.

92. I would like to thank Christopher Zurn for helpful comments regarding these issues.

93. In summarizing the empirical results of psychoanalytic and cognitive developmental psychology Habermas states, "I should like—very tentatively—to distinguish among (a) the symbiotic, (b) the egocentric, (c) the sociocentric-objectivistic, and (d) the universalistic stages of development" (CES, 100). What is the significance of his emphasis on the tentativeness of the hypothesis? Is this merely an expression of false modesty, or does it indicate that this is a "throw-away" hypothesis? On the one hand, he seems to be acknowledging that he is not an expert in developmental psychology. On the other hand, Habermas is not the sort of thinker to put forward theses carelessly, and he has the reputation of having an exceptional ability to understand and master wide-ranging theoretical traditions. I do not think this was meant to indicate that his thesis is a throw-away thesis, that is, one that he is proposing without much confidence.

94. Note that Habermas is here using "discourse" in his technical sense, referring to the practice of intersubjectively evaluating the validity claims made in speech.

95. It should be noted that the second of these essays, "Moral Consciousness and Communicative Action," was written much later, and with a different purpose in mind. In this essay Habermas is concerned primarily to provide indirect confirmation of his theory of discourse ethics. Nevertheless, his comments here are relevant to the asserted homology between moral consciousness and legal systems.

96. See esp. Lawrence Kohlberg, "Stage and Sequence: The Cognitive-Developmental Approach to Socialization," in *Handbook of Socialization Theory and Research,* ed. David A. Goslin (Chicago: Rand McNally, 1969); "From Is to Ought," in *Cognitive Development and Epistemology,* ed. T. Mischel (New York: 1971); *Essays on Moral Development* (San Francisco: Harper & Row, 1981).

97. Habermas distinguishes various responses actors can adopt with respect to an action conflict. In particular, he distinguishes between action conflicts that are resolved through force or strategic action, and those that are resolved discursively by the achievement of a consensus. The adoption of the latter orientation of resolution by achievement of consensus is what Habermas is referring to when he speaks of moral or legal regulation of action conflicts: "I call those action conflicts 'morally relevant' that are capable of consensual resolution. The moral resolution of conflicts of action excludes the manifest employment of force as well as 'cheap' compromises; it can be understood as a continuation of communicative action—that is action oriented to reaching understanding—with discursive means" (CES, 78).

98. To be sure, there is no equivalent phenomenon that results from the lack of recognition at the societal level comparable to schizophrenia that results from the lack of recognition at the individual level. Nonetheless, it is difficult to conceive how a society might achieve a substantive identity (an 'I') without recognition from other societies. Even xenophobic societies derive part of their substantive identity from the exclusion of the Other.

99. Cf. Charles W. Mills, *The Racial Contract* (Ithaca: Cornell University Press, 1997).

100. In this section, Habermas uses the phrase *Ich-Identität* in two senses. In the first sense, it is used to refer to the identity of the ego in general, that is, is to the identity of the

individual in contrast to that of the group. In the second sense, it refers to the third stage of ontogenesis in which the individuals reflectively constitute their own identity.

101. Habermas comments briefly that in modern societies this ego identity could be 'supported' by vocational roles (in Weber's sense), but that these seem to be "slipping away." While he offers no explanation of this phenomenon, he does say that feminism "is an example of an emancipatory movement that . . . searches for paradigmatic solutions to the problem of stabilizing ego identity under conditions that render problematic—especially for women—recourse to the vocational role as the crystallizing nucleus of life history" (CES, 110).

102. William H. McNeill, *The Rise of the West: A History of the Human Community: with a Retrospective Essay* (Chicago: The University of Chicago Press, 1991).

103. Habermas continues to maintain that the modern form of the nation-state is an inherently unstable solution because of the tension between the universalism of constitutional democracy and the particularism of "nationalism" (see BFN, appendix 2: "Citizenship and National Identity").

104. What Habermas means by "doctrines" and "forms of life" is that previously collective identities were grounded in metaphysical-theistic worldviews. These worldviews were comprehensive and unquestioned. But with the modern turn to a postconventional identity formation, collective identities are now generated reflexively, that is, based on fallibilistic assumptions and with a prospective orientation to who we want to be.

105. Strydom, "Ontogenetic Fallacy."

106. Honneth and Joas, *Social Action and Human Nature*; Klaus Eder, *Die Vergesellschaftung der Natur* (Frankfurt: Surhkamp, 1985).

107. Strydom, "Ontogenetic Fallacy," 66.

108. Ibid., 72.

109. This, of course, is not strictly a fallacy, since a fallacy involves a faulty inference, not arguing from a false premise.

110. Note that this is in addition to the systems-theoretic conception of social change as functional adaptation.

111. This section is adapted from David S. Owen, "Habermas's Developmental Logic Thesis: Universal or Eurocentric?" *Philosophy Today* 41, Supplement (1998): 104–111.

112. To be sure, a full defense of this argument requires more than the logical and conceptual analysis done here, it also requires empirical corroboration. But of course that is beyond the scope of this study and beyond the limits of my own expertise.

113. This line of thought was suggested to me by Barbara Fultner, "Habermas on the Lifeworld, Intelligibility, and Conflict Resolution," unpublished manuscript, Granville, OH, 1996.

114. Functionalist theories of social change explain social *evolution* in terms of the successful (i.e. functional) solution of specific, empirically describable system problems. In his well-known book, *Karl Marx's Theory of History*, G. A. Cohen presents a functionalist interpretation of Marx's theory of history.

115. Schmid, 1982.

116. Ibid., 174.

117. Ibid., 173.

118. Ibid.

119. Ibid.

120. Ibid.

121. Ibid., 173–174. It should be noted that Schmid asserts only a very tentative status to his suggested explanation. His point is merely to persuade that an explanation that does not involve a developmental logic is plausible.

122. Ibid., 174.

123. Rotenstreich.

124. Ibid., 369.

125. Schmid, 173.

126. Strydom, "Ontogenetic Fallacy," 72. William Outhwaite raises this same objection (*Habermas: A Critical Introduction* [Stanford: Stanford University Press, 1994], 62).

127. Strydom, "Ontogenetic Fallacy," 73. For more on his critique of Habermas's conception of collective learning, see Strydom, "Collective Learning: Habermas's Concessions and their Theoretical Implications," *Philosophy and Social Criticism* 13 (1987): 265–281.

128. Strydom, "Ontogenetic Fallacy," 73.

Notes to Chapter 5

1. To be sure, much more is involved in social critique, for instance, why a determinate social phenomenon is unjust or oppressive, or what real possibilities obtain for social change. My concern here, however, is only with the normative understanding of the concept of progress.

2. Since each dimension of development, the cognitive-technical and the moral-practical, expresses its own autonomous pattern or logic of development, each of these dimensions will likewise manifest its own learning levels.

3. Of course, Habermas is critical of the legitimacy of positive law since it is grounded in de facto legislative agreements (ideally). Legitimate law in his view must be grounded in rational agreement, that is, an agreement that meets the requirements of procedural rationality. See BFN.

4. This interpretation was first suggested to me by Thomas McCarthy.

5. The following quotation from that essay goes to the motivation of my project: "A dialectical theory of progress, which historical materialism claims to be, is on its guard; what presents itself as progress can quickly show itself to be the perpetuation of what was supposedly overcome. More and more theorems of counter-enlightenment have therefore been incorporated into the dialectic of the enlightenment, and more and more elements of a critique of progress have been incorporated into the theory of progress—all for the sake of an idea of progress that is subtle and relentless enough not to let itself be blinded by the mere illusion of emancipation. Of course, this dialectical theory of progress has to contradict the thesis that emancipation itself mystifies" (WB, 155).

Bibliography

Austin, J. L. *How to Do Things With Words*. Ed. J. O. Urmson and Marina Sbisà. 2nd ed. Cambridge, Mass.: Harvard University Press, 1962.

Baynes, Kenneth. *The Normative Grounds of Social Criticism: Kant, Rawls, and Habermas.* Albany: State University of New York Press, 1992.

Beard, Charles A., and Sydney Hook. "Problems of Terminology in Historical Writing." In *Social Science Research Council, Theory and Practice in Historical Study: A Report of the Committee on Historiography*. New York: Social Science Research Council, 1946.

Benhabib, Seyla. *Critique, Norm, and Utopia: A Study of the Foundations of Critical Theory.* New York: Columbia University Press, 1986.

Bottomore, Tom. *Sociology: A Guide To Problems and Literature.* 3rd ed. London: Allen & Unwin, 1987.

Bury, J. B. *The Idea of Progress: An Inquiry into its Origin and Growth.* New York: Dover, 1932.

Cohen, G. A. *Karl Marx's Theory of History: A Defence.* Princeton: Princeton University Press, 1978.

Eder, Klaus. *Die Vergesellschaftung der Natur*. Frankfurt: Surhkamp, 1985.

Flavell, John H. *The Developmental Psychology of Jean Piaget.* Princeton: Van Nostrand, 1963.

———. "Stage-Related Properties of Cognitive Development." *Cognitive Psychology* 2 (1971): 421–453.

———. "An Analysis of Cognitive-Developmental Sequences." *Genetic Psychology Monographs* 86 (1972): 279–350.

Flavell, John H., and Joachim F. Wohlwill. "Formal and Functional Aspects of Cognitive Development." In *Studies in Cognitive Development*, ed. David Elkind and John H. Flavell. New York: Oxford University Press, 1969.

Frankenberg, Günther, and Ulrich Rödel. *Von der Volkssouveränität zum Minderheitenschutz.* Frankfurt: Europäische Verlagsanstalt, 1981.

Fultner, Barbara. "Habermas on the Lifeworld, Intelligibility, and Conflict Resolution." Unpublished Manuscript, Granville, OH, 1996.

Gill, Richard T. *Economic Development: Past and Present.* 2nd ed. Englewood Cliffs: Prentice-Hall, 1964.

Habermas, Jürgen. "Technology and Science as 'Ideology.'" (1968) In *Toward a Rational Society: Student Protest, Science, and Politics.* Trans. Jeremy J. Shapiro. Boston: Beacon Press, 1970.

———. "Towards a Theory of Communicative Competence." *Inquiry* 13, no. 3 (1970): 370–376.

———. *Knowledge and Human Interests.* Trans. Jeremy J. Shapiro. Boston: Beacon Press, 1971.

———. *Theory and Practice.* Trans. John Viertel. Boston: Beacon Press, 1973.

———. "*Wahrheitstheorien.*" In *Wirklichkeit und Reflexion*, ed. Helmut Fahrenbach. Neske: Pfullingen, 1973.

———. *Legitimation Crisis.* Trans. Thomas McCarthy. Boston: Beacon Press, 1975.

———. *Zur Rekonstruktion des Historischen Materialismus.* Frankfurt am Main: Suhrkamp Verlag, 1976.

———. *Communication and the Evolution of Society.* Trans. Thomas McCarthy. Boston: Beacon Press, 1979.

———. "History and Evolution." Trans. David J. Parent. *Telos* 39 no. 5 (1979): 5–49.

———. "A Reply to my Critics." In *Habermas: Critical Debates*, ed. John B. Thompson and David Held. Cambridge, Mass.: MIT Press, 1982.

———. "Walter Benjamin: Consciousness-Raising or Rescuing Critique." In *Philosophical-Political Profiles*, trans. Frederick G. Lawrence. Cambridge, Mass.: MIT Press, 1983.

———. *The Theory of Communicative Action.* Vol. 1, *Reason and the Rationalization of Society.* Trans. Thomas McCarthy. Boston: Beacon Press, 1984.

———. "Remarks on the Concept of Communicative Action." In *Social Action*, ed. G. Seebaß and R. Tuomela; trans. Ruth Stanley. Dordrecht: Reidel, 1985.

———. "Questions and Counterquestions." In *Habermas and Modernity*, ed. and with an introduction by Richard J. Bernstein; trans. James Bohman. Cambridge, Mass.: MIT Press, 1985.

———. *The Philosophical Discourse of Modernity.* Trans. Frederick Lawrence. Cambridge, Mass.: MIT Press, 1987.

———. *The Theory of Communicative Action.* Vol. 2, *Lifeworld and System.* Trans. Thomas McCarthy. Boston: Beacon Press, 1987.

———. *Moral Consciousness and Communicative Action.* Trans. Christian Lenhardt and Shierry Weber Nicholsen. Cambridge, Mass.: MIT Press, 1990.

———. "A Reply." In *Communicative Action: Essays on Jürgen Habermas's "The Theory of Communicative Action,"* ed. Axel Honneth and Hans Joas; trans. Jeremy Gaines and Doris L. Jones. Cambridge, Mass.: MIT Press, 1991.

———. *Autonomy and Solidarity: Interviews with Jürgen Habermas.* Ed. Peter Dews. Rev. and enlarged ed. London: Verso, 1992.

———. *Between Facts and Norms: Contributions to a Discourse Theory of Law and Democracy.* Trans. William Rehg. Cambridge, Mass.: MIT Press, 1996.

Habermas, Jürgen and Niklas Luhmann. *Theorien der Gesellshaft oder Sozialtechnologie-Was Leistet die Systemforschung?* Frankfurt am Main: Suhrkamp Verlag, 1971.

Hegel G. W. F. *Elements of the Philosophy of Right.* Ed. Allen W. Wood; trans. H. B. Nisbet. Cambridge: Cambridge University Press, 1991.

Heller, Agnes. "Habermas and Marxism." In *Habermas: Critical Debates,* ed. John B. Thompson and David Held. Cambridge, Mass.: MIT Press, 1982.

Herzog, Don. *Without Foundations: Justification in Political Theory.* Ithaca: Cornell University Press, 1985.

Honneth, Axel. *The Critique of Power: Reflective Stages in a Critical Social Theory.* Trans. Kenneth Baynes. Cambridge, Mass.: MIT Press, 1991.

Honneth, Axel and Hans Joas, eds. *Social Action and Human Nature.* Cambridge: Cambridge University Press, 1988.

———. *Communicative Action: Essays on Jürgen Habermas's "The Theory of Communicative Action."* Trans. Jeremy Gaines and Doris L. Jones. Cambridge, Mass.: MIT Press, 1991.

Horkheimer, Max. "Traditional and Critical Theory." In *Critical Theory: Selected Essays,* trans. Matthew J. O'Connell et al. New York: Continuum, 1972.

———. "A New Concept of Ideology?" In *Between Philosophy and Social Science: Selected Early Writings,* trans. John Torpey. Cambridge, Mass.: MIT Press, 1993.

———. "The Present Situation of Social Philosophy and the Tasks of an Institute for Social Research." In *Between Philosophy and Social Science: Selected Early Writings,* trans. John Torpey. Cambridge, Mass.: MIT Press, 1993.

Horkheimer, Max, and Theodor W. Adorno. *Dialectic of Enlightenment.* Trans. John Cumming. New York: Continuum, 1944.

Hoy, David Couzens. "Taking History Seriously: Foucault, Gadamer, Habermas." In *Union Seminary Quarterly Review* 34, no. 2 (1979).

———. "Power, Repression, Progress: Foucault, Lukes, and the Frankfurt School." *Tri Quarterly,* 52 (fall 1981). Reprinted in *Foucault: A Critical Reader,* ed. David Couzens Hoy. Oxford: Blackwell, 1986.

Hoy, David Couzens and Thomas McCarthy. *Critical Theory.* Oxford: Blackwell, 1994.

Humphreys, R. Stephen. "The Historian, His Documents, and the Elementary Modes of Historical Thought." *History and Theory* 19 (1980): 1–20.

Ingram, David. *Habermas and the Dialectic of Reason.* New Haven: Yale University Press, 1987.

———. *Critical Theory and Philosophy*. New York: Paragon, 1990.

———. "Nussbaum's 'Habermas on Austin's Perlocutionary Effects.'" Paper read at the Central Division Meeting of the American Philosophical Association, 1995.

———. *Reason, History, & Politics: The Communitarian Grounds of Legitimation in the Modern Age*. Albany, N.Y.: State University of New York Press, 1995.

Jay, Martin. *The Dialectical Imagination: A History of the Frankfurt School and the Institute of Social Research 1923–1950.* Boston: Little, Brown and Company, 1973.

———. "Habermas and Modernism." In *Habermas and Modernity*, ed. Richard J. Bernstein. Cambridge, Mass.: MIT Press, 1985.

Joas, Hans. "The Unhappy Marriage of Hermeneutics and Functionalism." In *Communicative Action: Essays on Jürgen Habermas's "The Theory of Communicative Action,"* ed. Axel Honneth and Hans Joas; trans. Jeremy Gaines and Doris L. Jones. Cambridge, Mass.: MIT Press, 1991.

Kohlberg, Lawrence. "Stage and Sequence: The Cognitive-Developmental Approach to Socialization." In *Handbook of Socialization Theory and Research,* ed. David A. Goslin. Chicago: Rand McNally, 1969.

———. "From Is to Ought." In *Cognitive Development and Epistemology,* ed. T. Mischel. New York: Academic Press, 1971.

———. *Essays on Moral Development.* San Francisco: Harper & Row, 1981.

McCarthy, Thomas. *The Critical Theory of Jürgen Habermas.* Cambridge, Mass.: MIT Press, 1978.

———. "Reflections on Rationalization in *The Theory of Communicative Action.*" In *Habermas and Modernity,* ed. and with an introduction by Richard J. Bernstein. Cambridge, Mass.: MIT Press, 1985.

———. "Complexity and Democracy: or the Seducements of Systems Theory." In *Communicative Action: Essays on Jürgen Habermas's "The Theory of Communicative Action,"* ed. Axel Honneth and Hans Joas. Cambridge, Mass.: MIT Press, 1991.

———. *Ideals and Illusions*. Cambridge, Mass.: MIT Press, 1991.

McNeill, William H. *The Rise of the West: A History of the Human Community: with a Retrospective Essay*. Chicago: The Univeristy of Chicago Press, 1991.

Mills, Charles W. "Is it Immaterial that there's a 'Material' in 'Historical Materialism'?" *Inquiry* 32 (1989): 323–342.

———. *The Racial Contract*. Ithaca: Cornell University Press, 1997.

Nisbet, Robert A. *Social Change and History: Aspects of the Western Theory of Development.* London: Oxford University Press, 1969.

O'Connell, James. "The Concept of Modernization." In *South Atlantic Quarterly* 64 (1965): 549–564.

Outhwaite, William. *Habermas: A Critical Introduction*. Stanford: Stanford University Press, 1994.

Owen, David S. "Habermas's Developmental Logic Thesis: Universal or Eurocentric?" in *Philosophy Today* 41 (1998): supplement.

Piaget, Jean. *The Principles of Genetic Epistemology*. Trans. Wolfe Mays. London: Routledge & Kegan Paul: 1972.

Pinard, Adrien, and Monique Laurendeau. " 'Stage' in Piaget's Cognitive-Developmental Theory: Exegesis of a Concept." In *Studies in Cognitive Development*, ed. David Elkind and John H. Flavell. New York: Oxford University Press, 1969.

Rawls, John. *A Theory of Justice*. Cambridge, Mass.: Harvard University Press, 1971.

———. *Political Liberalism*. New York: Columbia University Press, 1996.

Ritter, Harry. *Dictionary of Concepts in History*. New York: Greenwood Press, 1986.

Rockmore, Tom. *Habermas on Historical Materialism*. Bloomington: Indiana University Press, 1989.

Rorty, Richard. *Philosophy and the Mirror of Nature*. Princeton: Princeton University Press, 1979.

Rotenstreich, Nathan. "An Analysis of Piaget's Concept of Structure." *Philosophy and Phenomenological Research* 37, no. 3 (1977): 368–380.

Sahlins, Marshall D., and Elman R. Service, eds. *Evolution and Culture*. Ann Arbor: University of Michigan Press, 1960.

Sennet, Julius, Jr. *Habermas and Marxism: An Appraisal*. Beverly Hills: Sage, 1979.

Schluchter, Wolfgang. *The Rise of Western Rationalism: Max Weber's Developmental History*. Trans. Guenther Roth. Berkeley: University of California Press, 1981.

Schmid, Michael. "Habermas's Theory of Social Evolution." In *Habermas: Critical Debates*, ed. John B. Thompson and David Held. Cambridge, Mass.: MIT Press, 1982.

Strydom, Piet. "Collective Learning: Habermas's Concessions and their Theoretical Implications." *Philosophy and Social Criticism* 13 (1987): 265–281.

———. "The Ontogenetic Fallacy: The Immanent Critique of Habermas's Developmental Logical Theory of Evolution." *Theory, Culture & Society* 9 (1992): 65–93.

Swindal, James. *Reflection Revisited: Jürgen Habermas's Discursive Theory of Truth*. New York: Fordham University Press, 1999.

Taylor, Charles. *Hegel*. Cambridge: Cambridge University Press, 1975.

———. *Human Agency and Language: Philosophical Papers I*. Cambridge: Cambridge University Press, 1985.

———. *Sources of the Self: The Making of the Modern Identity*. Cambridge, Mass.: Harvard University Press, 1989.

———. *Philosophical Arguments*. Cambridge, Mass.: Harvard University Press, 1995.

Thompson, John B., and David Held, eds. *Habermas: Critical Debates*. Cambridge, Mass.: MIT Press, 1982.

Toulmin, Stephen, Richard Rieke, and Allan Janik. *An Introduction to Reasoning*. New York: Macmillan, 1979.

Tugendhat, Ernst. "Habermas on Communicative Action." In *Social Action*, ed. G. Seebaß and R. Tuomela. Dordrecht: Reidel, 1985.

Weir, Allison. *Sacrificial Logics: Feminist Theory and the Critique of Identity*. New York: Routledge, 1996.

Wellmer, Albrecht. "Practical Philosophy and the Theory of Society: On the Normative Foundations of a Critical Social Science." In *The Communicative Ethics Controversy*, ed. Seyla Benhabib and Fred Dallmayr. Cambridge, Mass.: MIT Press, 1990.

———. *The Persistence of Modernity: Essays on Aesthetics, Ethics, and Postmodernism*. Trans. David Midgley. Cambridge, Mass.: MIT Press, 1991.

White, Stephen K. "The Normative Basis of Critical Theory." *Polity* (fall 1983): 150–164.

———. *The Recent Work of Jürgen Habermas: Reason, Justice and Modernity*. Cambridge: Cambridge University Press, 1988.

Whitton, Brian J. "Universal Pragmatics and the Formation of Western Civilization: A Critique of Habermas's Theory of Human Moral Evolution." *History and Theory* 31 (1992): 299–313.

Wiggershaus, Rolf. *The Frankfurt School: Its History, Theories, and Political Significance*. Trans. Michael Robertson. Cambridge, Mass.: MIT Press, 1994.

Index